AF_2

CARPENTER'S WORLD TRAVELS

—

Familiar Talks About Countries and Peoples

WITH THE AUTHOR ON THE SPOT AND
THE READER IN HIS HOME, BASED
ON THREE HUNDRED THOU-
SAND MILES OF TRAVEL
OVER THE GLOBE

"READING CARPENTER IS SEEING THE WORLD"

FROM TANGIER
TO TRIPOLI

IN THE LANDS OF THE DESERT

Like a rocky island in a raging sea, Islam stubbornly resists the waves of Western civilization, and the ancient Moslem traditions passed on from father to son have more force than the modern ideas of alien rulers.

FROM TANGIER TO TRIPOLI

*Morocco, Algeria, Tunisia, Tripoli,
and the Sahara*

BY

FRANK G. CARPENTER

LITT. D., F. R. G. S.

WITH 119 ILLUSTRATIONS
FROM
ORIGINAL PHOTOGRAPHS

GARDEN CITY   NEW YORK
DOUBLEDAY, DORAN & COMPANY, INC.
1928

ACKNOWLEDGMENTS

IN THE publication of this volume on the countries of North Africa I wish to thank the Secretary of State for letters which have given me the assistance of our official representatives in the countries visited. I thank also our Secretary of Agriculture and our Secretary of Labour for appointing me an Honorary Commissioner of their Departments in foreign lands. Their credentials have been of the greatest value, making accessible sources of information seldom opened to the ordinary traveller.

I acknowledge also the assistance and coöperation rendered by Mr. Dudley Harmon, my editor, and Miss Ellen McBryde Brown and Miss Josephine Lehmann in the revision of the notes dictated or penned by me on the ground.

While most of the illustrations are from my own negatives, certain photographs have been supplied by the French colonial officials in Morocco, Algeria, and Tunisia, the American Geographical Society, the American Red Cross, and the Publishers' Photo Service, all of which are protected by copyright.

FRANK G. CARPENTER.

CONTENTS

ix

CONTENTS

LIST OF ILLUSTRATIONS

xi

ILLUSTRATIONS

ILLUSTRATIONS

ILLUSTRATIONS

FROM TANGIER
TO TRIPOLI

FROM TANGIER TO TRIPOLI

CHAPTER I

JUST A WORD BEFORE WE START

THIS book is the story of my travels in Morocco, Algeria, Tunis, Tripoli, and the mighty desert that lies to the south of them. We start with Morocco, the land of the Moors, and end in Old Tripoli, or Italian Libya, as it is now called. The talks are given as they were penned in the heart of North Africa, with only slight changes to make them correspond more nearly with our interest in these lands and peoples as they are to-day. The work, therefore, partakes of the old and the new, my notes being modified only where absolutely necessary and retaining the original story and form.

For instance, during my stay in Morocco the Sultan Abd el-Aziz, one of the most picturesque of modern monarchs, still maintained his Mohammedan rule, and the robber Raisuli was still cutting his pranks under high heaven. The stories about these men and their people picture a civilization which promises soon to become a tale of the past. To-day a New Morocco is being born into the colonial family of France, while in Algeria the Republic is gaining fresh sustenance and strength. Tunis and old Carthage are of perennial interest, and the mighty

1

Sahara, invaded though parts of it are by the airplane and the railway, changeth not through the ages.

In these travels I have included my talks with the late Ranavalona, the former Queen of Madagascar, and Behanzin, once King of Dahomey, whom, through the courtesy of the French Government officials, I was able to meet. Both Dahomey and Madagascar are now included in the empire of France, and their domains henceforth will be part of the white man's burden as borne by the French, leaving these unique monarchs as milestones marking the progress of modern civilization.

The chief virtue of these talks, I believe, is that they are given in the open air, from notes made on the streets of city or village, while riding camel-back over the desert, or passing through the mountains and valleys on foot or in automobiles. The pictures of what I have seen are at times sketched in the blazing sun of midday and again in the soft twilight of the evening. But I have had the reader ever before me, and have tried to give him a radiographic representation of just what was passing under my eyes.

All of these countries, however, are changing to correspond with the revolution which began with the Great War in Europe and even now goes on throughout the world. In order to keep the reader in step with the trend of the moment I have added a chapter containing last-minute notes of their progress and more important events. The whole, I believe, gives a good picture of northwestern Africa as it is to-day.

In Tangier we are only a few miles from Europe and the Rock of Gibraltar, but we are centuries removed from modern life and civilization.

Water peddlers are common in North African cities. I might have bought the entire contents of the skin bag for a few cents, but contented myself with a little brass cupful, which I dared not drink.

CHAPTER II

IN THE LAND OF OTHELLO

COME with me this bright Sunday morning for a walk through one of the oldest cities of this land of Othello. The sombre-faced Moors are going to and fro through the streets and we shall meet with many a scowl. We shall not see the faces of their Desdemonas, for they are concealed except for slits for the eye, and we shall have to be careful lest we give offence. We must fight shy of the mosques, for Christians are not admitted, and we had best think twice before entering the door of a house, no matter how wide open it be.

We are in Tangier, at the end of northwestern Africa, so near Europe that by a short ride to Cape Spartel one sees the hills of Spain plainly in view. Gibraltar, with its mighty lion-head rock, is within a cannon shot of us, an hour or so of smooth sailing having brought us from that port to this nearest gateway to Africa. It is only ten days since we left the wharves of New York on a great ocean liner, and we have jumped, as it were, from the bright light of our Christian civilization into the semi-darkness of these Mohammedan Moors.

Tangier lies on the edge of the Atlantic Ocean, in a hollow or nest in these wild African hills. It has a big wall around it and its blue and white houses remind us of a lot of gigantic store boxes of all sorts of shapes thrown together

3

at haphazard. The highest part is the citadel, where the governor lives. There he holds court and there is his prison, where scores of half-naked, miserable beings are shut up, with chains around their legs. At night they sleep on the floors, all tied together by one chain which binds the necks of the whole crowd of criminals. They do their own cooking, but their friends must furnish the food or they will starve on the short rations of dry bread and water. There is no *habeas corpus* act here, so it is not hard for a man of influence to send a poorer brother to jail.

From the height near the governor's place one sees what a strange town is this so close to Europe! How out of date it seems in this twentieth century! The roofs are flat and there is not a chimney in sight. There are no smokestacks, and no smoke rises from the jumble of houses below us. This does not mean, however, that the sixty thousand people living in them do no cooking. They eat three meals a day, but their cooking is done upon fires of charcoal made in clay basins half the size of a wash bowl with a hole at the side for the draft. Some of the larger establishments have little brick ovens built into the walls of their kitchens. As the land about here is treeless and there is no coal, the fuel is expensive, an armful of fagots as big as broom handles costing a dollar, with charcoal proportionately high. For this reason about all the washing is done in cold water. We can see the clothes hanging out on the roofs of the houses. There are but few yards and the women often dry their wash near the streams outside the city where they clean the garments by pounding them on the stones.

As we go about the streets we realize that Tangier, like almost every Moroccan city, suffers from a scarcity of water. The streets are sprinkled by men who go through them with goatskin bags on their backs, bending half double as they scatter the drops here and there. Each bag holds about ten gallons, and the water comes from the sea. Other carriers go from house to house with fresh water, which they bring from the wells or the streams outside the city. They ring bells as they go, and have little brass cups in which they will give you all the water you can drink for less than a cent. I should, however, as soon think of drinking a cup of pure typhoid bacteria as of tasting such water, although I stopped one of these ragged old water peddlers to-day and bought a cup, while my guide, Mohammed, snapped my camera. If I had bought the whole skinful I should have had to pay only four or five cents. Much of the water for cooking and washing is brought into the city in little five-gallon kegs, two or three of which are slung on each side of a donkey, with the peddler sitting on top or walking behind. At a rough guess there are five hundred water carriers of one sort or another in this town of Tangier.

"And why do they not have water wagons?" I hear someone ask.

Open the eyes of your imaginations and see. These streets are so narrow that a hand cart could not be pushed through them. In some I can stand in the centre and touch both walls with my hands. There is not a wheeled vehicle inside the whole town, there is not even a hand cart or a wheelbarrow, but there are so many donkeys that one has to jump from side to side to keep out of their way. They go along without bridles or halters, directed by the cries and the sticks of the donkey boys who follow behind.

5

The donkeys are the drays of Tangier and carry enormous loads. I saw two little fellows to-day, not much higher than my waist, almost covered by an upright piano, which rested on their backs as they walked through the main streets of the city. Everyone knows that six men are required to lift a piano in our country, yet the two little beasts carried this one in its pine box on their bare backs. It was steadied by two porters who walked at the sides. The animals had enormous ears and their rat-like tails, shaved close, made me think of abbreviated black snake whips. Both were ragged and knotty and scarred with sores where their masters had cut away the skin in order that they might the more easily hurry them onward by goading the raw flesh. This afternoon I met a donkey caravan, each animal loaded with two heavy bags of flour. The little fellows had to brace themselves while the men threw on the bags, and then they went off staggering. One of them stumbled and threw his load over his head. It took two lusty porters to replace the sacks.

My heavy trunks were brought from the boat to the hotel upon donkeys, and I have seen donkeys without number carrying sand in baskets, bringing in charcoal and wood, and even loaded with stones and brick for building material.

Some freighting is done by mules. I saw two going along the street to-day with the iron girders for a building strapped to their backs. Mules serve also as riding animals, and I have travelled for miles upon them through the country about. The saddles are great red cushions a foot thick with stirrups so big that they rest the whole foot from the heel to the toe. The natives ride their donkeys or mules sitting far back with their long legs

6

Because of the seclusion of their women, the Moors are specially
dependent on each other for companionship. One often sees two men
going along hand in hand.

In the grand Sok, a desert market outside the Bab-el-Sok gate of Tangier, we see an Arab singer playing on the gimbri, an instrument much like a mandolin.

hanging down. The native women ride astride, looking like rag bags tied to the saddles. Their covered heads bob up and down as the beasts jog along. Morocco has also many fine horses of Arabian blood. Some belong to the Moorish cavalry, as may be seen by the rifles carried by their riders, who use short stirrups, so that their knees are high up on the saddle.

But turn now and look at the people as they pass by. These Moors are unlike any Africans we have in America. They are tall, straight, big-boned, and broad-shouldered, moving about with a grace and a dignity not found in our land. They wear long white gowns with hoods at the back, which are often pulled up over their turbans, making them look taller. Their bare feet are clad in bright yellow slippers. The men are all bearded, for the razor touches only the hair of their heads. Nearly every other man has a white skin, while most of the dark-skinned Moors even have features like ours. Their noses are large and straight, their foreheads are high, and their eyes as fierce as those of Othello. They walk with a haughty stride, swinging their arms, and two men frequently go along hand in hand.

The people are very polite, even the poorer classes and the Berbers from the country being free from any roughness or rudeness of manner. Observe how friendly they are with each other. Those two old men on the corner have been gossiping for more than an hour. A little later these streets will be bordered with groups of men sitting on the ground or upon low stools, leaning back against the walls as they chat. They spend a great deal of time in the tea houses and are fond of entertaining each other. Since this is a Mohammedan land no one ever introduces his

7

wife or daughter to his friend. The two sexes are kept wide apart. This throws the men together and makes close friendships among them more common than in our part of the world.

Most of the other Mohammedan nations drink coffee. The Moors drink tea and are especially fond of it when flavoured with mint. It is served in tumblers at tea houses all over the country. The Moors drink it boiling hot, sitting cross-legged on the ground as they do so. Most of the tea comes from Japan via England, London alone sending as many as twenty thousand chests in one year. The Moroccans are fond of sweets, and their consumption of sugar is so great that it has almost ruined their teeth. This one can see whenever a man opens his mouth.

Besides the white-gowned Moors, we meet other odd characters at every step. There are rough fellows in gowns and hoods of dark gray or brown, fierce-looking mountaineers with brown faces, and Negro slaves as black as a stove. There are many mulattoes. We see also men from the desert and beyond, travellers from Fez and other interior cities, and labourers, some of whom are almost in rags.

One queer character of Tangier is a beggar who claims to have visited America. He is jet black with hair standing out like woolly wires over his head. He goes about with cymbals, dancing and singing and asking for alms. He accosted me to-day, saying:

"Master. You American. I been in America. I been Shecago, Buffo, San Lowie, Umweho, Philadelphweya, and Wasingtone. I Sudan man with Barnum circus. We two American. Suppose you give me money."

"Wasingtone" is my home when in the United States,

8

and it was in its honour that I handed him a half-dozen coppers. He bowed to the ground, then danced away, jingling his cymbals.

The women are among the strangest sights here. One does not see much of them, except an eye or so, but they look out nevertheless. If an American girl will take a well-worn blanket of thin, white flannel and drape it about her body over her clothes, so that it hides the whole of her person, wrapping a fold or so about the head and leaving only a crack for one eye, or perhaps both, she will present a fair likeness of the average Moorish girl as she goes along the streets. The only bare skin one can see is the little section about the eyes; at least, that is, until the lady gets by. She shows more at the rear than the front, for from behind one sees quite an expanse of bare leg. The rosy heels of these maidens can always be glimpsed, rising and falling in their red slippers, as they hasten along. The women do not loiter and chat on the streets, and though they often visit their friends, they spend little time at the doors greeting each other, and there are no front gates to hang over while they discuss the servant question or retail the last scandal.

Some of the lower class Moorish women go about with their faces exposed, and an old woman may, now and then, drop the covering which hides her features. The young and the pretty are always kept hidden, and I notice that many have a cloth of some kind wrapped closely about the lower part of the face, in addition to the outside covering, which they hold tight as they go.

Moorish girls are said to be fond of fine clothes, and these ghostly wrappings often hide costly garments. Over the *kaftan*, a sort of waist and skirt reaching to

9

the feet, they wear a garment of sheer material through which the bright *kaftan* shows. They have belts of leather or sashes of gold thread. They sometimes have hand-kerchiefs about their heads held up by cardboard. They like jewellery and load themselves with earrings, bracelets, and anklets. They paint the eyebrows, lips, and cheeks, but are not tattooed.

About the only women's faces one sees are those of the Jewesses. The younger girls are often good-looking. They have fine dark eyes and ivory-white skins, with cheeks tinged with the hue of a dark moss rose. The older women run to much flesh and seem coarse. The dress of the Jewish women is much like that worn in our country save that the richer ones use gold embroidery for trimming. They wear silk handkerchiefs tied about the head, half conceal-ing the forehead and covering most of the hair.

I wish I could show you some of the Moorish children who are flocking about me. They are just as sweet as our American little ones, although they seem different. They dress somewhat like their parents, the boys wearing red fezzes and long white gowns. While playing in the streets many go bareheaded, and if you will imagine a crowd of little Americans of say six, eight, and ten years, dressed in white nightgowns, playing on the streets and thoroughly enjoying themselves, you will have one of the common sights of this city. You must make the faces, however, white and yellow and even black, and must shave the heads close with the exception of spots here and there where long locks are allowed to grow. The little girls have at first only a single lock on the crown of the head. Later this is allowed to spread out until it finally covers the whole head. The hair is then braided.

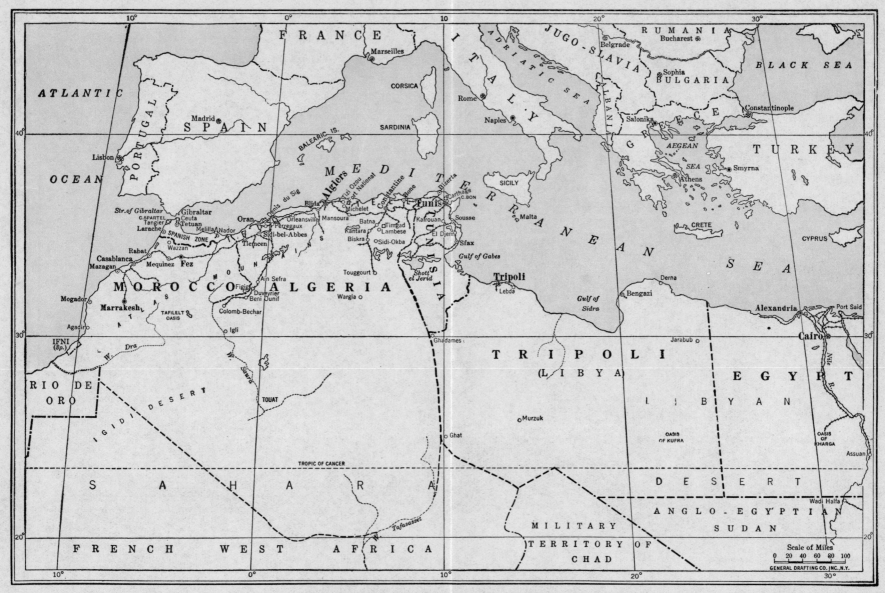

NORTH AFRICA AND THE MEDITERRANEAN

This map shows why, with the development of modern transportation, the countries of North Africa must inevitably become increasingly vital factors in the statesmanship and trade of Europe.

NORTH AFRICA AND THE MEDITERRANEAN
This map shows why, with the development of modern transportation, the countries of North Africa must inevitably become
increasingly vital factors in the statesmanship and trade of Europe

IN THE LAND OF OTHELLO

The boy's head is shaved as soon as he is born, and is kept shaved for the greater part of his life. Each rich family has its own barber, who, until he is married, keeps the head of the boy in order for nothing. At that time he receives a present and is well paid thereafter. Every man is shaved regularly, the whole head being scraped, except the lock left on the crown, by which as a handle the Mohammedan thinks he may be pulled into Heaven. The man being shaved sits upon the ground, the barber soaping and lathering him as he bends over him. The hair is cut close to the scalp, a good job leaving it like the skin of a drum head sprinkled with pepper, or, better, gunpowder.

CHAPTER III

THE shops of Tangier are full of interesting features. The trade is mostly in the hands of the Jews, and the American salesman who comes to Morocco must expect to carry on his business largely through them. There are Moorish bazaars, it is true, in Tangier and all of the cities, and there are Moorish commercial houses with large capital in Fez, but the Jews are everywhere, and they deal with all classes. As business men they are the equals of any of their race.

Coming to this country along about the thirteenth century to do business with the Moors, the Hebrews have been here ever since. They are despised and at times ill-treated by the other races. When they first came they were required to wear black clothes and shoes and to go on foot as they passed through the cities. To-day they wear black skullcaps, black slippers, and long black coats belted in at the waist. I am told that in the Berber districts they have curls hanging down in front of their ears, but otherwise they dress like the Berbers.

In some of the Moroccan cities of the interior the Children of Israel still live in their own sections, and in some they are shut off at night from the rest of the town. These quarters are known as *mellahs*. They are among the most squalid parts of a city. Their streets are narrow and dirty. The front doors are little more than holes in

12

the walls, and most of the houses contain many small rooms in which the people are herded together like cattle. The homes of the rich are much better.

In local matters the *mellahs* are governed by the Jews themselves. The rabbis are about the most influential of all. The people are religious and attend their synagogues regularly. They do no business on Saturday, their Sabbath, on which day many of them will not even open a business letter. I attended one of their synagogues here. It was a dark little room surrounded by dwellings.

The Hebrews now have their own schools in which their children get a sort of modern education, although much of the time is devoted to Hebrew and Spanish. The schools teach also French and English, geography, and other subjects.

I have made a hunt through the bazaars here to-day for American goods, visiting among other places the largest fancy grocery store in Tangier. I told the Jew clerk to show me samples of all the American articles he had, and he brought out kerosene oil, corned beef, and corn meal. The corn meal was in a pasteboard package labelled Chicago, and the oil in a square can from Philadelphia, while the corned beef was in a flat tin box from a packing house in Kansas City. At another store I saw canned salmon from Seattle and pickles from Boston. All of these goods came via London.

I imagine the store has not had any great demand for the corn meal and I am sure the average Moroccan stomach would be surprised at American flour. The bread of the country is made of meal ground at home. Every family has its own mill, consisting of two rude grind-

13

stones, one on the other, the grain being poured through a hole in the top stone. These mills are turned by the women of the family, and as the stones are worn, bits of them come off and mix with the flour, leading to broken teeth and bad digestion.

The Moroccan bakeries are interesting. There are scores of them here and baking is a regular profession, for very few people do any baking at home. They make their flour into dough for bread and cakes, and send it to the nearest bakery to be cooked. Often a baker will have his regular customers and will send out his boys, little long-gowned, dark-faced urchins, to bring in the dough. They usually carry it upon boards which rest upon their heads, and a few hours later take back the baked article. The baker gets ten per cent. of the amount of dough sent and a loaf of that proportion is always put in for his pay.

The bake ovens look like caves. They are found here and there along the main streets of the cities. One steps first into a dark cellar-like room, where the proprietor, a white-gowned, turbaned Moor, sitting cross-legged, watches the count and bosses the labourer who has charge of the oven. This man is none too clean. He has a long paddle upon which he puts the loaves of dough and places them upon the oven floor. This is on about the level of the floor of the room, while the baker stands in a pit at the front of it. The ovens are long. Each has a fire of twigs in one side, so arranged that by means of draughts the smoke is carried away.

The loaves are of the size of a tea plate and about two inches thick. They taste good. The baker sells the extra loaves which he takes in trade. There are bread peddlers in every market. They are usually women, shrouded in

14

Throughout North Africa are these sidewalk cafés, the Arab clubs.
Unlike most other Mohammedans, the Moroccans prefer tea to coffee.

On account of the scarcity of fuel in Morocco almost no bread is baked
in the homes of the people, and bread peddlers are found in every market.

American goods are scarce in the bazaars of Tangier, though some of the grocers sell our canned corned beef and kerosene oil.

white blankets, who hide their faces from the men as they sell, but nevertheless keep a sharp watch through the peep-hole in their head shawls for their change.

In my tour of the shops I saw no American tables, chairs, or beds for sale, nor did I see on display any quantity of furniture from any other country. It will be a long time before the ordinary Moroccan will want furniture. The poorer classes sleep on the floor; they are so hardy that a man will wrap himself in his gown and lie down anywhere for a snooze. There are men sleeping on the stones out in the streets here every night, and by the hundreds. Many houses are guarded in this way.

Spring beds are unknown to such people and they seldom have chairs. When they sit they do not hang their legs down but double them up under them or lean back against the wall with their long beards resting on their knees. If they use a bench or divan it is to sit cross-legged upon it. The tables are rude, often being simply low, round brass pans upon legs. Some of them are beauti-fully carved. Candles are in demand and many thousands of dollars' worth are imported every year.

I notice, too, that there are few socks and stockings and no American shoes, so popular in Europe, for sale in Tangier. The men want a loose slipper of soft leather with a counter that can be bent over. As a usual thing, they take their shoes off when they enter their homes, and never wear them inside the churches or mosques. The black of the American shoe looks strange to the Moroccan, for every Moorish gentleman likes a delicate pale yellow. As to the women, they wear red slippers of soft Morocco leather, the better class having their foot-wear embroidered with gold and silver. In the house most of the girls go barefooted, while no one wears a French heel. Indeed, no heels are worn here, and even fine Morocco boots are heelless. All of the footwear is handmade.

The Moors do not want stockings. Most of them have never even heard of them, and I should say there are not ten thousand women in the whole country who wear them. Only the very well-to-do or those who have been affected by foreign influences wear them on occasions.

If one would see all classes of these people, he can do so in the big market on the edge of Tangier. It is in a space covering ten or more acres, which on two or three days of each week is filled with people buying and selling. There are dignified Moorish merchants. There are hooded men in from the country moving about with bare legs. There are peasant women with great hats, and veiled Mohammedan ladies. There are Jewish men in their caps and long coats and Jewish women with their heads bound up in bright-coloured handkerchiefs. There are swaggering Moorish soldiers on foot and on horseback. A great, lumbering camel shuffles along here and there, while countless donkeys carrying loads as big as themselves push their way through the throngs. There are peddlers of all sorts, from those selling water from goatskin bags on their shoulders to those hawking sweet cakes and candies. There are women loaded with fagots and men carrying charcoal. There are bread peddlers and vegetable peddlers and other odd-looking men and women selling almost everything under this African sun.

CHAPTER IV

BANDIT DAYS IN MOROCCO

EVERYWHERE I go in Tangier I am reminded that I am in the wild and turbulent land of Morocco. There are ten Mohammedans to every Christian, and the men who would laugh or sneer at the Prophet in a public place would be in danger of death. The town is surrounded by walls and guarded by soldiers. The country outside is filled with brigands and bandits. Rumours of a holy war against the Christians are rife; and it is said that in the oasis of Tafilelt, where the Sultan's family comes from, troops are preparing to invade Algeria and attack the French.

On my way here I called at Algeciras, Spain, where the conference of the Powers was held in the hope of bringing some sort of order and safety into Moroccan affairs. But the Algeciras conference, far from settling things, has stirred up the people; and the police force of twenty-five hundred men under foreign officers, which it provided for the eight ports of Morocco, is insufficient. There is already trouble at many of the ports. Since I landed one of the mountain tribes besieged Mogador on the Atlantic and attacked the French Jews. The Jews, who compose nearly half the population, have been making a great deal of money and some of them have been gradually moving out of the *mellah* and renting houses in the Moorish section of the town. This, I am told, was the cause of

17

the trouble. The chief of one of the Mohammedan tribes near by was called in and drove the Jews back to their own quarter, telling them they should know their place and keep it. A reign of terror exists in Marakesh, the southern capital of the Sultan, and His Majesty cannot control any part of his dominions outside of Fez.

Right here around Tangier, within a short distance of the fortifications of Gibraltar and just over the way from Spain and southern France, the country is full of wild and warring tribes, most of whom are fast losing their fear of the foreigner. As I write this, it is impossible to go five miles east of the city without soldiers to guard one. The Berbers of the region are up in arms. The governor of Tangier, the former cattle thief, Raisuli, refuses to take any risks and will not send an escort of soldiers with me to the town of Tetuan, which is only two days' journey from here. I can look out of my hotel window and see the villa of Walter B. Harris, the well-known London *Times* correspondent, which is situated near here on the shore. It is not more than an hour's walk from where I am writing, but its owner dare not remain there over night for fear he may be kidnapped and taken out into the mountains to be held for ransom as was the American citizen, Ion Perdicaris.

Mr. Harris was the first of the foreigners to be kidnapped by Raisuli. He was living in his beautiful home on the seashore, just three miles from Tangier, when twenty-five hundred brigands, with Raisuli at their head, carried him off. They held him in captivity for more than three weeks, but released him without ransom. During this time Mr. Harris had a close view of Raisuli. He describes him as a handsome and rather fascinating man

We found sentries at every few feet and passed through an encampment
of soldiers at the edge of the city.

Fez, formerly a great seat of learning, is still sacred to Moslem pilgrims. Its Mosque of Mulai Idris is considered so holy that the streets leading to its entrance are closed to Jews, Christians, and four-footed beasts.

of strong character and a great bluffer. He says that the Sultan has but little power, that he is afraid of the two rebel leaders, Raisuli and Bu Hamara, and that he has bribed them to keep the peace. Bu Hamara has now about one fifth of Morocco under him, and Raisuli, with comparatively few soldiers, is growing rich off the country around this city. He is, I understand, laying up money since he got the seventy thousand dollars in ransom for Perdicaris, and is buying business properties here in Tangier.

In his rooms at the Cecil Hotel Mr. Harris talked with me about the situation. He thinks it rather hard lines that he dare not live at home although the British have a treaty with the Sultan which provides for the protection of foreigners. His villa is within fifteen miles of the fortifications at Gibraltar and within an hour's walk of the walls of the Sultan's chief port. Nevertheless, its owner has to stay at one of the hotels in the city for fear of kidnappers. The governor of Tangier keeps fifty soldiers guarding the villa and its contents, but still it is unsafe.

At the same time Morocco insists on all the rights that she has under her treaty with foreign nations, and the foreigner is allowed no favours. The other day Mr. Harris attempted to send two white peacocks to a friend who was living at the hotel at Algeciras, across the Strait. He brought them to the Custom House, but was told that they could not be sent out of the country, as there was nothing in the treaty with Great Britain about the exportation of peacocks.

Mr. Harris has resided in Morocco during the greater part of the last sixteen years and has gone by caravan over most of it. He has travelled widely also in other Mohammedan countries; he has ridden on camel back over Arabia, and he speaks Arabic fluently. During his stay in Fez he was a great friend of the Sultan and has now an intimate acquaintance with some of the most powerful of his ministers. He is also closely associated with Si el-Mehdi el-Menehbi who was for a long time minister of war, and who, as such, through his influence with His Majesty Abd el-Aziz, practically controlled Morocco. Menehbi lost caste when he failed to quell the rebellion of Bu Hamara, and was forced to leave the Sultan's cabinet.

I asked Mr. Harris some questions about railroads. He told me that the Moors object to them on the ground that they are a foreign innovation and also because it is feared they may put the donkeys, mules, and camels out of their jobs. As it is now, the trade of Morocco goes by caravan, or by sea from port to port. The freight rates per animal in the interior are comparatively low and the charges for board and feed at the Moorish hotels are almost nothing. In Fez it costs about four cents a day to feed a camel and less than three cents a day for a horse or a mule. The ordinary native can be taken care of for a little more. The expenses on the road are also small, but the loads carried are so small that an animal will soon eat up the value of its freight.

As to the transportation of foreigners, the cost is enormous. The distance from Tangier to Fez is about one hundred and seventy miles, and in the United States a railroad journey of that distance would cost, including baggage, about eight dollars, and the time required would be only about five hours. The ordinary foreigner cannot reach Fez in less than a week, and the cost of the journey from Tangier will be from twenty to thirty dollars a day.

I thought of making the trip, expecting to spend a month on the way there and back. One of Cooks' dragomans said that I would have to pay thirty-five dollars per day for all the time of my absence, making my one month's journey, including a stay of two weeks at Fez, cost me ten hundred and fifty dollars. For this trip I would have had to employ a soldier or so and would have required about three mules to carry my baggage, as well as mules for myself, a guide, and a cook. I should have had to camp out every night, and should have been lucky had I reached Fez in one week. Connected with the American legation at Tangier I found a dragoman who offered to give me the same accommodations for six hundred dollars. Moreover, there was great danger of being captured by brigands on the way and held for ransom; so, on the whole, I did not think the trip worth the risk.

Our American minister, who made the journey from Tangier to Fez a month or so ago, spent twelve days on the way. He had a large company of soldiers, furnished by the Sultan, who paid all his expenses, amounting to many thousands of dollars.

"It takes a thief to catch a thief." This old maxim holds good here. At present the country west of Tangier is quiet, because the Sultan has bribed Raisuli to take care of it. This same brigand, who captured an American citizen and made the Sultan pay a ransom of seventy thousand dollars before he would let him go, has been appointed by the Sultan the governor of the Tangier district, and his men are the only guards of this city.

I find Raisuli's soldiers in every street and they are patrolling the main roads outside the town. We took donkeys yesterday and rode out over the hills to the villa where Mr. Perdicaris was living at the time of his capture. I was accompanied by my son Jack and my turbaned guide, Hadj Mohammed Breck. We found sentries at every few feet and passed through an encampment of soldiers at the edge of the city. The soldiers wore red fezzes and gay Moroccan uniforms, but many were bare-legged and bare-footed. They were armed with Mauser rifles and their fierce eyes gleamed out of their bearded faces at us without smiling. They were not at all friendly, and so when they objected to being photographed I did not insist.

In the meantime, Raisuli holds a peculiar position in Moroccan politics. He has bluffed the Sultan and his officials and has, as it were, held up the government and the army. He has made the nominal rulers of the country give up a lot of hard cash as well as one of the fattest of fat jobs. He knows that he has many enemies and the Sultan would welcome his assassination. As a result, he is badly frightened and is trying to guard against accident. These Moors are wonderfully friendly with one another. They are among the most polite people on earth. When two of them meet they embrace and each kisses the head and the hands of the other. I am told that Raisuli has discontinued all such greetings for fear he may be entertaining a Judas whose kiss may be accompanied by the heart thrust of a dagger or the drawing of a knife across his throat.

Indeed, the way Raisuli is now handling his callers is somewhat in the style of Russell Sage after he was almost blown up by dynamite. Mr. Sage made his visitors talk to him through a little window like that for general letter delivery in a post office. Raisuli makes all strangers stand

Most of the inhabitants of Fez prefer water from the muddy river to that from the pure springs in certain parts of the city, one of which supplies this fountain of marvellous mosaic.

Since they first came to Morocco in the thirteenth century, the Jews have controlled the bulk of the business. Formerly required by law to wear only black garments, most of them still do so.

at the door while they talk and he remains at the other end of the room.

Raisuli is now at war with the tribes on the other side of Tangier, and the fighting goes on even in the city itself. These rival Berbers sometimes pepper one another across the market space, foreigners being advised at such times to keep out of the way. As Raisuli now holds the town, this condition makes it difficult for the tribes of the eastern mountains to do their buying and selling in Tangier, which is their chief marketing place. They have been hard up for supplies, and only yesterday they sent in their women, knowing that on account of their sex Raisuli would not attack them. The women brought in their wares upon donkeys, expecting to carry back food. The bandit's gallantry, however, did not extend to the beasts of burden, so he captured the donkeys, and sent home the women, old and young, weeping and wailing. The result of this will be a truce sooner or later, but there may be a pitched battle before that occurs.

At present, every traveller carries a gun and every native who goes about the country has his rifle and knife. I am told, however, that the Moroccans look upon life as of but little account. They are always fighting with one another. Families have feuds which last from generation to generation and there are feuds also between the tribes. The only rule is that of the stronger and the country is fast approaching a state of anarchy.

Indeed, these conditions make me think of what Colonel Pettit said to me during our war with Spain when I had landed at Zamboanga in the Philippines to see something of the Moros there. I had called at the military headquarters and had asked the commander if it would be

23

safe for me to go through the Moro villages. **Colonel** Pettit replied:

"I think so, my boy, but I would advise you first to tie your head on with a string."

It is about the same here. One is safe enough if one does not get into the wrong combination; and there are plenty of wrong ones. These Mohammedans are more fanatical than our Moros. They call all Christians dogs, and the Moor does not want them in his school, his home, or his church. A Frenchman who tried to enter a mosque at Fez not long ago was shot dead at the door.

Since it is against the law of the Koran to have one's picture taken I find it dangerous to use a camera. The average Mohammedan scowls when he sees one pointed at him; and many of the Moslems would fight rather than be photographed. Just yesterday, for instance, my son Jack, a husky young fellow of twenty-one, who is making this trip with me, tried to enter a *fondak*, or Mohammedan hotel and stable combined, which was near the market. He happened to have his camera open at the time. Inside there was a crowd of Moslems made up largely of men from the interior. Catching sight of the camera, they thought Jack intended to take their photographs, and rising in a body they jumped for him and our dragoman, Hadj Mohammed. Both fought them back with their sticks, and after a time we made our way off.

One cannot really understand the situation in Morocco until one considers the people. These Moors are not like our Negroes, whose ancestors came from across the Sahara in the lands bordering the Gulf of Guinea. Those people are as black as your boots, and as barbarous as any tribes on the face of the earth. They are low in intelligence and

24

are terribly debased, while the Moors have brains which will compare with our own. About the only black Afri-cans here are those who have been brought across the desert from the Sudan to be sold as slaves. There are, however, many mulattoes, the offspring of Negroes and Moors.

The population of Morocco, all told, is perhaps about six millions. A census has never been taken, and by some the number is estimated to be much higher. The majority of the people are Berbers, or Kabyles, and after them come the Arabs and the Jews.

The Berbers have a language of their own and once had their own religion. To-day they are about all Moham-medans and, like true believers in the Prophet, resent the foreign invasion. They do not want to pay taxes, and not long ago, when one of the Sultan's officials demanded the tenth of the crop of a certain tribe, the chief replied:

"If the Sultan wants taxes let him come himself for them. We will mould them into silver bullets and deposit them in his person." That tax has not yet been collected.

The Arabs came in with the Mohammedan invasion many centuries ago and have mixed more or less with the Berbers. Some are nomadic Bedouins, living in the oases of the Sahara or on the edge of that desert, while a large number are farmers on the rich plains of Morocco. Arabs are found also in the cities.

The Jews number perhaps two hundred thousand. They live in all the cities and here and there in the villages. As I have said, they are the real business men of the country, doing most of the banking and having the prin-cipal wholesale and retail shops. Many of the chiefs of the large tribes are financed by Jews, who lend money to the Moorish officials as well. Most of these Jews came originally from Spain, and some belong to families which have lived hundreds of years in Morocco. They are universally despised, are sometimes stoned by the Moorish boys in the streets, and are forced to do certain menial work. The name *mellah*, given to the Jewish quarter in the Moorish town, means "salt" and may have been given because of one special job which the Jews have; that is, the pickling of the heads of rebels before they are fastened up over the gates of the cities as a warning to traitors.

Almost every Moroccan city has three parts: one belonging to the government, where the officials live; another containing the stores and the homes of the Moors; and the third, the quarter of the despised Jews. There are but few large towns and all are of about the same character as Tangier, being made up mostly of box-like, flat-roofed buildings surrounded by walls. These walls are entered by gates, so that the city can be tightly closed at night. The business is largely done in markets, although all towns have shops and bazaars.

The cities of Morocco, however, contain but a small part of the population. The masses live in movable tents or in villages of huts of stone chinked with mud and thatched with straw. Many of the huts are altogether of straw, while not a few are of sun-dried brick.

How squalidly these people live one can see by riding a few miles out into the country. The average village is like a collection of falling straw stacks, each surrounded by a hedge of cactus, the leaves of which have thorns as sharp as fine needles. Each house stands alone and no foreigner dares peep in through the gate or look over the hedge. The cactus usually encloses a small bare yard into which the cattle, sheep, goats, horses, pigs, camels, and chickens belonging to the family are driven at night.

Such villages have no streets and no pavements whatever. After sunset they grow as dark as a pocket, except where the houses are lighted by candles or perhaps by American kerosene. The villagers are farmers who own lands near by. No one lives on his farm, and in looking over the landscape one sees no barns or fences. There are only bare fields or the crops.

In the pasture lands the sheep, goats, pigs, and other animals are watched by a shepherd, who is often employed by several farmers at so much for each animal, the flocks thus feeding together. At night, when he drives them all to the village, every one makes a bee-line for its own individual home. No one would think of leaving even a goat outside the town after dark for fear of thieves.

Often a half dozen or more of the villages make up the home of one tribe. Such a tribe is governed by a chief who collects certain taxes and acts as the leader in the wars with other tribes. This is the condition throughout the Sultan's empire, which is rather an aggregation of wild pastoral and agricultural tribes than a kingdom or empire in our sense of the word. Each tribe cares only for itself and its own particular region, and there is, I am told, no such thing as a real country or state of Morocco. The only binding cords between the tribes are those of religion. They are one in fanatical hatred of the Christian and all that belongs to him. They want nothing to do with him and resent his presence here.

Morocco is in a sad state. The army has dwindled to a few hundred troops, and the Sultan has no soldiers to speak of outside of Fez. When Menehbi was minister,

27

His Majesty had about sixteen thousand troops, and his power was such that the various tribes sent in tribute and presents worth many thousands of dollars. Every tribe sent one or more horses, many sent large sums of money, and there were other gifts of value. Now the government has practically no control over the tribes, and the people are refusing to pay taxes or to send in tribute to the Sultan.

Such are the conditions within a mile of Tangier, the chief seaport of Morocco. In the interior they must be far worse. There are many families in tents, but all are on a constant lookout for thieves and brigands and nearly every tribe is at war with its neighbours.

CHAPTER V

BEHIND THE SCENES WITH THE SULTAN

COME behind the scenes with me and take a look at Mulai Abd el-Aziz, the Sultan of Morocco. He is the ruler of the best part of northwestern Africa; his empire is almost one twelfth the size of the whole United States and more than five million Berbers and Moors look upon him with reverence.

The Sultan is just twenty-six years of age, with all the strength of full-blooded youth. He has a muddy white complexion and his slightly bloated face bears the marks of smallpox, which he had years ago. He has a straight nose, a large mouth, a long upper lip, and a somewhat receding chin. Like all his people, he never shaves his face, but his curly black full beard is so thin that it does not show much in the picture. He has rather a blasé air, wearing in ordinary conversation a somewhat bored look. He seems to have sucked dry the orange of power and luxury and to care more to take things easy and have a good time than to rule. Indeed, I understand that he would be glad to leave the throne, for he thinks the game of governing a country as turbulent as this is not worth the candle. He is fast losing prestige with his own people by consorting with foreigners, and were it not for his position in the Mohammedan hierarchy he would ere this have had to step down and out.

29

All the rest of the Mohammedans of the world acknowledge some kind of allegiance to the Sultan of Turkey.
This is true of our Moros and of the fifty-odd million
Mussulmans of India as well as of the lesser number in
Turkey and Egypt. But these Moors will not let the
Turkish Sultan send a representative here. They acknowledge no allegiance to him, considering that only the family
of this young man has the right to the title of Commander
and Ruler of the Faithful.

Indeed, the sultans of Morocco are perhaps the most
blue-blooded monarchs on earth. Abd el-Aziz, the thirty-
fifth lineal descendant of Ali, the uncle and son-in-law of
the prophet Mohammed, is the fifteenth monarch in his
own dynasty. His father was the famed Mulai Hassan,
who was sultan for twenty-one years, during which he
ruled with an iron hand. When about to die he chose as
his successor Abd el-Aziz, his son by a Circassian slave
imported from Turkey, although he had other and older
sons.

The Sultan is the high priest of the religion of this
country as well as its chief executive. He is called the
great Imam, or "Prince of True Believers," and he prays
for all. One of his chief elements of strength is the power
of conferring blessings, which has come down to him
from Mohammed. He is supposed to have this direct from
God, but if any other man of his family could make
the people believe that he had this power in a greater
degree, he could easily raise a rebellion and oust Mulai
Abd el-Aziz from the throne.

This was attempted by Bu Hamara, the so-called son of
the She-Ass, who falsely claimed to be an elder brother
of Abd el-Aziz, and who, by sleight-of-hand tricks, made

Sultan Mulai Abd el-Aziz with his extravagant dissipations led the powers a merry dance in Morocco before France succeeded in dethroning him.

Airplanes carrying passengers and mail operate regularly between Toulouse, in southern France, and the Atlantic coast of Morocco. This photograph shows the Lyautey stadium in Casablanca, the Moroccan terminus of the trans-Mediterranean air service.

The present Sultan of Morocco is permitted to have his council, but the word of the French Resident-General is the real law of the land.

the people think he was performing miracles. He started a revolution, and the soldiers broke out into an insurrection, notwithstanding the fact that their officers gave them a flogging and dusted out their mouths with red pepper for speaking against His Majesty. This Bu Hamara was eventually put down, but the rebellion was quelled by a compromise whereby the son of the She-Ass has, like Raisuli, been bribed with a fat office. He is now ruling a large section of the country. This would seem to put a premium on a second rebellion.

Like the old emperors of China, the Sultan makes sacrifices for his whole nation. This he does by killing a sheep on every Bairam, or Mohammedan Easter. At this time every good Moorish family is supposed to offer up sacrifices, and it is estimated that as many as thirty thousand sheep are killed on that day in the city of Fez. The sheep are brought in from the surrounding country, and mutton prices rise to such an extent that a good fat ram or ewe will bring thirty dollars. If there were such a custom in America the market would surely be cornered.

The sheep killing is started by the Sultan, surrounded by a large concourse of people. One of the holy preachers first sings out a sermon, after which the sheep is handed over to His Majesty. He cuts its throat, and as the blood gushes forth the bands play and the cannon thunder. The news is sent out all over the city, whereupon the sacrificing begins, extending to every part of Morocco.

Bairam is the great festal occasion of all the year. The Moors come out in their good clothes, the soldiers have new uniforms, and the people who, like pious Moslems everywhere, have been fasting throughout Ramazan, which is their Lent, give themselves up to rejoicing. The chiefs of the various tribes are then supposed to send presents to the Sultan, and in the past vast sums have been received. Some tribes bring money, often running into thousands of dollars, some horses, and some slaves, a Negress being a common gift.

During the present year the gifts were few and the horses poor. This was the result of the recent rebellions, and was brought about by the association of the Sultan with Europeans and the jealousy and distrust with which his people regard him.

Indeed, the monarch's tastes seem to be Christian rather than Mohammedan. He is so fond of Western methods that he would, if he could, introduce them into his empire. He has made some attempts to do so, but his people object, and this is one cause of his unpopularity. He is, notwithstanding, an independent young man and persists in courting the favour of the foreigners. I am told that he spends a part of every day with Europeans, and that he is not at all exclusive in his selection of them. One high-class Moor here complains to me that His Majesty allows common merchants and other tradesmen to come to the palace, while others tell me that he has spent millions on all sorts of foreign knickknacks which some of his Christian friends have begged him to buy.

One of his extravagances is a camera of solid gold which cost him ten thousand dollars. At the same time he bought two thousand dollars' worth of printing paper and thirty-three thousand dollars' worth of other supplies. His photographic outfit, in addition to the camera, cost him, all told, thirty-five thousand dollars, a large part of which went, as a matter of course, into the pockets of those who ordered it.

Another recent purchase is a bedstead of crystal mirrors with pendants like a chandelier. The story goes that he sees three images of himself whenever he crawls into bed, and that the pendants jingle when he turns over. He has bicycles made of aluminum on which he delights to play bicycle polo with his friends. He learns all sorts of games easily, and can do no end of bicycle tricks. He will ride up a steep plank and down again, and he has ruined several fine wheels by crashing into the walls.

The Sultan has a number of automobiles, a London hansom, and a coach of state. His gold coach, which cost many thousands of dollars, now stands outside the palace at the mercy of the weather.

In the meantime, the Sultan's foreign friends who have ordered these things for him are making fat fortunes, and are working the young man for all he is worth. Every foreign thing he buys costs him ten times what it is worth, and his ministers and friends absorb the profits. They are already rolling in luxury. In fact, everyone about Abd el-Aziz steals both from him and his people. I am told that the whole income of Morocco has gone into extravagant expenditures. The taxes bring in something like five million dollars a year, yet Morocco is now several hundred thousand dollars in debt.

One of the Europeans here tells me he thinks that the Sultan has salted down a pretty penny for a rainy day, while another courtier says that he is, strange to say, almost mean in the expenditures which come out of his own immediate treasury. He will quibble about an outlay of one hundred dollars if the money is to be paid down on the nail, and, at the same time, will dash off without thinking an order for one of his custom houses to pay over a sum of ten thousand or more in taxes.

Any one who understands the jealousy and hatred which the Moors feel for Christians can easily see how unpopular such actions on the part of their ruler must be. The better classes are no fools, and it is hard for them to respect even a sultan who does such foolish and irreligious things. As I have said, they are opposed on religious grounds to pictures and photographs, so the Sultan's golden kodak is particularly offensive to them, while the fact that he is really a good photographer does not better the matter. They do not approve of his buying a yacht and having it carried inland to Fez to be played with on the little river near there. They are angry about the crown he ordered at a cost of a hundred thousand dollars or so, for it is against the Mohammedan religion for the Sultan to wear a crown, and his people objected especially to his coronation coach.

As a Moor's home life is not supposed to be known outside his immediate family, no European ever sees the Sultan's harem. I doubt whether any Mohammedan man except his own eunuchs has ever crossed its threshold, and it would be improper to question His Majesty as to the health of the multitudinous ladies of his household. Nevertheless, the gossip gets out in one way or another, and I am able to give you some idea of this feature of the Sultan's establishment.

According to the Koran every man has the right to four wives and no end of concubines. The palaces are large and the Sultan himself lives on the first floor, in a suite of big rooms, at the four corners of which his wives have their apartments. Each wife has her own quarters and

34

Some splendid examples of the finest Moorish architecture are to be seen in the houses of wealthy Arabs. They are especially rich in carved woods, mosaic, and tiling.

Wealthy Moors love luxury. In their homes the light falls through curtains embroidered in gold and silver upon beautiful hand-woven rugs and deep, soft divans.

servants, but all are subject to the rule of certain slave women called *arifas*, Negro concubines who were especially favoured by Mulai Hassan, this sultan's father. The ruler's real wives must be chosen from the different branches of the royal family, so that he is forced to marry his cousins.

The Sultan of Morocco is frequently presented with secondary wives or concubines by his tribal chiefs. The girls are often sent up for his approval, especially at the feast of Bairam, and he can select for his household such as may take his fancy. In addition he has a large number of coal-black Negresses, purchased from time to time in the local slave markets, and also other women imported from the Orient.

This potentate has many palaces. He has quarters in nearly every town in his dominions, and the governor's home here in Tangier belongs to him. He has four different capitals: one in southern Morocco, one in central Morocco, one at Tafilelt, and another at Fez. This last is the largest, and everything there is managed on a vast scale. The palace is surrounded by walls. It is in the Dar-el-Makhzen, where all the government officials live. The buildings contain no end of bedrooms and living rooms, as well as a large kitchen and dairy. They swarm with servants, both male and female. The kitchens are managed by Negro cooks, and among the other manservants are the "men of the bath," "men of the tea," and "men of the water." There are also "men of the bed" and "men of the mat." The bath men have to do with the imperial chamber, the tea men make the royal tea, using the best of the green leaves and mixing them with mint. The bed men have charge of the Sultan's tent when he camps, and the mat men bring his prayer rug and spread it out for him at the hours for prayer. In addition there are Negro men slaves who take charge of the Sultan's horses and mules; there are others who walk behind him, when he goes out for an airing, to flick off the flies, and a third set that carries the imperial parasol to shut out the rays of the sun.

In the harem itself, or rather in his own private apartments, the Sultan is attended by women only. His servants are concubines and slaves. Like the manservants, they are organized into classes, each slave having her special job. He has "girls of the wash basin," "girls of the soap," and "girls of the towel." There is one set of females who help him at his bath and another whose business it is to serve his meals. His Majesty now eats alone, although, as long as his mother was alive, he took his meals with her. He eats with his fingers, and I doubt not in so doing considers himself more cleanly than you or me. The Mohammedans have a saying that everyone knows whether one has washed his fingers, but no one can tell who has washed the knives and forks.

Before eating the young sovereign laves his hands in scented warm water, repeating this performance at the close of his meal. His food is so cooked that it can be easily broken, and much of his meat is served in small bits. His chief meal is at midday. He also takes something on rising and a light supper in the evening.

As far as I can learn, the Moorish ruler has a soft snap. He works only in the morning, devoting the afternoon to his foreign friends, to playing polo, billiards, bicycling, or any other amusement which may suit him. His evenings are spent with the numerous members of his family. He rises early, drinks a cup of coffee, and then says his prayers. In doing the latter he faces toward Mecca and goes through all the motions prescribed by the most rigid Mohammedan rules. He has a mosque in his palace grounds which he attends every Friday.

At the close of his morning devotions His Majesty goes from his palace to the great buildings where he holds his court and where the various officials have their offices. Here he enters a small room off by itself and sends for such of his ministers as he desires to see. He leaves his work largely to his officials, doing no more of it himself than he can help. At noon he stops for dinner, after which he takes a smoke and a nap, rising about three o'clock. He frequently has music in his palace and is said to play well on the violin and guitar. He has more than one hundred musicians and all sorts of instruments. He has a piano upon which he drums at times, his mother having taught him to play.

From a Moorish standpoint, the Sultan is well educated. He can recite a great part of the Koran and is well up in Moslem law. He gets papers from all parts of the world and has a clipping bureau, which furnishes him with extracts on all matters relating to Morocco.

He has a cabinet, consisting of a grand vizier, a secretary of state, a secretary of the interior, and a secretary of war. He has also a chief chamberlain, a chief treasurer, and a chief administrator of customs. He has had an army of ten thousand or fifteen thousand men, and at times as many as twenty thousand troops in different parts of Morocco. The soldiers are said to be armed with good weapons and to have a few batteries of field guns.

Within the last year the army seems to have grown

weaker and weaker. The rebellion of Bu Hamara, the capture of Perdicaris and the ransom forced from the Sultan by Raisuli, together with the foreign complications, have made His Majesty so unpopular that his support is drifting away from him.

One of the big mistakes Sultan Abd el-Aziz made was in dismissing his minister of war and chief adviser, Si el-Mehdi el-Menehbi. He was in high favour and the real ruler of Morocco until the rebellion of the so-called Son of the She-Ass, who claimed to be the elder brother of the Sultan, but after that was forced to resign. Menehbi's excuse for leaving Fez was that he wanted to make a pilgrimage to Mecca. He went there via the Mediterranean, and after getting back settled in Tangier, becoming a British subject and thereby protecting himself against any possible persecution from his enemies who had taken his place with the Sultan.

It is said that Menehbi saved a lot of money while he was one of the Sultan's chief officials, and that instead of burying it in the walls of his house at Fez or under its floors, as is sometimes done by the Moors, he deposited it in the Bank of England to his own order. This prevented his enemies getting possession of his fortune. After his settlement here in Tangier he withdrew the money, and invested a great part of it in a large apartment house and other buildings. His own home is one of the finest in the city, and I doubt not will compare favourably with any private home in the country.

It was in Tangier that I had an interview with this interesting character. Travelling upon my mule through the narrow streets, I rode with my party by the *Kasbah*, or the governor's palace, past the soldiers and officials

Rabat is the real capital and administrative centre of Morocco under the French, and the headquarters of the Resident-General.

France began the opening up of Morocco with light military railways which are now being replaced with permanent standard-gauge construction.

Even in the doorways of their own homes, the Moorish women are
quick to cover their faces if a Christian chances to pass by.

sitting at the gate of the city, and on into the country. About a half mile from the city gates we came to a walled inclosure with a plain, unpretentious door. We knocked upon this and it was opened by Negro slaves, who took charge of our mules. Passing in through a sort of porter's lodge, where a half-dozen other slaves were sitting, we found ourselves in a great court or park surrounded by Moorish buildings, the rooms of which looked out upon it. This park was made up largely of gardens filled with beautiful flowers and semi-tropical plants and trees. One section of it contained a tennis court with a cement floor as smooth as marble, where the ex-minister delights to play tennis with his European friends. There is a central path through the gardens down which we walked until we came into two great reception rooms, where the war minister receives his men friends. Passing through the first set of parlours, which are floored with mosaic and luxuriously furnished, we came into a large room walled with glass looking out upon the Atlantic Ocean. The house is built on a high bluff overhanging the sea and the mountains of Spain were in plain sight across the waves. We could hear the surf roar as it dashed itself against the rocks below.

At the entrance to this room stood two tall clocks of the kind that sell in the United States for five hundred dollars apiece and play chimes at the striking of the hours. The tiled floor was covered with oriental rugs, the great divans were upholstered in rich red Morocco leather, while about the walls were cases containing rare china, swords, rifles, and other weapons, inlaid with gold and silver. The surroundings were those of a man of taste, and this was my impression of the ex-minister when he appeared.

39

Si el-Mehdi el-Menehbi is a typical Moor of the better class and of a kind one does not expect to find in what is generally known as one of the black spots of this black continent. He would make one of the handsomest Othellos who ever trod the stage. He is tall, straight, and fine looking, his Moorish costume making him look even taller than he actually is. He has a light complexion and, like all Moorish men, wears a full beard, his whiskers being brown and curly and as fine as spun silk. A broad forehead with large hazel eyes may be seen below his white turban. His nose is straight and his cheek bones are high. His costume consisted of a long white woollen gown, or *burnouse,* with a hood at the back, and sleeves so wide that they showed his forearms to the elbows. The skin was as white as yours or mine. As we watched, he now and then smiled, showing a good set of strong teeth, and he twice perceptibly yawned.

In the course of my brief interview with him, I asked Mr. Menehbi whether his people made good soldiers.

"Both the Berbers and Moors are brave to an excess," he replied. "They have excellent fighting stuff in them, and if the time comes when the tribes can be organized and welded together, an army of a hundred thousand men could be raised. As it is now, each tribe furnishes a certain quota of mounted men and these altogether make up the army. One large clan may furnish two thousand soldiers, a second a regiment, and a third only a company. Such soldiers are officered by the tribal chiefs, who are subordinate to the general of the Sultan. There are so many quarrels among the different divisions that it is difficult to harmonize and organize them. They are always warring among themselves, and it would be only through religious feeling that they could be formed into a compact army organization."

In closing our conversation, I asked Mr. Menehbi to send, through me, a few words of greeting to the American people, saying, "Your Excellency is about the most progressive man in Morocco, and I should like to take from you a word of greeting to what we consider the most progressive nation of the Western world."

The Sultan's ex-war minister smiled at this. His face, however, soon grew serious, and he said:

"I have a great admiration for you Americans, and I hope I shall be able to cross the Atlantic to visit you. The only message I have for you is that you should study this country, and cultivate closer trade relations with it. We have here some six million inhabitants, and we are now large consumers of cottons and other things which Americans make. Our homes are lighted chiefly by American petroleum, and our people wear clothes made of stuff grown by you. Your raw cotton, however, goes to England; and the English do the weaving and sell us the goods. I understand that you have cotton mills of your own. Why not make the goods yourselves and get all the profit? We Moroccans are friendly to you, and we would be glad to trade with you; but as it is our chief supplies come from the various countries of Europe, mostly from England, Spain, Germany, and France."

CHAPTER VI

IN SPANISH AFRICA

I AM in what is about the last of Spain's colonial possessions. In the sixteenth and seventeenth centuries she owned the best part of the New World. If we include the Louisiana Purchase, which we bought from France after Spain had let it slip through her fingers, she had the cream of North America. She had almost the whole of South America excepting Brazil. The best of the West Indies were hers. Cortez poured the treasures of Montezuma into her royal coffers, and Pizarro, shoeing his horses with solid silver, robbed the Incas of Peru and sent gold-freighted galleons sailing across to his Spanish sovereign. The Philippines added to these sources of wealth, and for a long time two great golden streams rolled across the Atlantic and the Pacific to Spain's treasure chests. In her colonial possessions she was then the richest of all the Powers. To-day by mismanagement and oppression she has become the poorest, and since her war with us, when she lost Cuba, Porto Rico, and the Philippines, there have been "none so poor to do her reverence."

Indeed, all the land which Spain has left outside her own boundaries is in Africa, and even here her territories are the ragtag and bobtail of the continent. They cover a bit over a hundred thousand square miles but are largely desert sand or fever swamps, and the tillable lands

42

suitable for white men which they contain are not as big as some counties of Texas, while their total population is only about that of Cleveland.

In contrast with this, two of the great Powers of Europe have been quietly gobbling up the fat things of this mighty continent. France has the lion's share, if we include the Island of Madagascar. She has more than one third of all Africa. A vast deal of her territory, however, is in the Desert of Sahara, being made up of stone and sand which might form good building materials, but which are of no value where they lie. Great Britain comes next among the national landowners, with close to another third of the continent.

Spain owns in Africa the Island of Fernando Po and a small tract on the mainland on the Gulf of Guinea. Her country there contains about nine thousand square miles, or a little more than the area of the state of Massachusetts. The land is swampy and so unhealthful that it has become known as the "White Man's Grave." It is covered with a luxuriant vegetation and produces some India rubber and palm oil. The only foreigners are a few Spanish, French, and English merchants. The natives are among the most degraded of the Africans. They are Negroes of the lowest type, and slavery is common. Fernando Po itself has convict settlements from which the criminals seldom return.

North of the Gulf of Guinea, between Morocco and French West Africa, Spain has a wide strip of land ruled by the governor of the Canary Islands. It stretches for several hundred miles along the Atlantic, but it is one of the worst parts of the whole Desert of Sahara. It has neither rivers nor oases of any value, and is very thinly populated. This region of Rio de Oro is golden only in name.

Spain's northern zone in Morocco is a mountainous strip stretching from Larache on the Atlantic to Melilla on the Mediterranean, and from Ceuta in the north to Wazzan in the south. Ceuta is just across the way from Gibraltar. I passed it on my way to Tangier. It can be reached from Algeciras by a government steamer which takes over dispatches and mail every day. It consists of a rock on which the town stands and where the fortifications are.

Ceuta was where the Moors embarked when they first crossed over from Africa to invade Spain many centuries ago, and they dwell in all the country about it to-day. They still so dislike the Spaniards that it is impossible for the Ceuta people to go back into the interior unless accompanied by soldiers. There are stories that the Moors never mention the Spaniards without adding in parenthesis "whom Allah curse."

Melilla, which I visited, is the chief town of what is called Spanish Morocco. It lies on the Mediterranean several hundred miles east of Ceuta and about thirty-six hours by steamer across the way from Malaga.

Melilla has long been noted for its Spanish military prison. There are eight thousand soldiers stationed here, a large number of whom have come as punishment for desertion or other transgressions of military discipline. Spain has often had to fight the Moors to keep her hold on this little patch of Morocco, and at such times has had tens of thousands of soldiers in Melilla and its vicinity. I cannot imagine a worse place. It makes one think of the inscription over the door to Dante's hell, which reads:

44

IN SPANISH AFRICA

"All hope abandon, ye who enter here."

The town is built upon a mighty bluff which runs out into the sea.   There are thirsty hills all about, each with a great white round fort upon it, and large iron-barred barracks in and about the city.   Outside these large buildings the houses are one- and two-story structures of brick and stucco painted all colours of the rainbow.   They are built Spanish fashion in blocks, with iron-barred windows as prison-like as their surroundings.

The inhabitants are chiefly Spanish Jews and motley Moors.   The Jews have little stores in the city and the Moors sell in bazaars just inside the walls, where each turbaned merchant stands in a sort of hole with his goods piled around him.   There is a Moorish encampment near by, and a caravan trade is carried on with all western and southern Morocco.

I have not found the natives here any too friendly. When we landed and showed our passports describing us as Americans the soldiers scowled and were none too pleasant, although I succeeded in getting some excellent photographs of them during my stay.   In the town, when it became known that we were Americans, the boys and men gathered around us with a hostile air.   One of them threw a stone the size of a man's fist at our carriage and narrowly missed hitting me.   As it was, it struck the door handle and bent it.   Our coachman jumped down and ran after the boy, but we concluded not to give the offender over to the police, and indeed were rather glad when we were safe out of the town.

It seems odd to think of pirates carrying on their trade in the twentieth century, but piracy is a regular business with certain of the tribes of the Riff Mountains near here. They do not go out with large ships and attack the vessels of the Mediterranean as they did at the beginning of the last century, but they rob and sometimes kill the sailors of the smaller craft when the bad seas drive them upon the shore. About a century ago the whole coast of Morocco was infested with pirates, and there were sea robbers all the way from the Strait of Gilbraltar to Tripoli. Just before entering the Strait one sees on the north coast the town of Tarifa with its old Moorish forts, from which the Moors swooped down upon passing vessels and made them pay tribute. From that town and that practice came our word "tariff."

About the same time the Moors of Morocco and Algeria were preying on all the commerce of the Mediterranean, and nearly every great nation submitted to their exactions. We did so for some years, but in 1815 declared war upon these pirates, and were the first to bring them to time. We had trouble with the Dey of Algiers and sent Commodore Decatur over to tell him that Americans would pay him tribute no longer. The Dey insisted until Decatur pointed his guns at the city of Algiers. Then the Dey began to weaken. He sent out word to our Commodore suggesting that if he would pretend to storm the town, using powder only, the tribute might be omitted. Commodore Decatur replied that cannon balls always went with American powder, and that if the Dey received the one he must take the other. Soon afterward Decatur captured some of the Algerian ships and the Dey finally had to pay him damages to the amount of about sixty thousand dollars and to conclude a treaty which renounced all tribute from Americans for the future.

Time was when the Barbary pirates not only seized the

Through years of fighting the tribesmen, Spain has clung to her small slice of Moroccan territory, the chief port of which is Melilla.

There are always Spanish soldiers in Melilla, the base of military operations against the natives of the interior.

In proportion to the area he rules, the British Governor of Gibraltar is one of the highest paid officials on earth. His principality covers two square miles and his salary is $25,000 a year.

So violently do the Moors hate the Spaniard that mention of him in their café political discussions is always followed by the phrase: "May Allah curse him."

ships but enslaved their captives. Captain John Smith served as such a slave. Shortly after our refusal to pay tribute the English did likewise and bombarded Algiers. The French followed in a war with the pirates, and in 1820 they threw the Dey from his throne and took the ten million dollars in gold and silver which they found in his treasury.

I saw a blind beggar going through the streets here this morning. His eyes had been burned out with red-hot pokers by one of the Berber chiefs of the mountains near by, and he presented a horrible sight. I learned that this was done as a punishment for stealing, and that it is not an uncommon practice in certain parts of Morocco. At the first theft the man's hand is cut off, while at the second his eyes are burned out. Sometimes a foot is also cut off, after which the thief must move about upon crutches with a boy to lead him.

During my stay in Tangier I rode one morning out into the country and made some photographs of a village which had taken summary vengeance upon an under official who had been unjust and oppressive in collecting taxes for the *basha* who held office prior to the present governor. This official was caught as he passed through the village and his eyes were burned out. That was not long ago, and it shows that such crimes are still possible in this land of Morocco.

On the other hand, a recent sultan of Morocco, Mulai Hassan, inflicted punishments on his subjects which were horrible to an extreme. One of these might be called "salting to death." It consisted of cutting four great gashes out of the palms of the hands of the offender and filling them with salt. The fingers were then bent inward and fitted tightly into the holes or cuts. After that each hand was sewed up in green rawhide which shrank as it dried, causing terrible pain. In some cases the rawhide was sprinkled with lemon juice, which, it is said, rapidly accelerated the shrinking of the hide, often forcing the finger nails clear through the palm and out of the back of the hand. After this the criminal was taken to jail and left without water. The torture was such that he usually died within a few days.

Despite the wildness and disorder of her Moroccan possessions, Spain clings to her foothold in North Africa and talks of running a railway tunnel under the Strait of Gibraltar as part of a line to extend southwestward to the coast of Africa at Rio de Oro. Perhaps, too, she hopes some day to regain Gibraltar, her old stepping stone to Africa. I spent some time at Gibraltar on my way to Morocco and had a good chance to inspect the outside of the fortifications and the harbour improvements. The largest of the naval war vessels can be drydocked there, while the deep harbour is big enough for the whole British Atlantic fleet.

The rock of Gibraltar lies at the end of a narrow neck of land connecting it with the Spanish peninsula. One could walk across this neck in a few minutes. The town of Gibraltar, which contains something like thirty thousand people, is situated upon it with its houses extending along the lower sides of the rock itself.

This rock is a gigantic piece of solid limestone rising almost straight from the water on the side facing the Mediterranean Sea to a height nearly as great as that of the Blue Ridge Mountains in Virginia. If you could put two Washington Monuments one on the top of the other and on the top of these a spire as tall as the dome of the Capitol, you would have just about the height of Gibraltar. The rock is about three miles long and less than a mile wide at its greatest width.

Approaching it from the sea, one sees many portholes here and there along the sides. They come from the tunnels within. The whole rock has been tunneled. It has eighty miles of galleries burrowed through it until it is a honeycomb of chambers. The fortifications have, of course, the finest of modern guns and other war machinery. Only a few parts of them are shown to visitors, and only the British soldiers and War Office know just how the works are constructed and defended. There are undoubtedly many big guns, some of which would land shot in Africa across the way, for the strait is only about twelve miles wide at that point.

As Gibraltar is practically a free port, tobacco and everything else is cheaper there than in Spain, which is some two miles away across the isthmus. The land between is called "the neutral ground," and there is now a high woven-wire fence across it, which is guarded day and night by the Spanish customs officers. The fence was put up in order to prevent tobacco being carried across without duty being paid. The smugglers had trained dogs to carry parcels from one side to the other. The way they did it was to dress up one of their number as a Spanish customs officer, and then, having tied a bag of tobacco to the neck of the pup they wished to train, they would drive him in the direction of this bogus official. As soon as the dog came near, the man in the customs uniform would run for him, and if he caught him would give him a good thrashing. The pup, soon learning that all men so dressed were his enemies, naturally gave them a wide berth for ever after. The dogs were brought from the Spanish side to Gibraltar and there loaded with tobacco. They would start home on the run, and until this fence was erected no customs official could get within a mile of them.

The British always keep several thousand soldiers at Gibraltar. The place is a crown colony with a governor-general, who is also commander-in-chief. In proportion to the area which he rules the Governor of Gibraltar is one of the best paid officials on earth. His principality covers about two square miles and his salary is twenty-five thousand dollars a year. Our president must look after about three million six hundred thousand square miles. If he were paid at the same rate per square mile as is the Governor-general of Gibraltar he would be receiving the enormous sum of forty-five billion dollars a year.

In her forests in the Atlas Mountains, Morocco has an asset of great value which the French expect to develop in the years to come.

Every house in Oran has a view of the Mediterranean. This second largest city in Algeria is built on hills rising in three great terraces from a beautiful bay.

CHAPTER VII

IN ORAN

I HAVE left Morocco and am now travelling in Algeria, another important part of African France. The richest of the French colonial possessions lie along the southern shores of the Mediterranean, and of them all Algeria is perhaps the best. It is a winter garden for France, furnishing vegetables for all of her cities, besides being the granary which supplies a large part of her flour.

Many look upon this country as a little strip of mountain and desert. The truth is that the part of it lying along the sea and running back up the foothills of the Atlas has some of the richest soil upon earth. This is the Tell, which includes a territory about as large as New York and Massachusetts combined, running clear across Algeria and on into Tunisia. The Tell for centuries has grown the wheat of this part of the world. The Phœnicians and Carthaginians built empires upon it and it was for a long time one of the principal bread baskets of imperial Rome. It was fought for by the Greeks and the Vandals. It became a Mohammedan land in the eighth century, when it was conquered by the Arabs

Algeria consists of these rich lands of the Tell, of the high plateaus of the Atlas just south of them, and of the foothills running down into the Sahara. The country is just about as long from east to west as from Philadelphia

51

to Cleveland and as wide as from Washington to Boston by way of New York. It contains as much land as all New England, with New York, New Jersey, and Louisiana added thereto. Northern Algeria, or Algeria proper, is divided into three departments, each beginning at the Mediterranean and cutting across to the Sahara. The largest of these is at the east and is known as Constantine. It is almost as big as Minnesota and has about the same number of people. The next is Algiers, which is not far from the size of Missouri, with a population of sixteen hundred thousand, and the other is the western province of Oran, where I am writing. Oran is just about the size of Pennsylvania, and contains more than one million people. Southern Algeria consists of the four territories of Ain Sefra, Ghardaia, Touggourt, and the Saharan oases.

The population of Algeria is a mixture of Spaniards, Italians, French, Maltese, Jews, Negroes, the white Africans known as Kabyles, or Berbers, and Arabs. The Mohammedan Arabs predominate. The Negroes were originally brought across the Sahara as slaves and sold in the market of Algiers. In some of the Algerian oases the people are nearly all Negroes, and I see many in the towns. The Negro women often act as shampooers in the Moorish bath houses, while many of the men are beggars some of whom dance about singing weird songs to the clashing of queer iron cymbals. One such followed my carriage today. His dance was a sort of a nautch dance, consisting of a continuous contortion of the hips and a twisting of the waist.

Oran has a fine harbour in a beautiful bay with a high, ragged mountain looking down upon it. East of the mountain there is a ravine or canyon with low hills extending eastward, while in and on the sides of this is the town of Oran.   There is some flat ground for the wharves, but back of them the buildings of the city climb the hills in three great terraces, giving every house an outlook over the Mediterranean Sea.

The port has all modern landing facilities, including steam cranes and electric lights.   A long breakwater has been built out at the west against which the stormy Mediterranean dashes itself in vain.   From the wharves one rides up smooth roads, which have been cut out of the sides of the mountain, to the upper parts of the city and the best hotels.

Down near the port are great warehouses filled with alfa grass, bags of wheat and oats, hogsheads of wine, and other stuff ready for export.   The wharves are piled high with such wares which are hauled up and down the hills by mules in immense drays, each carrying four or five tons.   I have seen seven huge hogsheads of wine on one dray drawn by four mules hitched tandem, and other drays carrying loads that would seem an impossibility in the United States.   Most of the traffic here goes upon two wheels, from the load of five tons on a cart with a bed twenty feet long, to a bushel or so hauled in a little store box on wheels by a donkey not much larger than a Newfoundland dog.

The Algerian mule has an odd harness.   The collar ends in three horns.   Two of them are as long as cows' horns and extend out from the shoulders.   The third, about two feet long, is just over the neck and is shaped like the horn of a rhinoceros.   These horns are hung with bells, which jingle as the animals move.   I observe that the mules have leather blankets tied on their backs. They may be for hot weather or rain. Some of the better animals have the hair clipped from their backs and sides. Many wear shoes that stick out about half an inch beyond the hoof all around. The shoes of the donkeys are made in a triangle with no opening at the back as in our horseshoes at home.

About four fifths of the people of Oran are Europeans, and were it not for Moors, Negroes, and Berbers sprinkled through every crowd, a person might imagine himself in one of the smaller cities of France. The buildings are just like those of French towns. They are usually of an even height of five or six stories, built of brick and plastered with stucco of a creamy hue. They have stores and shops on the ground floor and apartments above. Most of the people live in flats or apartments. In nearly every block there is a restaurant or café, with little round iron tables on the street outside it about which a motley crowd sit drinking coffee, wine, or some other liquor as they gossip and chat, play cards or dominoes, or read the newspapers. At the same time there are little Arab bootblacks moving about begging custom, and Arab newsboys who are selling copies of the Oran daily for about two sous apiece. The city has a number of newspapers that publish dispatches from all over the world. It has schools, libraries, and a museum. There are parks scattered throughout the town, and under their trees French peasant girls are sitting and knitting; there are many bareheaded French women moving about, and now and then a Frenchman in a blouse is pushing a cart just as in France.

If one would see the African side of this French town he

The Negro juggler is always sure of a spell-bound group of children
watching his antics.

The gentlemen of Tlemçen take great pride in their costly high hats made
of straw here in their own home town.

must go back of this modern section to the hills above it. There is what is known as the "Village Nègre," which may mean Black Village or Negro Village, as one wishes to translate it. The houses in this quarter are flat-roofed and of only one story. Arabs sit on the streets chatting. Others lie at full length upon mats on the pavements wrapped up in their gowns. There are Moorish coffee houses where Arabs and Berbers sit cross-legged on the floor drinking together, and there are Arab women moving about, each seeing her way only through a peep-hole about as big around as a wedding ring, which she has made in the white, sheet-like gown wrapped tight about her. There are Berber girls with big earrings, their cheeks and chins blue with tattooing.

In addition to these figures are the jugglers and story-tellers, with crowds of Arab men and boys watching their antics or listening to their tales; shoemakers and tailors working out on the streets; water carriers and peddlers, and all the other features of the life of the native. Such black villages or native quarters are found connected with all Algerian towns. The French quarters are almost altogether French, but one has only to go to the outskirts to find all the motley crew that inhabits North Africa.

I have spent some time looking for the old Oran. The French have wiped out all vestiges of it. It was probably a port in the days of the Romans, and it must have had a long history. We know that the Mohammedans founded a town here a thousand years ago; and about fifty or sixty years before Columbus was sailing about through the West Indies, trying to find a new way to the Orient, a Spaniard wrote that Oran then had six thousand houses, one hundred and forty mosques, and schools equal to the colleges of Cordova, Granada, and Seville. Some time after this the city was taken by Spain, but it was later recaptured by the Moors and finally acquired by the French in 1831.

CHAPTER VIII

THE DELHI OF NORTH AFRICA

JOIN me and my Mohammedan dragoman, Mustapha, for a walk through the Delhi of North Africa. We are in a city that was famous when Agra was at the height of its glory, and one that has mosques and tombs containing Moorish decorations which will compare in beauty with those of the famed cities of India. There are doors of bronze in the Mosque of Sidi Bou-Medin as beautiful as those at the entrance to the Capitol at Washington, and equal in their fine workmanship to those of Ghiberti at Florence. There are temples of Mohammedan worship hundreds of years old, which have a beauty greater than the mosques of Cairo and Constantinople. Yet all were constructed when Europe was still semi-civilized and a hundred years or so before the New World of America was dreamed of. Not far from these mosques are the remains of a ruined city which surpassed Pompeii in extent and glory, and in another direction is the tomb of the man who built that city, with the Arabs praying in and about it to-day.

All this is not in Italy, Greece, or India, the countries to which we look for the monuments of the past, but in this wild continent of Africa, on the edge of turbulent Morocco, thirty miles south of the Mediterranean and about one hundred miles from Oran, the chief seaport of western Algeria. It is so far out of the line of travel that strangers

57

seldom come here, but it is one of the most interesting places on the continent.

The Tlemçen of to-day is a small city situated in a beautiful valley at an elevation about as high above the sea as the average height of the Alleghanies. It has behind it great, bare, rugged mountains, which are capped with huge rocks, making them look like fortifications thrown up by the gods, and their strength as fortifications was probably one of the reasons for the site of the ancient cities.

Another reason was the rich Tell region lying below. Standing upon the walls of Tlemçen one sees as far as the eye can reach nothing but vineyards and orchards and rich fields of grain. There are hundreds of thousands of olive trees loaded with fruit. There are fine gardens and fields of potatoes making a patchwork of green of different shades, which extends on all sides below the city until it meets the hills on the horizon. White roads, cut here and there through this expanse of green, all lead up to the walls of Tlemçen.

The city is entered by gates. It was a fortified town in the past and the French have fortified it to-day. The high walls have portholes at every few feet through which rifles and other guns can be thrust; companies of soldiers are always moving to and fro through the streets, and the citadel, where the sultans of the past had their gorgeous residences many centuries ago, is now a barracks, prison, and hospital for the Algerian troops. Its old walls and gateways still stand, and the minaret of its mosque, ninety feet high, overlooks the rest of the city.

About five hundred years ago this citadel contained some of the wonders of the world. It had a clock which

58

was celebrated two centuries before that on the Strasburg Cathedral was made, while in one of the galleries paved with marble and onyx stood a solid silver tree upon which were many species of singing birds made of gold and silver.

Within a stone's throw of the citadel, surrounded by buildings that would not look strange in any country town in France, rises the mighty mosque Djama el Kebir. It was built in A. D. 1136, but it is to-day in as good condition as when the Moors first worshipped in it eight hundred years ago. The buildings of this mosque cover about an acre and the roof is supported by a vast number of columns bearing up great arches hung with many chandeliers. The buildings surround the court in the centre of which is a fountain of onyx, where, as I passed through, the Mohammedans were sitting and washing themselves before going in to pray. We were allowed to enter the mosque, but had first to put on slippers. We then walked about through the worshippers, who were kneeling on their prayer rugs and bowing again and again as they looked toward Mecca.

When Tlemçen was in the height of its glory it had seventy mosques. One of the most famous was built in honour of a confectioner saint who preached to the children as they gathered around his candy stall. I doubt not that he attracted them by giving them sweets. He became so popular that the Sultan made him a tutor to his three sons. This angered the Grand Vizier, who had the candy saint condemned as a sorcerer and beheaded outside the gates. Shortly after this the ghost of the candy saint appeared before the Sultan and made a complaint, and the Sultan tied the Grand Vizier hand

and foot and threw him into a vat of cement. As the cement hardened the Grand Vizier hardened with it until he was buried alive in a solid block of stone. After this the Sultan built the mosque, which remains to this day. This is said to have happened just one hundred and thirty-odd years before Columbus discovered America. I have no doubt the story is true, for I saw the mosque here with my own matter-of-fact American eyes.

Another mosque in Tlemçen, built in 1208, was in honour of an Arab lawyer. It contains some of the most exquisite Moorish work of the world, and is perhaps the finest monument any lawyer has ever had. The lawyer it commemorates is said to have been a man of truth.

One of the most interesting of the mosques lies several miles from Tlemçen, on the side of the mountains. It is that of Sidi Bou Medin, one of the most famous scholars of the Moorish civilization of eight hundred years ago. This man studied at Granada and Fez, and then travelled to Mecca. He lectured at Bagdad, Seville, and Cordova, and ended his career by lecturing here. The mosque is a wonder of fine workmanship. It is floored with mosaic, its doors are of bronze, and its decorations are of Moorish lace-work of wonderful patterns. Near it there was a famous Moorish college, and there is a school here to-day. While I walked through the mosque I heard the boys singing out their Koran as they swayed back and forth, going over and over the Arabic sentences written on their wooden slates. I found many worshippers at prayer inside, and the red-faced keeper grew quite angry when I asked if I might take their photographs.

On my way back to town I stopped at an Arab café and drank coffee with half-a-dozen black-faced Berbers who

had just left the mosque. They were bearded and turbaned. They had taken off their slippers as they sat down
to drink, and I observed that their bare feet were clean
and the toe nails almost as well cared for as though a
manicure, or rather a pedicure, had worked upon them.
The men looked strangely at me from under their turbans,
evidently thinking me as much a curiosity as I considered
them. Nevertheless, they were friendly and we drank
our coffee together. The coffee was brought in steaming.
It was as black as ink, somewhat thick, and very sweet.
The price was one cent a cup.

I drove on to the ruins of Mansoura, on the other side
of Tlemçen. That city, which was built when Tlemçen
was great, had a population of one hundred and fifty
thousand souls. It was noted as a city of light and genius.
Its kings were lovers of art, science, and literature. They
had their own armies of disciplined soldiers, a police force,
judges, and courts. They coined their own money, and
had schools and colleges. This was several hundred years
before America was discovered.

Mansoura sprang up on the plains almost in a night.
An Arab general, Abou Yakoub, had besieged Tlemçen,
encamping with his army about three miles from the city.
The siege lasted seven years, and Mansoura was constructed by Yakoub during the intervals of fighting.
For many years it was a rival of Tlemçen. Its walls and
forts inclosed a space of something like three hundred
acres, and it had a magnificent mosque, with a minaret
one hundred and thirty feet high. This tower was
decorated with green porcelain tiles, and was a wonder of
beautiful workmanship. Most of the tower is intact,
but the mosque has long since fallen to dust.

The great walls of Mansoura are still to be seen in some places as solid as when first built, and in others broken and crumbled. The whole space covered by the city is now a rich vineyard, the vines growing close up to the walls and hugging the foot of the tower. A crowd of Berbers were picking the large white grapes into great baskets as I drove through the ruins which I tried to people with the army and the gay throng of six hundred years ago. It was impossible amid such surroundings to rebuild, even in imagination, the immense edifices, the magnificent palaces, the great houses, and the gardens traversed by streamlets as described by the historians; but the scenes recalled to me some of the verses of Omar Khayyam about the evanescence of all things earthly:

> They say the Lion and the Lizard keep
> The courts where Jamshyd gloried and drank deep
> And Bahram, that great Hunter—the Wild Ass
> Stamps o'er his head, but cannot break his sleep.

Yakoub's soldiers finally conquered Tlemçen, but he himself was assassinated just before its surrender. After that the city of Mansoura began to decline, and its greatness was soon swallowed up in that of Tlemçen.

But, after all, a live dog is better that a dead lion, and the Algeria of the present is more interesting than that of the dead centuries of the past. I like the swing and go of this French colony, the jaunty air of the soldiers as they strut about in their bulgy red pantaloons and short jackets and their tall caps of bright scarlet; the stately walk of the Arabs as they go on slippered feet through the streets; and above all the long gowns and tall hats of some of the native gentlemen of Tlemçen. We think

The mosques of Tlemçen were famous for their architectural beauty when Europe was in the Middle Ages. These bronze doors of Sidi Bou-Medine are among the finest in the world

One of the seventy mosques of Tlemçen was erected by the Sultan to the popular confectioner who taught his three sons.   For killing this candy saint, the wicked Grand Vizier was thrown into a vat of cement.

five dollars much to pay for a derby and ten dollars a big price for a black silk tile, but these Tlemçen natives pay quite as much for straw hats. Their hats are, however, gorgeous beyond description and stand from twelve to eighteen inches above the crown of the head. They are made of straw as finely woven as a Panama and of several different colours. The brims, which are covered with silk embroidery, extend for six inches all around the hat. These hats are large enough to be worn over turbans and so big that I was able to put one over my cork helmet.

One of the industries of Tlemçen is making such hats. The town is quite a manufacturing centre. The natives— I mean the Berbers and Moors—seem to be engaged in house industries of one kind or other. I went through street after street lined with little shops, lighted only by the doors at the front, containing men and boys weaving cloths, embroidering caps for women and hats for men, sewing on slippers and shoes, and working at the various other trades of the country. The weaving is all done with native wool upon rude hand looms. In the dirtiest of shops the most beautiful of white *burnouses* are made, and little round caps covered with velvet and embroidered with gold and silver are turned out in places no better than dog kennels.

The whole of the native quarter is a mixture of the gorgeous and the squalid. A man will wear an eight-dollar hat and at the same time go about in a dirty white gown with his feet and legs bare half way to the knee. A woman will go along wrapped in a white flannel blanket much the worse for wear but on her head will be one of these gold-embroidered caps just about as big around and of the same shape as the tin funnels used in our kitchens. The cap will be hidden by the blanket which she keeps so tight about her face that only a hole the size of a postage stamp can be seen. Through this hole will peep a liquid black eye, and it is only when she stumbles or when the amorous wind tears open her garments that you may see any other part of her person. Even little girls are often so draped, although some show their faces.

At home the ladies either go barefooted or in slippers of velvet embroidered with gold. They plait their hair in long braids and arrange it in knots behind the head. They wear the little gold caps I have described, tying them on with cords of gold thread under the chin. Those who can afford it are loaded with jewellery. They have bracelets and anklets and some have gold rings in their ears. Even the children are decked with jewellery. I see little girls with earrings almost as big around as the bottom of a tea cup and anklets of silver as thick as their own little fingers.

The Arab men wear gowns of white woollen material striped with silk and bound in by sashes at the waist. Under the gown there are baggy trousers while over it is a white woollen *burnouse* of fine texture. The richer men sometimes wear over this another *burnouse* or sort of overcoat of navy blue cloth embroidered with silk. Some of them wear stockings and some, riding horseback, have long red boots of the finest Morocco leather, which are almost as soft as wool. Over the foot is a shoe covering the boot to the ankle, and to this shoe a spur is attached. The poorer Arabs wear *haicks*, long gowns shaped like nightshirts, made of camel's hair and wool in white and black stripes.

Many of the native garments are made in Tlemçen. The town has long been noted for its fine workmanship, its lace, hats, shawls, and blankets being famous. Among other garments are some made for the Jews, especially the bright red shawls which they use here for mourning.

The Tlemçen of to-day is composed largely of new French buildings. The streets are French streets. There is a square in the centre of the town where the people meet to walk about, and there is a park outside it, filled with great plane trees and wild olive trees, which is known as Tlemçen's Bois de Boulogne.

On my way here I stopped at Sidi Bel Abbes, a rapidly growing French settlement named after a Mohammedan saint. It still has its Arab quarter. The city is built in the shape of a rectangle with great walls about it, and like most of these Algerian towns has a military quarter inhabited by several companies of the foreign soldiers employed by the French to garrison Algeria. The troops are composed of such riff-raff from Europe as can be enlisted at a few cents a day.

In this hidden corner of Africa the Europeanized little town of Sidi Bel Abbes has its regular concerts by the military band, a theatre, and also a "Café Chantant," where the songs and dances are even more wicked than those of Paris itself. Indeed, things are moving fast in this French section of the African continent.

CHAPTER IX

THE TELL AND ITS FARMS

THE French have done good work in colonizing Algeria, and have greatly increased its value as a farming country. The colonization department has laid out new towns and farm sites. Some of the lands are given away and others sold at auction on long time. There are agricultural banks for the benefit of the farmers and special inducements to settlers in low steamship and railroad rates.

There are eight hundred thousand Europeans settled in Algeria. More than half of these are French, but there are also many Spaniards, Italians, and people from Malta, Sicily, and other islands of the Mediterranean Sea. Already about one seventh of the whole population is of European origin and the best lands of the country are being rapidly bought of the Mohammedans by these invading Christians. The European population has doubled within thirty years.

The cities are growing. There are French towns all over the country and the Christian element is everywhere in control. Perregaux, where I am writing, contains more than five thousand European inhabitants and has all the surroundings of a rural city of France. Its streets are wide and well shaded and it has a large public garden in which the band plays several times a week. Its stores are like those of France and it has no end of cafés and restau-

The giant cactus of the Atlas Mountain regions combines with thorny
shrubs to make an impenetrable hedge between the farms.

North Africa was once the granary of the Mediterranean world. Many of the natives still store their wheat in great baskets beautifully woven by the patient hands of old men.

rants. There are scores of other such cities throughout the Tell, many of which, like Blidah, Tlemçen, and Orleansville, are populous and prosperous.

The Tell of northern Africa has been noted for many generations as one of the granaries of the world. It fed Carthage from the time when it was founded by Queen Dido, eight or nine hundred years before Christ. It was the bread land of Rome in the days of her glory, and the Arabs and Moors grew fat upon it for centuries before the French came. It comprises the valleys between the mountains running along the coast and the high plateaus of the Atlas which fall away into the Sahara, as well as a rich coastal strip here and there. It runs clear across Algeria and Tunisia, and, in round numbers, is seven or eight hundred miles long from west to east and from thirty to one hundred miles wide. It contains altogether an area almost as large as New England and fully as large as the state of Illinois. It has between thirty-five and fifty million acres of excellent lands, but this is in patches, some large and some small. I have gone through regions such as Oran, where the soil is as rich as the Mississippi Valley, and through others where the vineyards grow in a fat, red loam, like that of the best coffee plantations of São Paulo, Brazil.

As it is now winter, only the stubble is left on the great grain fields, but there are strawstacks dotting the landscape everywhere and the trains are loaded with wheat and other cereals. The wheat is handled in four-bushel bags piled high on freight cars and then covered with tarpaulins. The straw is carefully saved, for it is the chief stock food, "long feed," as some of our farmers would call it. The stacks are covered with a thatch as carefully put on as the roof of a house. In the department of Oran, where the soil forms a natural cement when mixed with water, the whole outside of the stack is plastered with mud. I have seen hundreds of stacks, larger than any haystack in our country, so covered.

Some of the Algerian regions through which I have been travelling for the past week or so remind me of California. The sun here is just as bright and it is so strong that the clouds paint velvety blue shadows on the fields and hills. The sky is the same heavenly blue and the clouds are as fleecy white. The same fruits grow here as in California and the crops look much the same.

In other respects, however, Algeria is far different from any part of the United States. There are no fences anywhere and but few barns, for the cattle can be pastured all the year round so there is little need of stables. I have seen no haystacks since I came into the country, though I did observe some alfalfa fields near Tlemçen. The country people live in stone structures covered with stucco and washed with the brightest of colours. I saw a sky-blue farmhouse yesterday and stopped at a rose-pink one the other afternoon. There are excellent roads, but no four-wheeled wagons on them. Almost every vehicle is of the cart variety, and there are more mules and donkeys than horses. Oxen are largely used for ploughing. Now and then one sees a great awkward camel stalking sourly onward, and not infrequently there passes a caravan of mules or a drove of donkeys loaded with grain.

Not a little of the Tell is irrigated. There is an enormous dam near the town of Perregaux, which holds back a lake containing fourteen million cubic meters of water, and another not far away, near St. Denis-du-Sig, which contains six millions more. Wherever the water can be stored it is conducted over the lands, and a great deal of irrigation is done by means of wells, the motive power for drawing up the water being a blindfolded donkey, mule, or ox, and sometimes a camel.

These Algerians are a nation of farmers. Over one half of the Europeans and more than three fourths of the natives are engaged in agriculture and there are in addition an enormous number of native stock farmers. The Arabs own a great deal of land in the plains, while such of the mountains as are fertile are covered with little farms, some of which are not much bigger than a city backyard.

A large part of the Tell is devoted to grain. Algeria produces millions of bushels of cereals every year. There are about four million acres annually planted to wheat and something like three million acres to barley. In addition, some oats and corn are raised. The corn, however, does not grow nearly so well as in our country.

Wheat is by far the most important grain crop, and a large part of that grown is suitable for making macaroni. Both the French and the natives cultivate wheat, but among the latter it is done in a most slovenly way. There are but few modern agricultural implements, and only the foreigners who run big farms plough more than two or three inches deep. They have French ploughs with wheels in front. The shares cut well into the soil, but it requires a team of six or eight animals for each plough. Such a team is usually composed of oxen, though sometimes it is a combination of oxen, horses, and mules, and not in-quently a donkey aids in the work.

The native plough is little more than a forked stick with

a sort of iron shoe, shaped like a trowel, as a ploughpoint. This shoe is about ten inches long and a quarter of an inch thick, and serves only to turn the earth to a depth of two or three inches. It is not as good as a single shovel plough by any means. Such a plough has but one handle, and the native does not press down upon it, but merely steadies it with one hand as he walks behind in the furrow. The tongue is fastened to a stick which rests under the bellies of the two horses forming the native team. This stick is fastened to the horses by breast straps, without traces of any kind.

Since the natives are unable to do deep ploughing with such implements, much of the grain is planted in and out amid the bushes and undergrowth. Along many of the foothills of the Atlas Mountains the fields contain more bushes than wheat, while in places the wheat grows among thistles each of which has a head as big around as a pint cup.

The average wheat yield is not much more than one half as great as that of the United States and less than one third that of France. It is only about eight bushels per acre.

These Algerians do nearly all of their reaping by hand, and that with the sickle. It would be impossible to run a mower and reaper through the fields covered with brush, and it is only on the large farms that threshing machines are employed. Most of the grain is trodden out by oxen or other animals. I see threshing floors everywhere near the straw stacks. They are circles of well-pounded earth upon which the animals are driven around over the straw until the grain is ground out. After that the straw is raked off and the wheat, barley, or oats is

Sometimes North African farms are irrigated by clay jars attached to a wheel which is turned in a well, a horse, mule, or camel supplying the motive power.

Though the primitive farming methods of the past are still widely used, the rich lands of the Algerian Tell are feeding France to-day just as they once fed Rome and Carthage.

Both sheep and goats are pastured out of doors the year round in the Tell and in the foothills of the Atlas Mountains.

Algeria produces enough grapes each year to furnish every American with several gallons of wine. Blue grapes, crimson grapes, and white grapes as big as damson plums are sold everywhere.

thrown into the air against the wind to remove the chaff. The straw is then stacked and the grain put in large bags for shipment. If it is to be carried to market upon camels, the bags used will contain six or eight bushels each, as two bags of grain make a load for one camel. If it is to go upon donkeys or mules, each bag will contain half as much. There are no elevators in the farming districts nor at the stations. The grain is frequently hauled on great wagons with five, six, or seven mules to each wagon and a snarling dog on top to guard the load. The driver, who is usually an Arab or a Kabyle, walks alongside. A donkey will carry only one bag of wheat at a load, thousands of bushels being thus transported. The bag rests on the little fellow's back without being fastened and the donkey, as usual, moves along without bridle or halter, its Arab master following behind.

Most of the farm labour is done by the Kabyles. The Arabs and Moors are lazy, but these white Africans like money quite as well as their American cousins and will work for it. I see them everywhere: in the grain fields, in the vineyards, and in the orchards and gardens. They are employed by the French farmers, who come down in gangs from their homes in the Atlas Mountains to aid in the harvest. At such times they live in little straw shacks built for the purpose. They cook their own food on fires out of doors and sleep on the ground. Wages are best at the time of picking the grapes when many European labourers are attracted from across the Mediterranean.

The vineyards of the Tell are quite as important as the grain fields. I have never seen grapes grow so luxuriantly or produce so abundantly anywhere else. The vines are cut back every year, making their stems knotted and

71

gnarled. The main stems are not knee high. From these stumps long branches put out from season to season, and these bear the fruit. Some of the grapes are of a rich navy blue, not large, but full of juice and sweetness. Others are crimson and others white. The latter are as big as damson plums and surpass in flavour and colour the finest Malagas. I measured some that were served for dessert at the hotel here at Perregaux last night. They were three and a half inches in circumference, or more than an inch in diameter. They tasted as sweet as maple syrup and their flavour was delicious. The best of the grapes in the markets sell for about one cent a pound.

I have seen excellent vineyards everywhere I have gone. Algeria has thousands and thousands of acres devoted to them, and they extend from one end of it to the other. The French are careful as to the introduction of fruit diseases into the colonies, having passed stringent laws to safeguard the importation of trees, plants, and vines, as well as of flowers and fresh fruits.

The country is now producing more than enough wines every year to give several gallons to every man, woman, and child in the United States, yet her grape-growing lands have scarcely been touched. I see vast areas of vacant lands among the vineyards and new vines are being set out. It is said there is not a place in northern Algeria which cannot be made to raise grapes.

Wine is cheaper here than mineral water. I have two bottles every day on my table at the hotel, and if I buy a lunch at a railroad restaurant a quart is thrown in without extra charge. The wine is good, too. It is the pure juice of the grape.

THE TELL AND ITS FARMS

Algeria raises all sorts of fresh garden stuff. At our hotel we have green peas and beans, as well as asparagus, celery, and lettuce. Radishes are raised in great quantities, eggplants and tomatoes thrive, while onions and potatoes yield two crops per annum. Vegetables by the shipload go to France throughout the year, and Paris, Lyons, Marseilles, and other French cities rely upon this country for their winter supplies of fresh fruit and garden stuff. Fast steamers carry the fruit and vegetables across the Mediterranean in a day, so that within thirty-six hours they may be spread out for sale in the Halles Centrales in Paris.

The Tell can produce almost everything grown in the United States. It has apples, peaches, and pears, also figs and olives, oranges and lemons. The olive thrives well up into the Atlas Mountains. Many of the trees are centuries old. They live so long that the people have a saying that he who plants an olive is laying up treasures for his children's children. The natives consume large quantities of olive oil. Even the Kabyles make it in a rude way and store it in their huts for the winter. It is used for cooking, and has much the same place that butter has with us.

Enormous quantities of figs are grown and fig orchards are to be seen everywhere. The fruit is fine although not equal to that raised in Smyrna. Some of the varieties are white and others blue. Figs are as common here as apples in America and quite as freely eaten. The natives dry them and store them away for winter use and millions of pounds are exported.

Algeria does a great deal of stock farming. Not only in the Tell but in the ranges of the Atlas Mountains and on

73

the high plateaus upheld by them are large flocks of sheep and goats. They are to be found also all along the edges of the Desert of Sahara. Of the numerous cattle, donkeys, mules, and camels, more than nine tenths belong to the natives.

The sheep here are fine, large, long-woolled animals. They weigh, I should say, more than either our Southdowns or Shropshires and seem free from disease. They are white and brown in colour, many of the white sheep having brown faces. Their ears are long and silky and hang down somewhat like those of a spaniel.

Thousands of pairs of our American shoes are made of Algerian goatskins. The goats are black and brown. They are of good size, but in their milking qualities do not compare with those of Morocco. The goats are always grazed with the sheep. I have yet to see one flock which did not contain both animals, and I have passed millions on my way through Algeria. The flocks are always watched by shepherds, white-gowned, barefooted men or boys, who live out in the fields with them. On the edges of the desert there are many nomadic shepherds who live in tents, driving their sheep, goats, and other stock from place to place to find pasture.

The horses here are largely of Arabian origin. They are well made and tough, many of them being fine riding animals. Some French horses have been brought in for heavy draft, and many of those about the wharves of the cities show a strain of Percheron or Norman blood. Draft horses are usually worked single file, and a long team of five or six horses, harnessed up tandem, is not uncommon. Sometimes they are harnessed three abreast; a team of seven will often have two leaders tandem and behind them two abreast, with three abreast next the wagon.

Algeria has enough national roadway if stretched out in one line to reach from San Francisco to New York. Furthermore, these roads are better than most of those we have in the United States. They are as smooth as asphalt and are so laid out that the slope is everywhere along the easiest possible lines. This facilitates fast travel and the hauling of big loads. Indeed, I doubt whether these roads are surpassed anywhere in the world. One can easily travel over the country in an automobile and there are frequent motor-car excursions from Algiers into the wild scenery of the Atlas Mountains. These roads, which were begun by the French as a military necessity, are still kept up for the army. Everywhere the troops go new roads have been made, until they are now extended into the more settled parts of the Atlas and down to the very edge of the Sahara.

CHAPTER X

IN THE HEART OF THE SAHARA

I AM at Beni Ounif in southwestern Algeria, in one of the wildest parts of the greatest desert on earth. On all sides of me, stretching to the west, south, and east for hundreds of miles is the Sahara. It is so big that if you could lift up its sandy, rocky surface like a quilt and carry it across the Atlantic, it would cover every bit of the United States and hide a part of Canada and the Gulf of Mexico as well. It is longer than the Mediterranean Sea and larger than all Europe. In some places it is two thousand miles wide. Here at Beni Ounif I am more than four hundred miles south of the port of Oran and about twelve hundred miles from Timbuktu on the Niger, where the great fertile belt of North Central Africa begins.

This little town is on the very edge of the French Sahara. Just west of it are wild, rocky mountains as bare as the asphalt of our American city streets and as thirsty as was Dives when he begged Lazarus to cool his parched tongue. They mark the boundary between Algeria and Morocco. But the desert goes on farther westward, and on the southwest it does not stop until it reaches the Atlantic Ocean.

I came here from Oran on the military railroad built by the French to guard their people in Algeria from the brigands of Morocco. Railway travel in northern Africa is far different from that of the United States. In comparison with us these people are still a century or so behind the times. Express trains do not make more than fifteen or twenty miles an hour, and the railroad clocks at the stations are purposely kept five minutes behind other timepieces in order that passengers may not get left.

The methods of ticket selling and baggage checking are such that one must be at the train at least a quarter of an hour before starting. Once there, he will have to wait his turn with a crowd of Arabs, each of whom consumes at least two minutes at the ticket office and twice that time with the baggage master. If the ticket is a return, the agent figures out a reduction off the regular fare and makes a memorandum of the amount in a ledger as well as on the ticket itself. The ordinary tickets are somewhat like ours, but the "returns" and excursion certificates are the size of a legal document and quite as imposing.

Everything must be weighed, and only about seventy pounds of baggage are allowed free. There is a tax of two cents for checking, and the agent registers the weight whether it is below seventy pounds or not. The checks are not made of cardboard or brass, as in our country, but are merely receipts on a thin tough paper so arranged that one half of each receipt can be given to the passenger while the other is doubled up and tied with a string to the baggage.

Most of the natives carry their belongings in bags not unlike coffee sacks, and much of the checked luggage is of that nature. At the stations the poorer Arabs throw these bags over their shoulders and march off with them. First- and second-class passengers may take numerous valises and bundles into the cars. I am now travelling with nine packages, all of which go into the compartment with me. At every change the porters take my stuff in and out for me, but at such low rates that the cost of handling is little. Four cents is a big enough fee for one man, and a single good husky Arab can carry all my baggage.

The first- and second-class compartments are comfortable. I can travel first class, sometimes having a whole compartment for myself and my son. The cars are divided into little box-like rooms by partitions running crosswise. They are usually entered from the sides, so that it is not possible to go through a whole train as in our country. The seats are well cushioned, and as the windows are large and clean, we can get a fine view of the country as we go along. The second- and third-class cars are divided up in the same way, the second class being almost as good as the first. The third-class seats are bare board benches, usually filled with Arabs, Moors, and Kabyles, with a sprinkling of soldiers. The latter receive such small wages that they cannot travel in luxury.

Some years ago dining cars were put on some of these Algerian trains, but many still stop at the stations for luncheon and dinner. At every station there is a lunch room, called a *buvette*. The usual rate for dinner is about forty cents, for which one gets an excellent meal with the customary quart bottle of white or red wine thrown in. Luncheons are often put up and brought to the cars at a cost of about fifty cents each. For that one gets two slices of roast beef or half a chicken, several boiled eggs, and also cheese, sweet cakes, and fruit, and, of course, the wine.

Among the nomadic Bedouins women do most of the work, grinding grain between round stones and weaving the tents of camels' hair or wool.

Station clocks in the Sahara are left five minutes slow so the Arabs will not miss the desert express, for which twenty miles an hour is considered fast time.

Camels are said to smell water three miles away. It is their broad, thickly padded feet that enable them to stand the burning desert sands.

Like the restless sea, the desert is never still! The shifting sand dunes, sometimes six hundred feet high, move, grain by grain, with the wind.

I have no recent figures of the railroad wages, but they must be exceedingly low. A cross-roads depot, which in our country would hardly be thought worthy of an agent, requires half-a-dozen guards and the large stations proportionately more. There are always a manager, a baggage master, a telegraph operator, a ticket seller, and a number of porters. It takes half-a-dozen men to start a train. The engineer blows the whistle, one of the guards rings a bell, and others run from car to car and shut the doors while they cry, "Get on, gentlemen, if you please." On the train itself there are many employés: engineers, firemen, and brakemen, in apparently excessive numbers. Every train has its mail clerk and its baggage man and often an express messenger as well.

We left Oran in the afternoon and as the night fell were still in the fertile Tell. Wrapping myself in my blanket, with my camera under my head as a pillow, I slept fitfully all night and awoke on the high plateau of the Atlas Mountains, beyond which is the desert. We were passing through a great plain of yellow sandy soil covered here and there with stones, and spotted everywhere with bunches of dry alfa grass. Only in one direction were there any hills to be seen, and they were bleak, barren, and rocky.

The alfa was growing right in the sands, a long wiry grass, which is gathered by the thousands of tons and shipped to Europe for the making of paper. It is cut by the Arabs and handled by French companies that have an immense capital. It grows in bunches, some of them not bigger than one's fist, while others sprout out of mounds that would fill a half-bushel measure. The clumps are about the height of my waist. The grass looks tough and dry, but nevertheless large flocks of white and brown sheep and black goats and camels feed upon it. I saw such animals scattered over the plains, each flock watched by a white-gowned shepherd who looked like a ghost as he stood among his stock in the early morning.

We passed many tent villages occupied by such shepherds and their families. The tents are of a coarse black-and-white cloth woven in stripes. They are so stretched out that one has to get down upon his knees and crawl in.

The cloth is made by the wives of the shepherds out of camel's hair and sheep's wool. Throughout the desert this is used for canvas.

Leaving the Atlas region we came into the Sahara itself. There was still some vegetation; but it was only in patches here and there or along the banks of dried-up streams. Now the land was flat, and now it rose into rocky mountains which were black in the morning. As I looked out over the plains I saw the sun rise. First came a faint streak of yellow away off to the east, which grew until it drew a sheet of light over the horizon. A few minutes later a pale yellow sun could be seen through this veil. As it rose the veil disappeared and a blazing white ball jumped out into the sky. For a time a thin, fleecy mist hovered over the sands, but this soon gave way to the clear air of the desert.

As we kept on with our journey the Sahara seemed always changing. We passed for miles over bare rock almost as smooth as a floor, and then through regions where the rocks were ragged and cut up into all sorts of shapes. At times there were boulders and again small pebbles of different colours, red, brown, and black. Here about Beni Ounif the desert is largely limestone, while farther south, along the Sousfane River, I passed through rolling dunes and plains covered with boulders.

The old descriptions represent the Sahara as a dreary waste of barren sand as flat as the sea, a vast wilderness where travellers must perish if they try to go through it. The real Sahara has wide expanses of sand; it has plains as big as a good-sized state of the Union which are covered with stones, but a great part of it is rolling. It is largely a plateau broken by lofty mountains and cut up by water courses called wadies which are dry the greater part of the year. Its average height above the sea is about as great as that of the Blue Ridge Mountains of Virginia, though in many places it is as high as the Alleghanies and higher.

In addition to its rolling character, the desert offers other obstacles to railroad building. One is the long stretches over which the track must go without available water, another is the enormous cost of hauling the fuel, while a third is the creeping sand dune.

The sand dunes are sometimes six hundred feet high, rising from the desert in the shape of a crescent with its horns turned away from the winds. The sand is rolled up by the wind from the bottom to the top, each grain going over and over until it falls inside the crescent. As this continues the dunes increase in size. They move along slowly and if a railroad be in their way they will swallow it up. I have seen similar dunes on the great Peruvian desert at the foot of the Andes and have been told that they are the chief obstacles to railroad building in that region. These dunes grow solid and hard as the wind blows against them. During my travels through them not far from Beni Ounif, I rode up them on horseback, finding the sand almost as firm as that of a sea beach.

81

There are vast areas in the Sahara which have no vegetation whatever, but in many other parts there is grass during parts of the year. Grass grows everywhere on the edges of the desert and along the dried-up water courses, the beds of which contain some moisture. In many places there is a slight rainfall in certain months. The smallest bit of water causes the grass to spring up, and the Arabs drive their flocks to such places to pasture. Where the grass will not grow there are sometimes thorn bushes which camels will eat. Along the railroad to the Atlas Mountains there is in places a thin growth of tough grass upon which thousands of animals feed. Strange to say, the flocks are fat, although it looks as though they were grazing upon the bare stones.

As I have said, the road to Beni Ounif was built for military purposes. It is an absolute necessity for the French control of the Sahara. The depots are all of red sandstone one story in height with a stone wall about the roof and a high wall of stone surrounding the station yard. At intervals of four feet all around these walls have portholes or slits three inches wide and a foot long. Through these openings rifles are thrust to defend the station in case of need. In the roof are other portholes and both gate and windows are barred, so that they can be securely fastened.

Often a station consists of nothing but this fort-like building, although there may be sometimes an oasis or a mud village near by. The stops at these places are not more than from three to five minutes, unless the engine has to take on water. The supply pipes, eight inches in diameter, are wrapped with straw to retard evaporation, and from these the train boilers and tanks are filled.

Sometimes the vast Sahara is a sea of wave-like sand dunes, sometimes it is covered with boulders; in places bare mountains rise in jagged outline, while in others it is floored with smooth and solid rock.

Exalted by religious fanaticism, the desert Arabs often suffer their shoulders, arms, or cheeks to be pierced with lances. This youth also took frequent bites of the thorny cactus held by his preceptor in torture.

The story teller, juggler, and general vaudeville entertainer can always draw a crowd in the desert village. On the scroll are various items of news which are read out as part of the show.

All sorts of fakirs are found in the oasis towns of the Sahara. The snake charmer uses a brass, jewel-studded ball on a stick to reduce the deadly cobras to meek and helpless creatures.

IN THE HEART OF THE SAHARA

At every good-sized station the coming of the trains is an event. Soldiers and officers, gorgeously clad, are there, colonels and lieutenants in uniform, soldiers with high red caps, wide red belts, blue or red jackets, and full red or white pantaloons. They are jaunty fellows and remind one of Athos, Porthos, and Aramis, the three musketeers of Dumas's novel. Guns are everywhere. Not only the soldiers carry them, but all the Arabs who come to the train; and the baggage man, the guards, even the hotel clerk, are armed.

Beni Ounif is within almost a stone's throw of the Moroccan boundary and at the gate of a pass through the mountains that separate it from Algeria. The brigands of these parts of Morocco still make raids upon the oases and attack travellers and caravans going to and fro over the desert. One base of such expeditions is the oasis of Tafilelt, not far from here, where are some of the worst scoundrels of this part of the world. These expeditions are known as *harkas.* They are often composed of hundreds and even thousands of camels and men. One which came through here some years ago had about four thousand men mounted on camels, and a *harka* of five hundred camels is not uncommon.

It was a *harka* like this that brought about the battle of Figig, named after an oasis about eight miles from Beni Ounif where it took place. Figig is one of the richest settlements of eastern Morocco. It has about a million date trees, and its people have always been noted for their prosperity and trade. They are also famous as haters of Christians, and until lately it was death to any Christian to enter their oases. At a time when the railroad had not yet reached this point, the governor-general of Algeria

83

made an expedition from the end of the road, then at Duvivier to Beni Ounif, and thence to Figig. He was accompanied by a detachment of *spahis*, the bravest of these African soldiers, and three companies of the Foreign Legion, under the command of General O'Conner. It was then well known that a Christian who went into Figig did so at the risk of his life, and one of the Arab officials of the town warned the governor-general that he had better keep out. He did not heed the warning and the result was a fight which lasted five hours, after which the French retreated.

This battle was entirely with rifles on both sides, and after their victory the Moors thought they were equal to anything the French could bring against them. A day or so later the Foreign Legion and three squadrons of cavalry appeared, their force all together numbering forty-five hundred. They brought with them some mountain guns and other cannon, and placing these more than a mile away, opened fire with melinite shells upon the oasis and its villages. The result astounded the natives. Their mud brick houses were blown to atoms and the minarets of their mosques cut in two.

The Moors, who had never heard or seen anything like this, soon came, almost on their knees, to beg the French to desist. Since then the railroad has been extended to Beni Ounif and beyond, and a thriving settlement has grown up here at the gate to the pass. The French have made the whole region peaceful, so that it is possible to travel almost anywhere through it. French troops are stationed at every large oasis, while camel soldiers scour the country and heliograph the least sign of disturbance. These camel police are natives mounted on *meharis*, beasts which can go one hundred miles day after day without tiring. Many of the camel police are Tuaregs, who find it pays better to be employed by the French than to rob the caravans, as they did in the past; others are Targhis, from a warlike tribe in the eastern part of the Algerian Sahara. These *mehari* troops patrol the country, act as scouts for the French officers, and are ready to fight bravely in time of trouble. A large number of them watch the pass at Beni Ounif. Patrolling at wide distances apart, they bring in reports of the conditions existing all along the desert frontier.

The French have established also a mail service for the Sahara. The Arab postmen carry mail bags on their fast *meharis*. Every military station is thus served, and in some places, such as Colomb-Bechar and Adrar, there are post offices where money orders are issued and a regular mail service is supplied.

Here at Beni Ounif is a branch of the Foreign Legion made up of adventurers and homeless and friendless men of all nationalities. There are also several companies of military criminals who have been deported from France and sent down from other parts of Algeria for punish-ment. These men are put to making roads and bridges and doing all kinds of hard labour. I met one of the Legion last night in a Moorish café who told me he was an American. His complexion was that of a mulatto, but as he wore the red trousers, blue jacket, and tall red cap of the *spahi*, I took him for an Arab. I was drinking coffee at one of the tables when, sitting down beside me, he began to speak English. He told me that he came from San Francisco, that he had served as a marine in the French Navy, and had finally drifted into the army. He said that the food and treatment were so bad that he could not stand it, and that his pay was only one cent a day. Finally, he deserted and succeeded in getting to the Mediterranean, where he had hidden himself away in the hold of a German steamer. Just as the ship was raising anchor the military police came on board and discovered him through a Hindoo cabin boy who pointed out his hiding place. He was then put in prison at the port of Namours, where the sheriff set him to cleaning his horses. One day, taking the best horse in the stable, he rode across into Spanish Morocco to Melilla. There he again tried to get off, this time on a Spanish ship. He was caught once more, however, and shipped down here into the heart of the Sahara. He is expecting to be sent on into the desert far from the railroad.

Of all the Arabs employed by the French, the Tuaregs are doing the best work. They are organized into companies equipped with good modern guns. They have practically abandoned brigandage, and now, mounted on camels, they sweep over the desert aiding the French to keep the natives in order. The French captain who is chief of the Arab bureau here tells me that the Tuaregs are by no means a bad people, their bloodthirstiness being largely a matter of imagination. It is true they have been robbers in the past, but now that they are employed by the government they make splendid soldiers. They are paid from twenty to twenty-four dollars a month, which is a fortune to them. Each man owns his own camel and takes care of it and of himself; but as the food for both man and beast costs practically nothing, he considers himself rich.

These Tuaregs are descendants of the Berber or white

The French have made the warlike Tuaregs and Targhis, once dreaded caravan-robbers, into a police and mail service patroling the desert on swift camels. Tuareg men always go veiled.

The hard-worked mothers of the African desert age quickly. When travelling with a caravan, the women walk and carry their children, while the men ride on their camels.

race of the Atlas Mountains, who have been crowded off into the desert. They once lived in the heart of the sands, so far south of the Mediterranean that most of them had never seen it, although for centuries they controlled all communication between it and the Sudan. They have long been noted as the robbers of the Sahara. They are tall, slender, and wiry in figure, with regular features and swarthy skins. They are especially distinguished by the fact that they wear veils night and day. Their veils are usually white, but sometimes black or blue. They wind them about their heads like a turban, passing them over the nose and mouth and across the forehead, so that only the eyes can be seen. A well-bred Tuareg never takes off his veil, either to eat or to sleep. This strange habit makes the French call them "the masked pirates of the Sahara." It is said that the veil was originally adopted to keep out the dust, but that it is now a mark of fashion and modesty. Another story told me is that the Tuareg men first put on veils from shame over a piece of cowardice. They were surprised by their enemies and were so frightened that they threw down their arms and ran, leaving their families. Thereupon the women picked up the swords, spears, and daggers, and defeated the enemy. From that day until now the men, to show their admiration for the conduct of their wives, have adopted the veil, while the Tuareg women still go with uncovered faces.

The Tuareg woman wears a long roll of cotton stuff wrapped around the body, a pair of cotton trousers, and a head shawl. She is fond of trinkets to hang about her neck, and it is said that an old sardine can is a suitable gift for an admirer to bestow on a Tuareg lady. The standard of beauty is fatness, and the only cruel custom among them is forcing the girls to drink great bowls of curdled milk to make them stout and therefore handsome. The women are said to be cultivated in their own way, even to the extent of writing poetry, and they are very sociable among themselves.

Many of the Tuaregs live in tent villages, moving about from place to place. They own camels and sheep, and some of them have gardens. As a general thing they are miserably poor, the money received by those in the French service being far more than most of them made when their sole profession was robbing travellers crossing the desert.

CHAPTER XI

I HAVE just returned from the great oasis of Figig, on the boundary between Algeria and Morocco. It lies here in the heart of the Sahara Desert, four hundred miles south of the Mediterranean and one thousand miles from Timbuktu in the French Sudan. If I should go westward through Morocco about as far as from New York to Pittsburgh, I should strike the port of Mogador, on the Atlantic Ocean, while if I took camels and travelled to the east, I should have to go through the Sahara for a distance as great as from Philadelphia to Salt Lake City before I found anything green and came to the valley of the Nile.

Figig was long a caravan centre, and even to-day the freight from a number of oases is shipped here on camels. The products of Tafilelt, in Morocco, whence come the best dates, and of Touat, a large collection of oases in the Algerian Sahara, three to four hundred miles to the south, were brought to Figig as a distributing point. Now a large part of this freight has been diverted to Colomb-Bechar and Beni Ounif, to be sent northward by the railroad.

Figig is about as far north as desert camels can come without danger of taking cold. If they go farther they get sick and die. For this reason the goods from other oases were once brought here and then sent to the Mediterranean on donkeys or mules. The exchanges were made at Figig and caused it to become a commercial centre. Its merchants were among the shrewdest of the Sahara and sent regular caravans to Tlemçen and to Melilla, in Spanish Africa, on the Mediterranean Sea. Since the French completed their railroad to Beni Ounif Figig has been losing its trade. In fact, the caravan trade of the Sahara has fallen off generally. The trains of one thousand or more camels, guarded by soldiers, which used to start across the great desert with perhaps half a million dollars' worth of ivory, gold dust, and slaves, have dwindled to bands containing one hundred camels or less, and the caravans diminish every year. Some European merchandise is carried across from Tripoli, Tunisia, and Algeria to the Sudan, but most of the goods for that section go to the ports of west Africa by steamer and are taken by railroad and river to the headwaters of the Niger.

We started out from this fortified town of Beni Ounif, where camel troops were making their way through the streets; officers in uniform were dashing about on Arabian horses, and companies of soldiers, in bright reds and blues, were marching in various directions. The French Government does not permit travellers from here to go alone into this part of Morocco, and it was only upon my showing Captain Pariel, the chief of the Arabian bureau here, a letter which I have from our Secretary of War to the governor-general of Algeria that two Arab soldiers were detailed to accompany us.

These men were armed with repeating rifles. They rode Arabian horses and kept right in front of or close behind us during our journey. In addition to them I had with me my son Jack and Mr. Pascalet, the proprietor of the Hôtel du Sahara and one of the leading merchants of this part of the world. Mr. Pascalet, who speaks Arabic as well as French and English, acted as our guide and interpreter during the day. He has a branch store in one of the largest of the Figig villages and has many friends among the people.

We started at daybreak. The sun was just rising as we left Beni Ounif. It came up a red copper ball out of the eastern horizon, and in a few moments took on a white heat, only to be shrouded half an hour later by the thick sky which sent down on us to-night the sirocco, or wind storm, of the desert.

We rode along single file. Each of the soldiers sat on a red Arab saddle, with a high pommel and back, and their horses were good. Mr. Pascalet rode a white Morocco mare, which he said had cost him a thousand dollars and upon which he had recently ridden seventy-five miles in one day. Jack and I were mounted with English saddles on two pure Arabian three-year-old colts, which belied the gentle nature commonly attributed to their breeding. They bucked, trotted, and galloped, and at irregular intervals acted worse than the average Western broncho when a tenderfoot rides him. We managed to keep our seats, however, notwithstanding the stony desert and the winding walls of the oases inclosures. It took us about an hour to reach the Moroccan frontier. Crossing it between two high mountains, we at once entered a beautiful valley filled with thousands of date palms.

This valley contains the oasis of Figig, which consists of great date plantations. Standing at the entrance, between Mount Taria and Mount Zenaga, each an arid, stony brown mass about six thousand feet high, we could see a forest of green-leaved palms, ranging in width from two to three miles and extending up a ravine for a distance of seven miles or more. On both sides and beyond were nothing but sand, rocks, and mountains, perfectly bare, dry, and thirsty. The palms formed a great green sheet in this setting, with the round brown watch towers made of sun-dried brick and the yellow minarets of the village mosques rising above it. On a hill in the centre we could see the mud houses of the village of Zenaga, but the other towns of the oasis were hidden in the forest of palms.

This oasis has about the largest number of palms in one solid block of any in the Sahara. Mr. Pascalet thinks there are more than a million trees, and I am sure I saw two or three hundred thousand in front of and below me as I stood on the Jorf, one of the highest parts of the oasis.

Many of the Sahara oases lie along dried-up water courses which are flooded during a part of the year. Figig is fed by hot springs which rise out of a hill almost in the centre and are conducted by underground drains about a foot square, made of stones and cement, through the fifteen or twenty thousand acres covered by trees. Some of these springs are lukewarm while others have a temperature of about one hundred and sixty degrees Fahrenheit.

The largest of the springs are found in the date plantations on the highlands of the town of El Abid near the centre of the fertile tract. Who first constructed these underground drains that carry the water from level to level no one seems to know. The Arabs answer the question by saying: "We do not know when they were built, but it was many, many years ago." It may have been two centuries ago and it may have been longer.

These drains are kept in order to-day and new ones are constructed from time to time. There must be hundreds of miles of them, for they reach every part of the oasis, being connected with great reservoirs in each of the village plantations where the water is stored when not needed for irrigation. Each tree gets a good drink at least twice a week.

I visited El Abid and its springs. The palms grow all about them. In some places they are only two or three feet apart so that the branches meet overhead and shut out the sun. Some of the springs are in great vats, some are in hollows or ravines, and others in wells or square tanks. During our visit the Arabs were bathing in one of them, and crowds of gowned men with rags about their heads looked out at me over their long beards as I took these notes. At one place Jack attempted to take a photograph, but the Arabs protested and looked angry, only to smile again when they were told that we were merely taking pictures of the palms and springs and that we had very good-looking men in France and America and hence did not need to take home pictures of the natives of Figig.

Fifteen thousand acres is a pretty big farm, yet, as I estimate it, that is just about the extent of these oases. This Figig farm, however, is like nothing you can imagine. It is divided into little pens or gardens, each of which is a date plantation. Many of the holdings are not more than a quarter of an acre in size and each is surrounded by walls from eight to twelve feet in height. These are of sun-dried brick plastered with mud. They usually face upon the roads, which are so narrow that as I rode through them on my horse I could easily touch the mud brick walls on both sides. Here and there, where a wall was broken at the top, I could look over and see the date trees and gardens within.

Many of the date palms reach high above the wall while others are not more than six feet in height, but still they bear fruit. They are about eight inches in diameter and seem to carry the same thickness from the ground upward. The highest were not over twenty feet tall, I judge. At the top the palms branch out in great fan-like green leaves, and from the roots of the leaves hang the clusters of red and yellow dates. The fruit is long, flat, and smooth and of much the same shape as a butter-nut with the shell on. I saw many clusters, any one of which, I am sure, held half a bushel of dates, and not a few trees bore half-a-dozen clusters or more. We ate them fresh from the trees. They were sweet as honey, and their flavour cannot be imagined by those who have tasted only the mushy, dark brown dates of our grocery stores.

Under these palms, apricots, peaches, pears, pome-granates, and fruits of like nature were growing; and below them in some places were beans, onions, and other vegetables, three crops being produced on the same soil at the same time. Outside the date plantations were unirrigated fields where grain had been planted to take advantage of the slight rainfall which comes during certain months of the year. These fields are also given some water from the springs.

As we went on with our journey, we could see how important the date palm is to these people of the desert. It is their bread, firewood, and lumber. Over the ditches that here and there crossed the streets were bridges of palm wood. I observed the doors in the walls of the date gardens. Each plot has but one door, and that not higher

94

I started at daybreak for the oasis at Figig with two Arab soldiers
detailed by the Governor-General to escort me.

Long caravans are less common than formerly. Through the folds of the gaudily striped fabric protecting her from the sun may peep the lovely brown eyes of the young wife or daughter of the rich caravaner.

Figig is said to have a million date palms—more than any other oasis in the world. I could believe it as I looked down upon these trees.

than my waist.   Indeed, some of the doors are cut so low that the common razor-back hog would lose his bristles if he should try to go through them.   These gates are of palm planks sawed out by hand and rudely pegged together.   The date tree forms the pillars that uphold the house roofs, it is used as beams and rafters, and it is made into ladders for the watch towers.   The towers are of mud brick, but there is more or less palm wood in them, and the platforms, on which spies sit at the time of date harvest to guard the crop against thieves, are of the same material.

I was much interested in the palms.   They look ragged and rough and on the taller trees there are no leaves except at the top.   I am told that each ring of bark represents a year's growth.   If this is true many of the palms must be a century old.   They begin to bear at ten or twelve years, yielding crops every two years thereafter.   The dates here are not as good as those of some other parts of the Sahara. They are better, for instance, in Touggourt and in Biskra.

Stranger even than the palm trees are the people of this out-of-the-way land.   Each of these oases has its little village, and every small desert settlement is a community of its own kind.   The villages of Figig are seven.   The first and largest contains more than three thousand people.   It is known as Zenaga.   The next largest is El Oudaghir, and the third is El Abid, which I have described as having the hot springs and as furnishing water for the greater part of the Figig plantations.   The four other villages are named El Maiz Foukani, El Maiz Tahtani, El Hamman Foukani, and El Hamman Tahtani.

These seven Figig villages have more than fifteen thousand inhabitants, but taken together they constitute a little "United States" of their own, with a congress but no president. Each village governs itself, while a common council of the combined villages governs the oasis. Each village government consists of a council of seventeen members, of whom five are landowners and twelve are labourers. The common council has twenty-one members elected by all the villages. It passes only upon matters relating to the whole corporation of Figig. The village councils regulate all things affecting their respective villages. They appoint the local judges and make the town laws. Matters of peace and war with villages outside Figig and all questions regarding the water supply are dealt with by the common council.

Come with me and look at one of these oasis communities. We shall go through the town of El Abid. The municipality contains about two thousand souls, but it is not in the least like any town of that size in our country. In the first place, I doubt whether it covers more than twenty acres; and as one looks at it through the palm trees he sees only the mud walls that inclose it, with the flat-roofed, windowless mud buildings rising above them here and there.

We enter El Abid by a gate in the wall, perhaps ten feet high and about five feet in width, which is shut at night by rough doors of palm wood hung on rude wooden hinges. There are two gates to the town, and outside one of them some camels, a part of a caravan which has just come in from the desert, are now lying on the ground chewing their cuds, while the Arab driver sits meditating in the midst of his freight, which he has unloaded for the time. As we go through the gate we pass donkeys laden with grain and sugar, and, turning this way and that, find ourselves in dark covered streets in which we might lose our way had we not guides.

The town of El Abid reminds me of the catacombs. There are houses built over the streets with only here and there a hole for the light. Outside is the fierce glare of the African sun; here in the main streets it is almost as dark as in some subterranean cavern or in the tomb of Ti, in the valley of the Nile above Cairo.

The streets cut the town at all angles. Some are too narrow for horses so that one must dismount and go through them on foot. In some of the wider streets ledges have been built along the walls upon which shrouded figures lie and sleep or sit crosslegged and chat. At intervals we see men squatting on the ground, hugging the walls while they work away at their trades. I notice several tailors making gowns, a cobbler or so sewing on yellow slippers, and one or two peddlers. There are many little boys with sore heads closely shaven, and sore eyes with flies buzzing about them. They stop and stare at us. As we go on many bearded Arabs scowl at our camera. There are no Arab women to be seen, although now and then I catch a glimpse of sheeted figures running out of our way. In the Jewish quarter I see some girls with earrings as big around as the bottom of a pint cup. The Jewish men are dressed like the Arabs.

The town of Zenaga, which we next visit, is very similar to El Abid save that its streets are a little wider and it has a business section. This surrounds a square which does not cover more than a quarter of an acre. I have seen many a stableyard quite as large. Around this are a number of small stores with a motley crowd of Arabs shopping and chatting outside them. Some of the men are buying wool and others sugar and tea. The average store is not much bigger than a good-sized dog kennel, and the customers stand in the street while they bargain.

We left our horses in the square in charge of the guides and visited one of the principal citizens, a merchant of wealth. He was worth probably five hundred dollars. We met our host in the square and went with him to his house. We were told to wait a short time in the street outside that he might go in and tell his women to go to their own quarters, as strange men were coming.

A moment later the door was opened. We entered first a courtyard roofed by the sky and surrounded by stables. In one stall was a loom at which a woman had been weaving a blanket. In another a boy was cutting up palm roots for firewood. This court was surrounded by mud buildings about forty feet high. They were of two stories with a gallery around the second floor. These buildings contain the living rooms of the family, all of which face on the gallery. Such rooms are used chiefly for sitting or loafing, the sleeping places being on the roof. Except when the weather is bad, all Figig sleeps with only the sky for a cover, the whole population practising the open-air cure.

Crossing the yard, we were taken up to the second floor into what was, I suppose, the best room of the house. It was some twenty feet square and perfectly bare, with a ceiling at least twenty-five feet in height. The walls were whitewashed and the ceiling was decorated with palm leaves dyed red and green. The room seemed well lighted although it had only one little window high up in the wall. This had no glass and was barred with iron. With the single exception of a rug about as big as a bed quilt there

Date growing goes on in the heart of the oasis towns. The palms
loom up over the high mud-brick walls enclosing each tiny holding, and
the narrow streets between are cut up by open irrigation ditches.

The Arabs say, "Plant a stick in the desert, water it, and you have a date palm." According to them, to make good dates the head of the tree must be in the burning sun the greater part of the year.

was no furniture. There was not even a divan built out from the wall as in some Moorish houses.

Nevertheless, our host seemed to think his house very fine, and I doubt not that the rug was better than those in many other homes in the town. He motioned us to sit down upon it, and then fearing that we might not be comfortable with our legs under us, he had several soap boxes brought in and asked us to sit upon them. We preferred the rug. After we had taken our seats, about half-a-dozen dark-faced, bearded men, relatives and friends of our host, came in and were introduced to us. They were all Arabs and we sat together in Arab fashion crosslegged upon the rug.

After a short time a slave appeared with a muskmelon and a bowl of ripe dates fresh from the trees. We ate them with our fingers while we watched the man of the house make the tea. First he put a handful of green tea into the pot and then a bunch of green mint leaves on top. He filled the pot with lumps of sugar which he broke with a tack hammer from a round sugar loaf as hard as rock candy. He then poured on boiling water from a kettle brought in by a slave and left the liquor to steep. As the sugar melted he added more from the loaf, and now and then put in more mint, tasting the tea from time to time until he thought it just right. He poured it carefully into little wine glasses, seeing that each glass was filled to just the same height. When all the glasses were even, he handed them around. We drank the tea slowly, chatting as we did so. Our host made a second pot and a third, and each of us took three glasses, as etiquette prescribes. The mint gave the tea a delicious flavour. It was not a mint julep but a sort of mint syrup, and on the whole it was about as good as any tea I have tasted.

99

CHAPTER XII

THE GARDEN SPOTS OF THE DESERT

VERY few of us appreciate the extent of the fertile spots of the Sahara. I have visited a number of the oases and through conversation with explorers and travellers of this part of the world have learned much about others. They are scattered at wide distances apart throughout the Sahara. Often for miles and miles there will be none, then again they will pepper the rocky wastes as though the Lord had sown patches of green from out of the sky. It is estimated that there are all together something like eighty thousand square miles of such garden spots scattered here and there upon this ocean of sand.

Eighty thousand square miles!

That means a territory about twice as large as the state of Ohio, and one infinitely richer. Suppose we could pick out of our country enough of its richest hot beds to cover Virginia and Kentucky, and patch them together. That will give some idea of the extent of the oases. To appreciate them, however, we must see them lying in the midst of a region larger than the United States, all the rest of which is absolutely sterile. We must imagine them surrounded by sand, stones, boulders, and all sorts of arid formations. There is no green of any kind for miles about, only a vast waste of blazing white, dazzling yellow, or eye-aching red. Off in the distance the mountains may be blue changing to a warm rose tint at sunset, but all is arid and bare.

Sometimes the oases form a string, or rather a chain, of green islands marking the route of some sunken Gulf Stream flowing through the sea of sand. Sometimes many of them are clustered in one place, showing the presence of a subterranean lake, or of springs or wells far from any other apparent water supply.

The desert has been described as a vast ocean with the oases as its islands. These Sahara islands, however, lie below and not above the level of their sandy sea. They are always found in depressions where the scanty waters have drained in and formed reservoirs.

Much of the desert has a bed of stiff clay under it. The water may sink down through a hundred or more feet of gravel and rock, but when it comes to this clay bed it flows on until it strikes a hollow, and if this hollow be high enough and deep enough the result is an oasis. In the district known as El Erg depressions of this kind furnish wells which can irrigate eight million date palms. The place where I am writing is in the Wady Saoora, a great underground stream that flows far below the surface for several hundred miles and then breaks out and supplies the oases of Touat, which are among the largest of the western Sahara.

I have already described the extensive date plantations of Figig. That oasis is not at all like the oasis of Tarla, which I visited during a thirty-mile horseback ride over the desert from Beni Ounif. Tarla is one of many islands of the desert scattered along the branches of the Wady Saoora. It is found on the Sousfane River, which unites with the Wady Gir near Igli to form the Saoora, the latter flowing on southward from there to feed the oases of Touat. From Tarla to Igli, a distance of more than a hundred miles, the river flows so far below the earth that there is no vegetation whatever.

Just east of Figig the Sousfane comes out in a trickling stream, and the result is a cluster of garden spots covering a distance of several miles. These green places are sometimes so narrow that one could throw a stone over them. They are often not more than one hundred feet wide, broadening out at times to three hundred feet or more. The river bed is frequently dry even at an oasis, but little pools of water now and then come to the surface, and near them date trees loaded with fruit grow out of the thirsty sand.

At Tarla such palms are to be seen for eight or ten miles up and down the river bed. I rode through them for at least six miles, under bunches of ripe dates all the way. I stopped near a village, which was inhabited not long ago, but is now deserted except at times of harvest. Its people have moved across the sands to Figig in order that they may be better protected from the brigands of the region, although they still cultivate their little date farms, and when the crop is ripe come back to their huts and towers to watch them.

The Arabs say that if you thrust a stick into the desert and water it you will soon have a tree. I can easily believe it. The sands of the Sahara are wonderfully fertile and if they could all be watered, this would be the garden spot of the globe. As it is, the rainfall of the whole region does not average more than five inches per year, though there are some places on the highlands that have occasional rains, and at certain seasons the water falls

Though they are but islands in a vast sea of sand, the total of all the oases of the Sahara is over 80,000 square miles—an area twice as big as Ohio.

Under much of the desert sands is a layer of hard clay. Subterranean waters flow along the top of this until they come out in a depression, which thus becomes an oasis.

there, off and on, for several days. When this occurs vegetation springs up as though by magic. The ground is carpeted with grass and wild flowers of many kinds burst into bloom.

In coming to Tarla I rode through patches of thorn bushes scattered at wide distances apart. Such vegetation is found all along this part of the Sousfane, the moisture not being sufficient for anything else. As I rode by I saw a drove of camels feeding on the thorn bushes and stopped and made photographs of them. Nearer the dry river bed, where the moisture was greater, were thick bunches of alfa grass and other desert plants and flowers; then came the region of date trees.

The soil of the Sahara is not like that of any country where rain is common. Indeed, the lack of rain is one cause of its great latent fertility. Other lands are leached by the water, the brooks and streams carrying a great part of their potash and other fertilizing matter out to the sea. This is not so here. The rocks may disintegrate more slowly, but the weathering goes on all the same. There is no place where the changes of temperature are more sudden and marked. The sun is red hot during the day, but after sunset the atmosphere becomes so cold that blankets are by no means uncomfortable. I always carry an overcoat in my rides over the desert and find that I need it. The changes are such that the rocks split and crumble under them. The desert winds are as strong as those of the sea, and when the sirocco blows, the sand cuts one's face. It dashes the sharp grains against the rocks and grinds them down without the action of water, so that all the rich fertilizing materials stay in the rock particles which make the soil.

The oases will grow almost anything that is grown in California. They produce luscious oranges, grapes, melons, and olives, as well as apples, peaches, pomegranates, and pears. In the northern Sahara they have wheat, barley, millet, and sorghum, and in the south tobacco and cotton. I see eggplants, onions, tomatoes, and cucumbers for sale in the markets, together with peas, beans, turnips, and carrots. The chief product, however, is dates.

The date palm thrives throughout the Sahara if it can only have water. It is the money crop of every oasis and the chief support of the people. Indeed, an oasis is known, not by the number of its inhabitants, but by the number of date palms it contains, and its inhabitants are rich or poor according as the dates produced are good or indifferent. In some places the people eat little else, and dates are fed to the camels and even to dogs. Such dates are not like those we have in America. They are a dry variety, which can be stored away and kept for years. Those sent to the United States are of a soft variety, so full of juice that they have to be drained before they are packed. Other dates might be called table dates. These are delicious when eaten fresh from the trees. We have them every day with our dinner and served at breakfast with the coffee and rolls. They are fat and yellow, as sweet as sugar and as plump as prunes before they are dried.

Among the oases fed by underground rivers those of Touat produce some of the best dates, although their product is not so good as the dates of Tafilelt. Touat is controlled by the French. Tuaregs on camels, under the employ of the Algerian government, patrol it to keep order and the people have become peaceful and thriving. It is not one oasis only, but is composed of five large groups of oases in the very centre of the Sahara, comprising three or four hundred petty states. It is scattered over a region as big as Indiana, and has all told a population of one hundred and twenty thousand Arabs, Berbers, and blacks.

Touat produces opium, tobacco, cotton, and some wheat and barley. A large part of its date crop is brought by caravans up the valley of the Saoora by way of Igli to the railroad at this point, to be shipped from here northward to Oran and thence to Europe.

The oases of Touat are a great centre of the caravan trade. They lie about eight hundred miles from Timbuktu in the Sudan and a like distance from Mogador on the Atlantic, from Tangier opposite the Strait of Gibraltar, and from Tripoli on the Mediterranean. The French are now diverting the Tripoli caravan trade to their Tunisian port of Gabes, the route to which is much shorter.

About the best dates known to the world come from Tafilelt. They are very large and sweet and are shipped in great quantities to Europe as tid-bits for the holiday season. Tafilelt, like Touat, comprises a number of separate oases, having all together three hundred fortified villages. Its chief town is Abuam, which has the biggest market of the western Sahara. It is a desert trade centre, sending two immense caravans every year to Timbuktu, almost a thousand miles directly south of it.

The people of Tafilelt are independent and warlike; they are fanatical Mohammedans and have caused no end of trouble. They occasionally declare a holy war and organize raids into Algeria. The population, which numbers more than a million, is about the worst in Morocco. Since the family of the Sultan comes from that region, the Tafileltites have a great influence in all parts of Morocco.

I am now at the town of Colomb-Bechar just south of Beni Ounif and at the end of the railroad, which runs up to Oran. It is proposed to push the line on to Timbuktu, a distance of eleven or twelve hundred miles farther. If this is done, the French will have a railway clear across the Sahara, and much of the trade which now goes on camels to Tripoli and to the Atlantic will be carried over this road. The track is a narrow gauge, but is well built and carries considerable freight. Though the trains are slow, they are infinitely superior to camels. Already a great deal of the caravan trade of the Sahara has been diverted to the Atlantic, the products of the western Sudan are carried up the Niger to Timbuktu and Jenne, and thence sent overland to the railroad which the French have built from the port of St. Louis to Kayes on the Senegal river. That whole territory is controlled by the French and there are French soldiers stationed in Timbuktu. The southern part of the Sahara is policed from that region and the chief imports come from Europe via the Atlantic Ocean instead of across country on camels. There is another scheme to extend the Biskra line, which runs down into the Algerian Sahara from Constantine not far from the Tunisian boundary, so in time we may cross the Sahara by rail.

The French are rapidly prospecting the desert. Their civil engineers have gone over it from here to Timbuktu and report that the chief difficulty in running a railroad between the two points will be the question of fuel. The fuel now used is briquettes made of coal dust, each being the size of an ordinary building brick, and the expense of transportation is already almost prohibitive. This cost will be increased as the line goes farther south. If we should discover, as Thomas Edison long tried to do, a way of getting the full energy of the coal without turning it into steam, that might solve the problem. As it is now, fully ninety per cent. of the heat energy is lost. By such an invention coal would be ten times as efficient as it is now and the Trans-Saharan railroad would be a commercial possibility.

The caravans which bring goods here from the oases are as clumsy a means of transportation as can be imagined. On a long trip each freight camel carries only about three hundred pounds, and the usual rate of travel is not more than two miles an hour. Every dozen camels have to have a driver, and each caravan is equipped with water bottles of pigskin and provisions for the people on the journey.

Many of these caravans stop for the camels to feed on the thorn bushes as they go over the desert. Others carry provisions for a part of the way. The routes are always along the lines of the oases, as a camel can go only from three to five days without water. On a long journey the beasts are kept from drinking for some time before starting in order that they may be thirsty and fill the reservoirs inside them just as they depart.

I find a great difference in the camels down here in the Sahara. There are some which go as easily as a gaited Kentucky saddler and others that jar one more than a hard trotting horse. The *meharis* seem to be all legs and to have the speed of the winds. They are well cared for and are as beautiful as camels can be. With the larger caravans there are usually some of these *meharis* ridden by soldiers or the chiefs of the tribes, armed with guns. Sometimes Tuaregs so mounted are employed as guards.

The freight camels, on the other hand, are dingy and scarred. They always look sullen and will bite at you as they pass. They groan, grumble, and even shed tears every morning when the loads are put on, and seem angry from daylight to dark. It takes two or three months for a caravan to cross the Sahara, whereas by railroad one could make the journey in three or four days.

CHAPTER XIII

AN AFRICAN CAPITAL

I AM in the blazing white, many-terraced city of Algiers. My hotel is the de la Regence on the Place du Gouvernement, next to the mosque of Djama el Djedid. It is within a stone's throw of the great palace occupied by the government offices and just off the Boulevard de la République, in the very heart of the city.

From my window I look out over the Bay of Algiers and the wide Mediterranean with its ships going out and coming in. The foothills of the Atlas Mountains line the opposite side of the bay, and the city rises from the water in terrace above terrace until it reaches the great white citadel that formed the residence and chief fortification of the piratical deys of the past.

Down at the wharves, where the city begins, are mighty breakwaters that extend out like arms at each end, embracing steamers and sailing vessels from all parts of the world. More than four thousand big vessels and twelve thousand coasters, aggregating over three million tons, pass in and out of those arms every year. There are great Atlantic liners which call here on their way from New York to Naples and Genoa, big steamers from China and Japan, and also fast ships from Marseilles which bring the mails on their five-hundred-mile voyage across the Mediterranean in less than twenty-four hours. These boats give Algiers daily communication with ports of France and are always loaded with passengers and freight. Their rates are so low that French labourers and mechanics cross over by hundreds.

Come with me down to the wharves and see something of the enormous trade that Algeria does with all parts of the world. Its commerce is worth having, for it amounts to many millions of dollars a year. So far, the balance of trade is with France, but the resources of the colony are being rapidly developed, so that in time Algeria will no doubt sell more than she buys.

But let us go down to the harbour. Running back from the water for a distance of perhaps five hundred feet is a level space covered with warehouses. We reach this by stone steps, making our way in and out through mountains of cargo. Enormous wagons hauled by from three to six horses are moving about, directed by drivers in turbans and gowns; the railroad engines are shunting cars this way and that, and an army of bare-calved, big-trousered Biskris are loading and unloading all kinds of goods. Cork bark, which is one of the chief exports, is stacked up like cord wood; hogsheads of wine numbering thousands are piled one on the top of the other, and there are great mounds of bags of wheat and other grain ready for shipment. Heaps of boxes, packed with dates, are waiting to start for Paris. There are also enormous quantities of goods coming in.

Both on the wharves and out in the harbour are immense loads of coal, for Algiers is one of the chief coaling stations of the Mediterranean. Nearly all the ships which call here take on fuel. The shipping arrangements are of the best. The trains from the interior come right down to

The vineyards of the Tell provide France with a second wine cellar
and keep the docks at Algiers crowded with casks awaiting shipment
across the Mediterranean.

The capital of the rich African province of France rises in terraces from one of the busiest harbours of the Mediterranean. Algiers is a popular winter resort as well as a great commercial city.

the sea so that freight can be taken on board the ships almost direct from the cars.

Now turn your back to the sea, and take a look at Algiers climbing the hills all about you. You must throw your head back and rest it well on your shoulders or you can't see it at all. The city begins with a wall about one hundred feet high. The wall consists of vaults and warehouses, with one of the fine boulevards of the world above them. The pavement of the thoroughfare forms the roofs of these buildings, and back and above it rises the rest of the city. The street is the Boulevard de la République. With the warehouses below, it cost more than forty million dollars. It was constructed on a long-time concession by an English company, and I understand that it has paid big dividends. It is a wide avenue with a stone balustrade along it facing the busiest part of the harbour. On the other side of the boulevard are buildings which contain some of the chief banks, shops, and business establishments of the city. The stores are on the ground floor only; above them are apartments with iron balconies across their fronts. The buildings are of yellow stucco of the even height of six stories, and so constructed that the ground floors open upon an arcade as in the Rue de Rivoli in Paris.

Foot passengers climb to this boulevard from the wharves by stone steps which wind their way up, while at each end are long inclined roadways up and down which a stream of vehicles steadily moves. On the boulevard itself gaily dressed Europeans, mixed with stately Arabs, walk to and fro. Street cars filled with passengers are continually passing, and riding in them one may have a magnificent view of the harbour and shipping.

Beginning with the Boulevard de la République is the French quarter, or what might be called modern Algiers, the white catacomb-like dwellings of the Moors and Arabs being on the hill higher up. Here the streets near the harbour would not be out of place in Paris or in any other city of France. They are smooth and paved with wood blocks. They are walled with French buildings, nearly all of which jut out over the sidewalks, so that the shoppers are protected from the fierce rays of the African sun. This is the case with the Rue Bab-Azoun, which runs just behind and parallel with the Boulevard de la République. It is the fashionable promenade of the business section, and from four to six o'clock every day it is filled with people buying and selling. The stores are like those of Europe. The goods are usually French, and their price marks show that they cost no more than in France. The best shops are along the north side of the street only. They have plate-glass store windows filled with beautiful goods, so that the avenue, walled in by pillars, looks like a museum.

The promenaders are stranger than those at any national exposition on earth. They comprise men and women of all classes, from the islanders of the Mediterranean Sea to the Orientals of the Atlas and the Desert of Sahara. Europe is well represented. There are French officers in their gay uniforms, jaunty French soldiers in high red caps, blue jackets, and bulging zouave pantaloons the colour of brickdust, and French ladies wearing the latest costumes from Paris. The French dandy is here, also the grisette.

The Mohammedan world walks along with the Christian. Veiled Moslem ladies who have just left the harem of some rich Arab pass by, wearing white trousers, each leg of which is as big around as a flour barrel. Their pantaloons hang in folds and I am told that it takes fourteen yards of stuff to make an ordinary pair. They are tied in at the calves or the ankles and are sometimes loaded with shot to keep them in shape. Unveiled Jewesses, dressed in gay colours and bright shawls, with thin black handkerchiefs glued to their foreheads, walk along in couples, and Kabyle women, bronze-faced and tattooed, ragged and dirty-gowned, come close behind. As four o'clock approaches the Rue Bab-Azoun is so packed that it looks like a great cave with a human stream of all colours flowing through it.

Another fine business street is the Rue d'Isley. This is the main road to Mustapha Supérieur, the fashionable villa centre on the hills high above the city. It has many new buildings; the old structures have been torn down, the fortified wall which once girdled Algiers has been removed, and other improvements have been made.

It is down in the French quarter that the city post office is situated. The French have given Algeria the best of postal facilities, and that at rates much lower than ours to Hawaii, Porto Rico, or the Philippines. All kinds of goods can be sent by mail at low cost, and there is an enormous mail-order business with France and Europe. The telegraph and telephone lines are controlled by the government and the tolls show the benefit of government management. They are as low as in France and less than half of our charge either at home or in our possessions. All the chief Algerian cities have telephones.

Algiers is a city of amusement halls, libraries, and schools. It has a city theatre subsidized by the govern-

ment, movie shows patronized by all classes, a casino
which is a kind of second-class vaudeville, and regular
concerts by the military bands in the Place du Gouvernement and at Mustapha Supérieur. It has many clubs, and
in the winter there are fashionable society gatherings.
The governor-general then gives balls and receptions, and
the French Army adds to the gaiety. Mustapha Supérieur, situated on the hills six hundred feet above the
harbour, has magnificent villas with tropical gardens
which are occupied at that time by rich Europeans, and
there are also large winter hotels filled with Americans and
English. There are street-car lines equipped with our
own electric service to all of the suburbs. Each car has
first- second- and third-class compartments, the fares being
regulated by the part of the car in which one rides.

The city has a university with departments of law,
medicine, science, and letters. This institution is magnificently situated on the hills overlooking the harbour.
It has about thirteen hundred students and is patronized
not only by the French but by the Arabs and the Moors.
There are also agricultural schools and technical schools of
various kinds throughout the colony, and Mohammedan
high schools, where Arab pupils are prepared for native
employment. There is a normal college in Algiers, and
not far from it a military school like that at West Point.

Between the ages of eight and fourteen all the children
of French citizens, and, indeed, all children except those
of the Arabs, are compelled to attend school. There are
common schools everywhere. I have found them on the
edge of Morocco, far down in the Desert of Sahara, and
also in Grand Kabylia, high up in the Atlas Mountains.
In most of the native schools both French and Arabic are

There is international competition between the bootblacks of Algiers, whose costumes range from the French beret, or pancake hat, and western "pants," to the fez and baggy trousers of the native.

Some public schoolyards have fountains in which the Algerian boy can take a plunge if things threaten to get too hot for him. Education is compulsory for children of French citizens up to fourteen years.

A pious pastime of the Algerian street urchin is "playing his way into heaven" on a one-stringed instrument, probably the ancestor of the violin.

taught, and in many places the little ones write texts from the Koran on their wooden slates and commit them to memory.

Foreign and native religious houses are found in all of the large settlements. There are Moslem shrines and mosques on all sides. The French have a cathedral in Algiers and the Roman Catholic Church has an archbishop. There is a Scotch Presbyterian Church in Mustapha Supérieur, and there are Protestant pastors and Jewish rabbis who share in the government grants for religious support.

One might think that the modernizing of their city would change the character of the Arabs, and that they would throw off the customs and costumes of the Arabian Nights and adopt those of our present-day world. They do not. Come with me into the native quarter, which adjoins the French section as closely as a patch on a quilt. We climb to it by a staircase of stone steps and enter another world.

Here the streets are too narrow for carriages or horses. With the exception of a few crossroads, the walls are so close together that the fat Jewesses are squeezed as they go through. In places such as the Rue de Diable, or Street of the Devil, the houses are built over the streets, and one climbs through dark pipes, as it were, from one level to another. It makes me think of the homes of the cave-dwellers.

The French city was gay and noisy. This old quarter is sullen and silent. Sober-faced men in turbans and gowns, and women with sheets of white linen fastened so tightly over their faces that they seem to be pasted on, shuffle along in slippers, their voluminous breeches billowing about them. The city is all uphill and most of the streets consist of staircases climbing from level to level.

The shops are in striking contrast with those of the Rue Bab-Azoun. On each side of us are holes in the walls in which grim-looking Arabs sit surrounded by goods or work away at their trades. Here is a shoemaker with four helpers in a boxlike cell not more than eight feet square; just above is a carpenter in a space hardly big enough for his bench, while farther on are men in similar quarters, making jewellery of horns, using their toes to hold the objects they are polishing as we use our fingers.

How strange the crowd looks! There are bare-legged Biskris who have come in from the desert to act as porters carrying great loads on their backs. There are Kabyles with turbans and big hats from the farms, and there are many fat Mozabites, the Jews of the Sahara, who have come to town to make fortunes by trading with the Christians and Arabs. Now and then a native soldier makes his way through the crowd, and a Jewish woman, unveiled, waddles along. Indeed, old Algiers is the same as it has been from century to century far back into the time of the deys, when these people had Christian slaves and their piratical bands were the terror of Europe. The scenes are those of the Arabian Nights and the Scriptures. At every few steps we pass a man who might be an Abraham or an Isaac, and are crowded against the wall by men who remind us of the Forty Thieves. The pious Mohammedan is also in evidence. Turbaned men are praying in business hours, while merchants are to be seen reading the Koran in their shops between sales.

Through scenes like this we climb up to the citadel,

which was both the palace and the fortification of the deys of the past. This rises high over the rest of the town, and is now occupied by French troops. There are soldiers at the gates, who watch us as we pass through.

The citadel is surrounded by walls, with great portholes, through which were thrust two hundred guns, commanding the city and harbour. There is one building which the dey devoted to his harem. Another was his mosque, which has been turned into a French church; and a third, a tower built right over the entrance gate, contained the throne room where the dey held court. Outside this room is a chain which hangs down over the entrance gate. Upon it were strung the heads of Christians and criminals beheaded according to orders from the court above. I am told that the heads were usually shown for twenty-four hours, after which they were taken down and given to the Mohammedan soldiers for footballs.

Such were some of the capers these Moslems were cutting before high heaven when John Quincy Adams was president of the United States. They played no such tricks on the Yankees, however, for Commodore Decatur had taught them better. Nevertheless, they were still bulldozing Europe and preying upon the shipping of the Mediterranean Sea. They enslaved and murdered Christians and insulted the Powers when they objected. One morning, late in the twenties, when he happened to be feeling especially bad, the reigning dey held an interview with the French consul. He may have been having trouble with his numerous wives, his breakfast may not have agreed with him, or he may have been dissatisfied with the number of Christian heads hung upon the chain below his judgment seat. At any rate, he grew angry during the interview and struck the French consul in the face with his fan. The blow was not heavy, but it cost him his kingdom. France immediately declared war. It conquered the army of the dey and since then Algeria has been a dependency of France.

An Arab cemetery of Algiers.   The devout Moslem fears not death,
for in his Paradise he lives in a palace served by his wives, all as beautiful
as young brides, and by seventy-two black-eyed houris besides.

Surrounded by his wives and retainers the former king of Dahomey, once commander of an army of African Amazons, ended his days in captivity near Algiers.

CHAPTER XIV

BEHANZIN, KING OF THE AMAZONS

THIS is the story of my audience with Behanzin, whose army of female warriors once sent cold chills down the backs of French soldiers and whose conquest gave France Dahomey. Behanzin fought battle after battle with the French and caused them no end of trouble. His wars with them cost millions. Indeed, at one time the Chamber of Deputies at Paris made a single appropriation of six hundred thousand dollars to carry them on. He made treaty after treaty with France only to break them, and it was long before the French were able to subdue him and take possession of his kingdom. After that he was held in close captivity and prevented from having any intercourse with his country and people.

Behanzin was first carried off to the West Indies and imprisoned in Martinique, the little island belonging to France. Later he was given a villa there and allowed to drive about with his favourite wife and one of his sons. Finally he was brought from Martinique to Blida, about thirty miles from Algiers. Here he died shortly after my audience with him. The cause of his transfer was largely his ill-health and his fear of the volcano Mont Pelée. When the great eruption occurred Behanzin became frightfully excited, and every earth tremor thereafter sent him into fits of terror that the volcanic disturbances might extend to his home. His nerves became so shattered that the French feared he would die; so it was ordered that he be transferred to Algeria and kept under surveillance at Blida.

Blida is a military station with barracks inside and a great fort on the foothills of the Atlas Mountains near by. It has the chief army stud of the Algerian cavalry, and its surroundings are such that it would have been useless for the king to try to escape. He was given a villa outside the city walls, but he was always surrounded by spies and police. Behanzin very well knew that it was out of the question for him to think of making his way off to the sea, and also that the two thousand miles of desert between him and Dahomey were patrolled by French soldiers on swift camels. While in Martinique he had made all sorts of promises of good behaviour if he were allowed to go back to his own country. He continued to make such promises here, and it is believed that the chief cause of his death was his homesickness for the land of the Amazons.

I have the honour of having had the last newspaper interview with this notorious monarch. The interview was not full of meat, for the king was too sick to talk much, and as to the honour, I doubt much if that term applies to the meeting with one who had probably offered up human sacrifices, who had killed many Christians, and who had most likely often sharpened his ivory teeth upon the human flesh of the Caucasian race. At any rate, I saw and talked with Behanzin in his prison villa at Blida. My way to the villa was over a road fenced in by high walls above which waved the green branches of olive and orange trees. We passed by gardens filled with roses, by vineyards loaded with fat blue grapes, and by enough fig trees,

I verily believe, to have clad the six thousand Eves of Behanzin's Amazon army.

Finally we came to a gate labelled "*La Paisible*"—"The Peaceable." It was indeed a facetious name for the dwelling place of this, the bloodthirstiest of kings. Nevertheless, it was there that Behanzin was living with his four wives and his numerous children. The villa was a large two-story structure surrounded by a veranda twelve feet wide, with the rooms opening out upon it, and standing in an orange grove of several acres. As I went up the walk I passed the two pet donkeys of the king's little ebony princes, which were feeding under the trees.

As I neared the house I was met by Behanzin's aide-de-camp, or the man who came nearest to being his high court chamberlain. He was dressed in white duck. He was a Negro of Martinique who had been with the king for some years and spoke French fluently. Taking my card, he asked me to stay outside while he learned whether His Majesty would receive my party. Within a few moments he returned and led us upstairs to the veranda. Here we waited while the "high court chamberlain" crawled in through one of the windows and passed out several cane-seated chairs to us, asking us to rest upon them until His Majesty was ready.

As we tarried, the crown prince, Oualino, an intelligent young fellow of eighteen, as black as your boots and with typical Negro features, came around the corner and we chatted with him. He spoke French well and understood a few words of English. He was only six years old when his father was carried away from his kingdom, and, like the old king, he said he wanted to go back to Dahomey. He was quite dignified, bearing himself with

121

what might be called an imperial air. He told me that
Behanzin had been ill ever since he came to Algeria, that
the weather did not agree with him, or with his four wives,
and that they all wanted to go back either to Martinique
or on to Dahomey. He said he feared his father would
die if a change were not made at once.

After a few moments word came that the king would
receive us, so we went with Prince Oualino around the
veranda to the other side of the house and were admitted
to the imperial presence. As the room in which the ex-
king of Dahomey was lying opened on the porch, we
came right upon him as we entered the door. He rested
on a sort of cot with a white pillow under his head. His
black body was covered with only a gray-blue cape which
fell back as he half rose, showing his skin almost to the
waist. He had on a curious black velvet cap covered with
gold embroidery, which fitted his head closely, coming
low down over the forehead, covering the ears, and falling
almost to the shoulders. As he talked with me he now
and then pulled his gown up, but it kept falling back,
exposing four or five square feet of oily black skin. Upon
my presentation he reached out a naked black arm and
shook my hand saying in French, *"Bon jour!"*

As we chatted I could see two of his wives who were
waiting upon him. One of these seemed to be undergoing
some kind of punishment, for she was on her knees, leaning over a chair in the back of the room. The other was
crouched low on the floor on the opposite side of the cot
from where I stood. Both were jet-black and of the
most pronounced Negro type. Their woolly hair clung
close to their scalps in small kinky curls; they had flat
noses and white teeth, and each wore great plugs in her

ears. Their black necks, arms, and shoulders were perfectly bare, their white skirts fitting up close to the armpits, where they were tied by twisted white bands knotted over the breast. At the time of his death Behanzin had only four wives, a paltry allowance in comparison with the days of his prime, when he had three fourths of the young women of his whole nation to choose from. All of his Amazons were at his command, and hundreds of them were young girls of eighteen or more years of age. The king was sixty-three years old when he died, and the women I saw with him were, I judge, each forty or fifty years old. No one knows how many children he had. He left several little ones in Algeria and some in Martinique, and he had in his family also several good-sized girls and the crown prince, whom I have described.

One of my first questions to the king was as to his health. He replied that he was ill and that he desired to go back to Dahomey, his native country. He said Algeria was too cold for him and that he could not keep warm. He asserted that he was not dangerous to the French, that his army was long since disbanded, that he would make no further wars, and that there was no reason why he should not go home.

I asked Behanzin to tell me something about his country, Dahomey. He described it as a beautiful land, rich in its resources, and basking in the tropical sun from one year's end to another. His eyes lighted up as he spoke of it and it seemed to me I saw his thick lips quiver.

I referred to the stories which have been published of his Amazons and asked him whether those girl-soldiers were as brave as they had been painted. At this the king's lips tightened and methought I could see the lust of battle come into his bleary old eyes. He replied that the Amazons were brave and faithful, but that the French had outnumbered and overpowered them, and that now he was only a captive in the hands of his enemies.

I told him that I was a journalist, that I would tell the American people I had spoken with him, and that I could carry a greeting from him to them if he wished. He replied: *"Amis, tous amis,"* "Friends, we are all friends." He then reached out his naked black arm from under the cape, again exposing his skin to the waist, and shook hands with me as I said good-bye.

As I went down the steps upon leaving, I saw the French white guard watching me and I was told that His Majesty was never alone for a moment. If he drove out with his wives, a soldier or a policeman went with them to prevent any possible attempt at escape. His captivity was, in fact, always before him. He was warned again and again that he would surely be recaptured if he attempted to run away, and that although there were in Algeria many Sudanese Negroes as black as himself, there were none like Behanzin. He was assured that the news of his loss would put the army, the police, and the spies on the search, and that at the same time his guards kept him always in sight.

Outside this surveillance the king was fairly well treated by his French captors. He had all his expenses paid by the Government. His villa was free, his French cooks cost him nothing, and his provisions and his scanty clothing were supplied without charge. He had in addition to all this an allowance of money of eighteen thousand francs a year, which means about thirty-six hundred dollars of our money, or just about ten dollars a day. This certainly ought to have sufficed to keep him in tobacco and to furnish now and then a new ear plug for each of his wives.

Everything goes by contrast, however, and such a sum was as nothing to this Negro king who once numbered his assets by millions of francs and his subjects by hundreds of thousands.

Since the conquest of Dahomey the French have turned things upside down and are fast developing the country. They have established schools in all the villages, and at Porto Novo, the seat of government, there is an experimental farm. Cotton plantations have been set out. Between four and five hundred vessels now call there annually and the commerce is growing. Two railroads have been built, and a telegraph line joins Kotonu with Behanzin's old capital, Abomey, and with the River Niger, Timbuktu, and the Senegal.

These Dahomey people are of the same race as our Negroes. Their country is on the Gulf of Guinea, where most of the slaves were caught in early days. They are of pure Negro stock, belonging to the Fan branch of the Ewe family. The people go about half naked. They believe in witches and have their witch doctors. When Behanzin was in the height of his power, travellers who passed through Dahomey gave vivid pictures of him and his army. They said he sprinkled his ancestors' graves once every year with human blood. He was then so great that when his people approached him they had to crawl up to him with their faces in the dust. The annual grave sprinkling, which took place in October, lasted several weeks. The Amazons acted as the executioners, the victims who supplied the blood being usually captives taken in war. When the time for the killing arrived these unfortunate wretches were dressed in white shirts, tied hand and foot, and placed in baskets on the top of a platform. The king first made a speech, and then the Amazons hurled the victims down into a crowd, where they met with a horrible death. I have seen it stated that their skulls were used to adorn the palace walls and that this king had a sleeping chamber paved with the heads of his enemies.

The army of Amazons was one of the strangest features of King Behanzin's outfit. Most of them were young women of from eighteen to twenty-five years of age, and many had been trained to fight from their childhood. Others were wives who had been unfaithful to their husbands, and others, women who had been divorced on account of their bad tempers, because of their failure to have children, or for some other reason which caused their husbands to want to get rid of them. They were thereupon handed over to the king, and if they had the requisite physical vigour were drilled for the Amazon corps.

These Amazons were armed with swords, battle-axes, and guns. They were wonderfully brave and were trained to endure pain of all kinds. They were the king's special guard, and fought better than the male warriors in the wars with the French.

It is also said that after a woman joined the army she was shut off from marriage, the virgins among them being bound to perpetual maidenhood unless they were desired by the king. They were trained to ferocity, and the French say that in battle their recklessness was increased by a liberal allowance of gin. The girls had just enough

Much of the work on the Tell farms is done by the Berbers. The girls and women go unveiled and are tattooed on their cheeks, foreheads, or chins.

The roads leading out of Algiers are shaded with trees, and pass through gardens of roses, rich vineyards loaded with fat blue grapes, and orchards of fig trees.

liquor to make them devilish without interfering with their fighting.

These famous black women warriors had a uniform of their own. They wore tips of horns on their heads and had sleeveless garments of blue and white cloth which fell to the knees. Under these were short trousers, which made it easy to distinguish them from the half-naked male warriors. In times of peace they also wore bells around their necks as a warning to all men not in the army to keep out of their way. The other sex was afraid of them, too, and fled upon their approach, as it was death to be caught paying them special attentions. The women took vows of chastity upon entering the army, being, in fact, regarded somewhat as were the Vestal Virgins of old Rome. I have heard that many of these Amazons were beautiful, but if so they must have been far different from the African queens I saw during my audience with their former commander and king.

It is said that these women warriors were at their best during the last war which Behanzin waged with the French. During that struggle he caused a number of them to be beheaded on a charge of cowardice, and tried in every way to make them perfectly fearless and indifferent to pain. Among the most terrible trials of their courage was a climb up walls of cactus bushes sixteen feet high to a roof several hundred feet long carpeted with cactus. These barefooted and barelegged girls climbed the bristling walls and passed over the roof covered with cactus thorns. Then, as the story goes, they ran back and showed themselves to the king, their faces wreathed with smiles, although their feet and legs were covered with blood.

One of the French officers told me that the Amazons always planned to take their enemy by surprise, and that they made forced marches at night so as to fall upon them early in the morning. They would dash in upon their foes before they were fully awake, and then, with a terrible cry, would spring to the fray. This man said that he once saw four thousand of them grouped around King Behanzin, and that they were as muscular as the male warriors and quite as soldierly looking.

CHAPTER XV

THE people of the Atlas Mountains are whites, with features like ours, and some of them have blue eyes and red hair. Many have rosy skins and complexions so fair that if dressed in European clothes they would not look strange in London, Paris, or New York. Others are darker, from their admixture with the Arabs and Moors, but they are still a distinct people and strong enough to impress their type on their offspring. This race is scattered through the mighty mountains of northwestern Africa. It is composed of the Berbers or Kabyles, who are numbered by millions and are found everywhere in these hills.

The Atlas Mountains begin opposite the Canary Islands, well down the Atlantic coast, and run from southwest to northeast for a distance of more than fifteen hundred miles, ending near Cape Bon, below the Island of Sicily. They are longer than from Philadelphia to Omaha and wider than the distance between Washington and New York. The region is more than one seventh the size of the United States proper, and, including the valleys, has a population of fifteen millions or more.

Fully one half of these people are made up of the descendants of this white race, and if we add the tribes which have left the mountains and gone down into the lowlands and desert, the Kabyles will number still more. The

Tuaregs, the fierce brigands of the Sahara, who wear veils night and day and scour the desert on camels and rob the caravans, are of Berber origin, and so are the Biskris and others who come from far down in the Sahara to do the heavy work about the wharves of the Algerian ports. There are several million Berbers in Morocco, where they have divided up into hundreds of tribes. They live in the mountains and are lawless and wild. The band of Raisuli, which kidnapped Ion Perdicaris, was one of these tribes.

The Berbers are the oldest white race upon record, and if we could trace our own forefathers back to the Stone Age we should probably find that they are our cousins. They are supposed to have come here from southern Europe, but if so, it was when Europe was savage and when our ancestors were still eating with their fingers and sleeping on skins in the wilds of the forests.

Indeed, the Berbers were here when Athens was in its infancy and when Rome was yet to be born. There are records in the Egyptian temples dating as far back as thirteen hundred years before Christ, which speak of them as having rosy cheeks, blue eyes, and red hair, and we find them fighting with the Phœnicians, the Carthaginians, the Romans, the Goths, and the Vandals. They were conquered again and again, but they fled to their fastness in the Atlas and have kept their individuality to this day.

When the Arabs came, the Berbers were once more overcome. They adopted the Mohammedan religion but modified it to suit themselves, and they have still their own ways and customs, as they had in the past. The Kabyle women do not veil their faces, and a man is satisfied to have but one wife. A large number, however, have intermarried with the alien races, so that there are now among them as many brown skins as fair ones. The fierce African sun darkens the lighter-hued Kabyles in the summer until they take on the brown, roseate complexions of Italy, Spain, and south France.

I have seen many of these fair-skinned Berbers or Kabyles since I came to the Black Continent. I met them first in Morocco and again in Spanish Africa, and I have found them everywhere during my travels in Algeria. I have spent a week in Grand Kabylia, where they are almost the sole inhabitants, and have gone from village to village investigating their customs and photographing them at work and in their homes. Within the last three days I have driven for more than a hundred miles through the wildest of these African mountains, crossing the Grand Atlas chain from Tizi-Ouzou, the capital of Kabylia, by way of Fort National and Michelet, over a pass almost as high as Mount Washington, and then coming down to this little town of Maillot, in the rich valley of the Tell, where I am now.

Our road over the mountains covered a distance of about sixty-five miles. It was built years ago by the French as a military highway, and it is so smooth that one can go over it in an automobile. Indeed, I was offered a car for the trip from Algiers at a cost of twenty-five dollars per day, but I found that I should have to pay one day's return fare for every day I used the machine, making the cost really fifty dollars per diem. As there was also danger of a breakdown in the mountains, I concluded to hire a carriage instead. This I got for fifteen dollars a day. I had an Arab driver and three horses hitched up abreast, and the carriage travel enabled me to make my way leisurely from point to point, now stopping at a village and now at the little fields where the Kabyles were working.

This road over the Atlas is a wonderful piece of civil engineering. It goes along the sides of the cliffs and has been actually cut out of the rocks. In places the drop to the valley below is something like two thousand feet. At times, when a caravan of camels passed by us, each beast loaded with two great, long bags of barley which tripled its width, we had to stop for fear we might be crowded over the rocks and dashed to pieces in the valley below. At other places we met droves of donkeys, which their Kabyle owners had to bring down to single file to enable us to pass, and again companies of Berbers, with loads on their backs, who walked in the same order.

The road is a limestone pike with frequent stone culverts and now and then bridges of stone and iron. Away up on the top of the Atlas there is a tunnel which has been blasted through the rock; and at the very top of the pass we went through a deep cut made for the road. Along the whole way are piles of broken stone, showing that repairs are going on all the time, and there are guard houses at every few miles where the men who take care of the road are stationed. This pass is, in fact, a military highway, and enables France to control the whole surrounding region.

The Kabyles are among the most insurrectionary of the population of Algeria. Like the Swiss, they live in the mountains, and have the same love of freedom. In 1871, when France had its war with Germany, some of these mountain tribes revolted and an army of them marched on Algiers. They were defeated by the French, and since then no Kabyle or other native, except in certain wild districts, is allowed to have arms. Another reason for denying arms to the Kabyles of the Atlas is the fact that these people are much given to deadly feuds among themselves.

At Fort National I found a battalion of zouaves, about eight hundred strong. The town itself is fortified in such a way that its guns command the many villages on the neighbouring peaks. On my way to Tizi-Ouzou I passed several regiments of French soldiers on the march, and I could easily see how an army of them with a road like this could keep the people in order. I found most of the Kabyles friendly, the contrast between them and their brothers in Morocco being most striking.

Before I describe my visits to the Kabyle villages I want to tell you something about the mighty mountains which form their homes. I have travelled through the Alps, the Himalayas, the Andes, and the Rockies. Each has its own grandeur. The same is true of these lofty African mountains, which in many respects have scenery surpassing that of any other range of the world. The air here is as clear as that on the high plateau of Bolivia and one can see as far as on Lake Titicaca. The sun is so bright that where it strikes the fleecy white clouds it paints patches of navy blue velvet on the slopes below. These high Atlas peaks rise from the plain in rugged majesty. They roll over each other, with great canyons and gorges, and may be seen a hundred miles or more away cutting the blue sky of the horizon. They are of as many colours as the mountains of Colorado and in places are quite as ragged and rocky. Almost everywhere they are cultivated high above the line of fertility of the hills of other countries. Their sides are cut up into patches of all shapes, some of which are no bigger than a parlour rug. About these patches are stone walls or hedges, or sometimes furrows or ditches. Some have fruit trees growing in them, but more often only bunches of scrub, among which the grain has been planted. Each of these little patches is a Kabyle farm. Nearly every family owns some land, to which it clings as its dearest possession. The men cultivate their little crops, making what they can from them, and then go down into the lowlands to work for the French farmers to piece out their incomes.

Along the lower slopes of the Atlas there are many big orchards, but these are owned mostly by the French. They are walled off from the road by hedges of cactus in which dried thorn bushes have been twined, to make a barrier impassable for man or beast. There are also olive orchards, and almost everywhere, even high up in the mountains, are groves of wild olive trees, with now and then a forest of the evergreen oak the bark of which furnishes our cork.

Others of the mountains, especially the slopes facing the valley of the Tell, are covered with scrubby oaks with light green leaves an inch long and of much the same shape as those of a rose bush. The trees are nothing like the grand oaks of America, but nevertheless they bear acorns which feed numerous hogs. Many of these oaks are trimmed of their branches every year in order that the twigs and limbs may be used for fuel. I am told that it is against the law to cut the trees down to the ground, and that most of the charcoal and firewood of Algeria are made from these switches. They are used by the bakers, the bread of a great part of Algeria being baked by them.

As one climbs up the Atlas Mountains the views widen

The Kabyle farms are tiny patches clinging to the mountain side. Nearly every family in the red-roofed hill-top villages owns some land, though most of the men also work out for wages.

The French have built a wonderful road through the Atlas Mountains, and into Grand Kabylia over which grain and other products are brought down from the farms on the backs of donkeys and camels.

The Kabyles belong to the oldest white race known. A Berber
has but one wife, whom he allows to go about unveiled—and also to do
all the heavy work.

so that the whole world seems spread out below. One can see so far that panoramas from such mountains as the Alps dwindle by comparison. The ragged hills stretch away for hundreds of miles on every side, and in the winter, when the Atlas is covered with snow, the views must be beyond expression magnificent. I saw one sunset at the very top of the pass which will remain in my memory as among the most wonderful of the cloud paintings of my life. During the day the sirocco had been blowing its hot blast from the desert and the sun had been hidden. When it set the sky was full of clouds which it gilded with a hundred roseate hues. We were high up on the mountain pass with great masses of fleecy gold overhead and beneath us. The mountains took on all tints and shades, their sides becoming a patchwork of many colours which we saw through a thin golden veil. On some hills the veil was a delicate lavender, on others a snow-white tinged with rose pink. As the sun disappeared a band of royal purple ran around the foot of the mountain peaks, while there were bands of burning copper above and below.

But far the most striking feature of the whole of these Atlas scenes is the human interest which shines out of their every picture. The Kabyle villages are everywhere. There are thousands of them in the Algerian mountains. Every great hilltop is spotted with them and they cap all the lower peaks. Right on the tops of the hills the people build their little huts of stone and plaster with roofs of red tile. The walls are whitewashed, so that every town makes a great patch of white and red on the landscape.

The villages are usually far off the road and are reached only by mule paths. I climbed up and visited some of them.   One was entered by a gate forming a sort of loafing place for the gowned, bronzed-faced, turbaned citizens. Passing through this, I was in the midst of the settlement. The houses stand close together, built along narrow streets with no pavements of any kind.   They are all of one story and look more like stables than homes.   The doors are rude although some have carving upon them. They open into a court upon which are sometimes two houses, both facing the street.   The average house is about fifteen feet square with a ridge roof which is seldom more than twelve feet in height at the comb.   Here in the Atlas these roofs are of red tile, but in other places they are of thatch.

The houses are entered by doors as rough as those in the walls of the courts.   The homes are absolutely without ornamentation.   They have no windows, and, except through a little hole about a foot square under the roof at one end, have no light but that which comes in at the door.

Let me give you a picture of one of these Berber homes which I visited yesterday.   My dragoman, Emmanuel Zammitt, who speaks the Kabyle language, acted as my interpreter, and through him the owner gave us permission to enter.   We had tried at several other houses, but the women ran from us as though we had the plague and the boys slammed the court doors in our faces.

Like all Mohammedans, the Kabyles are jealous, allowing their women to have nothing to do with strange men. In this case both husband and wife were at home, for the man was more liberal than most of his kind.   He did not introduce us to his wife, but she was with him in the hut and, as usual, unveiled.   She had a baby at her breast, while a half dozen more small children were sprawling over the floor. Indeed, we had to step carefully at first for fear of trampling a baby, but as our eyes became accustomed to the darkness we got along very well.

In this house there was no sign of what we call furniture. There were neither chairs nor tables. The members of the family were sitting around a pile of figs which they were sorting as we entered. At meals they sit on the floor and eat squatting about the single bowl which usually contains the main dish of each meal. They have wooden spoons and use a common knife. They eat most things with their fingers and often break up bread and soak it in the soup or stew. They have meat about once a week, but their chief diet consists of fruit and of bread made of wheat or other grain. They grind their meal themselves, sometimes in the family mill and sometimes in one belonging to the village in common.

In a little home like this the winter supplies of the family are stored. One of the receptacles I noticed was a stone jar for figs with a hole in the bottom to allow the juice to run out; another was a larger vessel of the same material for wheat or corn. The latter would hold perhaps twenty bushels. There was also a large clay jar for the olive oil made on the little home farm and pressed out by the family. When I asked where the cooking was done, the woman pointed to a hole in the floor in one corner of the hut. The floor is the bare rock, so that there is no danger of fire.

As I looked about me I heard a sheep bleating apparently right under my feet. Turning quickly around, I saw a long-horned ram and a nanny goat looking at me from under a shelf at the back of the hut. This shelf was the chief sleeping place of the family, while the space below it served as a stable. There were some chickens in the same place and at night the donkeys and other animals belonging to the family are brought in and all sleep together. These Kabyle sheep are tame, following their masters from place to place like dogs. The people have many sheep, which they pasture on the mountains in one common flock watched by a shepherd. The sheep and goats are brought into town every night. As soon as they enter the village each runs for its own home and remains there until morning.

Some of these Kabyle women are fine looking. The wife of my host was about twenty, and would have been considered pretty in any crowd of American maidens. Her cheeks were rosy and her features as regular as those of the Venus de Medici. She wore a dress of bright red calico which came almost to her feet but still showed the thick silver rings about her bare ankles. She had heavy earrings and bracelets. Around her neck was a chain to which many ornaments were hung, and her breast was covered with great pins of white metal set with bright-coloured stones. I should say that she had at least two pounds of jewellery upon her. Her eyelids were blackened to add to her beauty. Like nearly all the Kabyle women I have seen, she was also tattooed on the cheeks and on the forehead and the chin.

Although even the poorest of the women of Kabylia wear more or less jewellery, many are ragged. Those who go through the streets have their skirts so pulled up that they show a large expanse of bare calf. I see them doing all sorts of hard labour. They carry water from the village well in clay jars; they gather the wood needed for

138

cooking, and not a few labour out in the fields. Indeed, their situation makes one think of the vaudeville song—

> Oh, the women do the work, do the work,
> While the men do the standing around—

or of that other sweet and well-known ditty—

> Everybody works but Father.

The Kabyle men are a strange combination of thriftiness and laziness. I saw many of them loafing about the streets while the women passed by loaded with all sorts of burdens. When at home they let their wives do as much as they will, yet they hire themselves out to the French farmers of the Tell to aid in planting and harvesting the crops. They are accumulative, saving almost all their wages, and many of them amass small fortunes of a few hundred dollars or so.

Indeed, these people have many qualities which distinguish them from the Arabs and Moors by whom they are surrounded. Their white blood crops out in their desire for independence and self-government. They are ruled by the French, but regulate local matters themselves. Each town is a little republic, with its own council and a public meeting house where town affairs are discussed. It has its own municipal laws and elects its own officials. Each village has a mosque and a school. The school is supplied with teachers by the French, and the children are taught to speak and write French as well as Arabic. The mosques are rude affairs, but the Kabyles go to them regularly and face Mecca as they pray. They are naturally religious, though they have changed the Mohammedan faith to suit themselves and have their own ideas of morals, right, and justice.

CHAPTER XVI

AN EXILED AFRICAN QUEEN

ONCE the ruler of the third largest island of the world, a country bigger than France, twice as large as Italy, and more than three times as big as New England, the beloved queen of more than four million people, with all the money she could spend, an army of her own, the most brilliant royal court south of the Equator, and all that she could wish for in the way of luxury, pomp, and power. To-day, deposed from her throne, a pensioner on the bounty of the French Government, an exile in the hands of her conquerors, watched always by spies and guarded by a muscular French woman, who controls her conversations and actions. Such is the present condition of Ranavalona III, the famed queen of Madagascar, by whom I was granted the honour of an audience to-day.

Her name, Ranavalona, is an imperial cognomen meaning "The Granddaughter of God." She comes of the royal family which ruled Madagascar for many years. She is a descendant of Radama I, who became king of all Madagascar in 1810. He was a chief of the Hovas, one of the largest and most civilized tribes of the island, who, after conquering many of the other tribes, formed a union with the Sakalavas by marrying Rosalimo, a Sakalava princess.

King Radama was the first to introduce our civilization

into Madagascar. He welcomed the missionaries, and as far back as 1820 introduced Protestant Christianity among the Hovas. During his reign schools were established, churches were built, the Bible was printed in the Malagasy language, and numbers of the people were converted. After his death, one of his wives, Ranavalona I, assumed the throne. She opposed the missionaries, but her son, Radama II, again gave the people full religious liberty and after him Queen Ranavalona II, the aunt of this queen, carried on the good work. She was succeeded by the woman I talked with to-day who was at that time only a young girl. I think she is a widow, for, according to custom, when she took the throne she married the prime minister, who was then seventy years old, and who must have died long ago.

When Ranavalona was crowned she made a change in the coronation ceremonies of the country. Other monarchs had always been attended by soldiers. She made school children her chief guard of honour. She had picked out five hundred boys and four hundred girls from the chief schools of Tananarivo, her capital, and all the scholars, with their teachers, had excellent places to see the ceremony. The day before, the schoolboys drilled and went through their spear and shield exercises in her presence, and at the time of the coronation she was attended by regiments of boys in uniform and troops of girls dressed in white.

The Queen, when I met her to-day, wore a plain black silk skirt with a blouse of white silk beautifully embroidered. She had at her throat a star of diamonds set in old silver, while about her neck was a gold chain as big around as your little finger. Her clothes were like those any American lady might wear when receiving afternoon callers, being neither extravagant nor striking in any way.

When Ranavalona was crowned she wore a white brocaded silk robe heavy with gold, with a train of crimson velvet embroidered in gold. She wore a large gold crown of peculiar design which fairly sparkled with jewels. She is said still to have many beautiful jewels. In fact, when she left the island of Réunion, to which she was first banished, the statement was made that the precious stones she took with her were worth more than two million dollars.

As the crown rested upon the Queen's head, the people fell upon their knees and then burst forth into a shout of applause, while the soldiers flourished their spears and the cannon roared. There were cheers upon cheers from the boys and girls and from the two hundred thousand natives said to have been present.

After that the Queen made a speech to her people. She used Bible quotations throughout her address, saying, among other things: "The fear of the Lord is the beginning of wisdom," and "Righteousness exalteth a nation." She promised to defend her country and stand up like a man with her people against any one who might attempt to take even a hair's breadth of it. She urged her subjects to obey the laws, and said that she expected to obey them herself, closing her statement with the words:

"I wish no one's life to be taken. Whoever forsakes the paths of righteousness walks in the paths of darkness. Is it not so, oh! my people?"

That was the way that Ranavalona started. She kept up her good work but, nevertheless, got into trouble with the French, who had long proclaimed their right to the protection of Madagascar. War ensued, and at a cost of

Until deposed from her throne and brought a political exile to Algeria, Queen Ranavalona III of Madagascar, was the Christian ruler of the richest court south of the Equator and a country three times as big as Italy.

Playing house has the same fascination for the boys and girls of Algeria as for the children of America.

The origin of marbles goes far back into antiquity, and the game is played to-day in lands which were old when Rome was built.

many million dollars the French were at last victorious. They kept the Queen for a time on the throne but, finding she could not maintain order under the changed conditions, they finally took entire possession of the government. At this time they treated Ranavalona rather harshly. Instead of calling upon her, the general of the French Army made the Queen call upon him. When she did so it was to request that he be kind to her people and to say that she knew he would treat them well.

Shortly after this Ranavalona was taken away from the capital and exiled to the island of Réunion, where she remained until she was brought first to France and then here to Algiers. Upon arriving at Marseilles, she had expected to go directly to Paris. She was delighted with the idea of seeing the Parisian capital, and when she was told that she must again cross the Mediterranean to an exile home, this time in Algeria, she is said to have burst into a flood of tears, crying:

"Who is certain of to-morrow? Only yesterday I was a queen; to-day I am simply an unhappy, broken-hearted woman."

However that may have been, the woman I saw to-day bore no marks of sorrow and has, I judge, become reconciled to her situation. She may be a captive, but she has a gilded cage and sufficient money to satisfy all her wants. The French supply her with one of the finest villas of Algiers; she has horses and carriages, gives receptions and dinners, and holds a little court of her own. Her captors allow her enough money on which to live comfortably and she is permitted to go to Paris for a month every summer.

It was through a card of introduction from the American

consul that I met Queen Ranavalona. I took an interpreter with me and in a carriage climbed the winding ways which lead from the sea to the villas of Mustapha Supérieur on the height above the harbour. Here, surrounded by great hotels and magnificent homes, the former Queen lives with her aunt, her niece, and a Frenchwoman who is called her "companion but who is really a guard. Nominally she goes where she pleases, but really she is closely watched by the government, her every motion and every word being reported. When I first presented my letter the servant came back with the statement that Her Majesty could not receive me as Madame Depret was not present and the Queen was not allowed to hold any conversation with strangers in her absence. Ranavalona later sent word, however, that she would be glad to see me at ten o'clock.

When I called again I first met Madame Depret. I was admitted to the villa by a maidservant and waited for a while in the reception room at the right of the entrance where two Paris hats and two parasols of lavender and rose pink which hung on the rack showed that the ladies were home. When Madame Depret entered my interpreter performed the introduction and I presented my request for an interview. The madame replied that I could have an audience with Her Majesty, although it was contrary to her custom to receive newspaper correspondents. She gave me to understand that the Queen would not talk about politics and her own country, and from the way she uttered the words I saw that she meant them. The lady then led the way into the parlour, a large room floored with blue tiles and containing many sofas and chairs upholstered in fine white satin.

AN EXILED AFRICAN QUEEN

We had hardly taken our seats before Ranavalona entered. Her aunt, who was with her, remained during the audience. I arose as Her Majesty came in and Madame Depret introduced me. The Queen shook my hand, looking me straight in the eyes as she bade me welcome. She has a very small hand and large and beautiful eyes. She is a fine-looking woman who appears much younger than she actually is. She has a high and rather full forehead, a long, somewhat thin face and rather full lips, although they are by no means so thick as those of a Negro. Her complexion is of a chocolate brown. It seems to me that her features are almost typically Malaysian. Her hair, which is jet black, is straight rather than curly, and is put up in a great knot on the top of her head. I have already described her dress of a simple Paris-made white silk blouse and black skirt, and have referred to the plainness of her ornaments. Her manners were as simple as her dress, being entirely free from ostentation of any kind. In fact, her every act was that of a well-bred society lady, and her soft low voice that of the drawing room. Motioning me to a chair, she sat down on another near by.

I opened the conversation by telling her that I had written a book for the American public school children about the "Islands of the Seas," in which I had described Madagascar, and that I would take pleasure in sending her a copy. I then showed her some photographs which the governor-general of Madagascar had sent me to illustrate this book. She looked over the pictures and at once became interested, her eyes lighting up with pleasure as she recognized her far-away island home and the various types among its people.

"Ah, that was my palace," she said, as she held out a

photograph of Tananarivo, the capital of Madagascar, and pointed to a building in the centre, rising high over the others, upon which the French flag was floating.

"And these are Hovas," she continued, as she picked up another, showing a family of well-dressed coloured people, "and those Sakalavas," as she looked at a third, a group of blacks with features like Negroes. Each picture brought out some remark and before either she or her aunt was aware of it they were talking quite freely. Meantime, the French madame looked rather sour, and when I put a direct question as to how Her Majesty liked the change from Madagascar to Algeria, she gave a sign and the Queen replied that she could not answer that and that she would prefer to say nothing more about her own country, as the French Government objected to her discussing such matters.

A moment later, when for some reason Madame Depret was called out, the Queen's aunt said that no conversation could go on until she returned. Interpreting this to mean political conversation, I said a word or two about the weather, asking the Queen how she liked the climate of Algeria. To this she replied:

"It does not much matter. I have to like it. Nevertheless, it is a very good climate."

Afterward she spoke of Paris and mentioned the pleasures she had in the life there. When I suggested that she extend her travels to the other side of the Atlantic and visit America, she said she thought that she would like to do so but doubted if that would be allowed.

I had brought a copy of my Geographical Reader on Africa with me and made her a present of it, saying that its simple language might aid her in her study of English. She took the book and looked over the pictures, comparing the natives there represented with her own people on that great island not far away from the African coast. She told me she found the English language much more difficult to learn than the French. Ranavalona is a good French scholar and speaks, writes, and reads that language well. During our conversation, which was carried on in French, she never hesitated for a word or a phrase to express her meaning.

At the close of the audience I told her that I would consider it a great favour if she would allow me to take a photograph of her, as I would like to have a picture made by myself to show to the American people. At first she said that she did not think it would be permitted, but that she would ask Madame Depret, and that if there were no objections she would go outside and pose for the camera. At this moment her French guardian came in and the question was submitted to her. The madame replied that it was all in the hands of Her Majesty who could do as she pleased.

Upon being assured that the pictures were not for use in Algiers, Ranavalona and her aunt went with me into the garden back of the house and she stood in the sun while I made the pictures. I had one photograph snapped by my dragoman of myself standing beside the Queen. I am five feet seven inches in height and the queen is almost a head shorter. After taking the photographs I left, Her Majesty again shaking my hand as she said good-bye.

CHAPTER XVII

THE POMPEII OF AFRICA

TIMGAD, the wonderful ruined city of Roman Africa, which the French have dug out of the sand, lies about one hundred and fifty miles south of the Mediterranean and perhaps three hundred miles southwest of Tunis. It is just over the mountains from the Desert of Sahara, on one of the lower slopes of the Atlas Mountains overlooking a valley which in the days of Rome was enormously rich. Pompeii was in existence about three hundred years before Christ, and was destroyed by the eruption of Vesuvius 79 A. D. It contained only twenty or thirty thousand people and was not half the size of this ancient African city.

Timgad was founded just twenty-one years after the destruction of Pompeii. It was built by the Emperor Trajan, whose soldiers aided in its construction, and was then known as Thaumgas or Thaumgadi. Situated at the intersection of six Roman roads, it was a fortified camp as well as a great commercial city. The excavations show that it must have been a social capital besides, inhabited by many rich people and surrounded by all the luxuries of Rome at the height of its glory.

Later Timgad became a religious city. St. Augustine was born near it, and in the seventh century, when the Arab invasion occurred, it had a Christian church the ruins of which still exist. For more than a thousand years after Timgad was destroyed by the Arabs, the rain and soil of the Atlas Mountains and the dust and sands from the great Sahara close by drifted over it, burying its remains layer by layer until the greater part of it was lost from view.

For centuries only a few of the more prominent of the ruins rose above the surface. There were columns here and there apparently growing out of the soil. Great mounds covered the half-destroyed buildings, and it was not until the French began their excavations that any one imagined that a great city lay buried beneath. I saw gangs of men working at the ruins as I wandered about through them this afternoon, and I photographed them as they raised buried columns out of the earth. The covering soil rose far above the height of my head.

I came here from Algiers by railroad, a distance of about two hundred and fifty miles. The nearest station is Batna, a French military outpost at the entrance of the valley in which Timgad lies. There I hired a carriage and drove for twenty-five miles up this valley to the site of the excavations. The only town we passed on the way was Lambese, which also was prominent in the days of the Romans, and which has ruins that would be considered wonderful were they not overshadowed by the greater ones at Timgad. The road, which was built by the French, is as good as was the Appian Way when Timgad and Rome were still in their prime. The grades are so gentle that our horses went on the trot and we covered the distance in less than three hours. We met many soldiers at Lambese, but except for them we saw nobody save Arabs.

Sometimes we crowded a caravan of camels going sullenly

on their way, and sometimes passed villages of low brown tents, the homes of Bedouin shepherds feeding their flocks on the foothills of the Atlas. At places in the valley we saw Arabs ploughing; but the soil is now semi-arid, showing but little signs of the fertility it must have had when this region was the granary of Rome. I imagine that the rainfall then was much greater than now, and it may be that the cutting away of the forests has modified the climate of Algeria, as has been the case with Spain, Palestine, and other lands.

I have already been here for the better part of two days. I am living at the little hotel put up for the excavators and strangers, and have been going over the ruins with an old French soldier long connected with the work of unearthing the city.

I almost despair of giving any conception of the character and extent of the city uncovered. The old Roman houses, like the Jerusalem of the Psalms, were built compactly together, and, although Timgad included only one hundred acres, it was a beehive of humanity and its people needed less space than many an American town of one tenth the size. The chief business and residential centres were divided into streets about twenty feet wide crossing each other at right angles. There are miles of these streets, and one can walk over them on the same pavements as those on which the Romans rode in their chariots. I tramped much of my way in the ruts cut by the chariots, and I found the stones of the roads worn smooth by the feet of these people of fifteen centuries since. The main thoroughfares are flagged with great blocks of limestone about three feet wide and often four feet long fitted close together. Under every street is a deep sewer running from

The Decumanus Maximus led from the arch of the Emperor Trajan, who built Timgad, to the Forum. Ruts in the paving stones worn by chariot wheels are plainly visible.

In great houses, sometimes containing sixty rooms decorated with marble columns and paved with beautiful mosaics, lived the wealthy Roman officials of ancient Timgad.

The marble counters of the butchers' stalls still bear the marks of the cleavers used in chopping off the steaks and roasts of Roman times. Balls of stone were used for weights.

one end of it to the other, for the whole city is underlaid with drains. Nearly every house has its own connection with the sewer, and there are public conveniences in all parts of the town.

There are rows of curbstones along the streets and the principal avenues have great marble columns on each side of them, some of which are broken and some almost perfect. In some places one looks for a mile through ruined pillars, easily picturing the grandeur of Timgad in its prime.

We enter an avenue by a great stone gate decorated with carvings, over flagstones cut into deep ruts by the chariot wheels. There are pillars on both sides of the streets leading to the Forum, while beyond them on each side are acres upon acres of ruined buildings ranging in height from a few feet to far above my head. The ravages of time, of siege, and of the Mohammedan iconoclast have cut away the tops of the buildings; but enough of the walls are left to show one just how they were constructed, and one can walk from room to room, through house after house.

At the right side of this main street ran a covered passageway the top of which rested upon these pillars. This was for foot passengers, who could there move along without danger from the throng of chariots and horses in the roadway outside.

On the Via Decumanus Maximus, which leads from the great Arch of Trajan to the Forum, one side is lined with stores. The greatest number of stores are near the Forum, and these probably formed the chief mercantile houses of the city. Each establishment had a main room facing the street, with another in the rear, which was perhaps used as a warehouse or as a private room for its owner. The Decumanus Maximus has deep wheel-tracks in the flags from one end of it to the other, and it is easy to imagine it filled with the gay throng of the days of the Emperors Trajan and Marcus Aurelius.

After walking through store after store in this quarter I went to another part of the city where the Roman market used to be. The marketplace, which was surrounded by columns, still shows many evidences that it was an interesting and picturesque place when the people from all the country about came here to buy and sell. The stalls of the meat market were on a platform built in a half-moon facing the square. The marble counters behind which the butchers stood are still intact and still bear the nicks made by the cleavers used in chopping off the steaks of antiquity. These counters are slabs, each about a foot thick and five feet in length. Crawling under one, I stood in the place of the butcher, trying to imagine the customers who waited outside for spring chickens, roasts of lamb, and rump steaks fifteen hundred years ago. In my mind's eye I could see Mrs. Cæsar testing the breastbone of a fowl, and Madame Cicero telling the boy to cut her a steak off the loin and watching him to see that he did not cheat in the weight. Later I saw in the museum the weights which were used to weigh the meat. They are balls of stone ranging in size from as big as my head to no larger than marbles.

Some of the houses of Timgad were magnificent. They had marble benches, beautiful frescoes, and floors of mosaic. The museum has many mosaics equal to almost anything discovered at Pompeii. They are made of bits of stone, some of them no bigger than a baby's fingernail, so fitted together that they seem one solid block. They are of many colours and represent the famous characters of mythology.   One about fifteen feet square shows Venus riding through the sea on a centaur, while the dolphins swim about beside her.   Another represents the triumph of Neptune, and others show various scenes connected with the gods and the goddesses of old Rome.

Near the Forum I explored a palace which contained about sixty-odd rooms, some of which are still decorated with marble columns.   This house had a wide entrance porch, and the stones at the front showed plainly the marks made by the carriages as they were driven out and in.   When I walked in, the floors seemed to be nothing but plaster, but as I scraped my feet on them I saw the mosaic beneath.   Even the floors of the bathrooms were of beautiful mosaic.

If it be true that cleanliness is next to godliness, these old Romans were pretty nearly godly.   There are ruins of baths here which show that this old town of Timgad, of anywhere from fifty to one hundred thousand people, had better accommodations of that kind than our largest cities of to-day.   Just outside the chief entrance gate stand the remnants of an enormous brick building, covering almost two acres, which was devoted to bathing and gymnastics.

I spent some time in these baths.   A large part of the outer wall is still intact, and the rooms, although the walls are broken down in places, can be easily traced.   There were thirty-five of them grouped about a grand hall forty feet wide and seventy-five feet long, where the men went through their gymnastics or rested and loafed after bathing.   There were many hot chambers for steam and vapour baths and several cold plunges with large swimming pools.

The hot rooms had mosaic floors with underground flues and fires. The remains of the heating arrangements could even now be repaired and the baths used as in the past. In the southern part of the city are ruins of other public baths, while in many of the houses there are remains of private bathrooms.

Timgad had a theatre which seated more than four thousand people. This theatre was in the upper part of the city at the edge of the hills. I went through its ruins and sat for a time in one of the boxes which faced the marble rostrum forming the stage. The audience came in through a covered passageway made of stone, and there was a covered passageway for exit. The actors had their own entrance, which led direct to the stage. There was no roof over this theatre; the audience sat in the open, with a magnificent view of the valley and mountains ever before them. The seats, which are of stone, run around the arena in the shape of a half moon, rising tier above tier. The orchestra played in the crescent below.

I was also much interested in the library, or public lecture room, of this ancient town. I do not suppose that ancient Thaumgadi had an Andrew Carnegie, but its ruins show that this building would have been a worthy monument to any corn king of old Rome. It has the shape of a half circle, with steps around it, and shelves in the walls, where the scrolls of manuscript were stored. Another curious structure is the ancient flower market equipped with fountains to keep the flowers fresh.

The Forum of Timgad, which has been entirely unearthed, bears evidence of having been far larger and more beautiful than that of Pompeii. Its stone courts are almost intact, and many of the tall marble columns which surrounded it are still here. It was manifestly a magnificent place. It is reached by stone steps. About it on every side were covered passageways upheld by pillars of marble. At one end, behind marble columns, was a great stone rostrum, I suppose for the speakers, and there was an extensive lobby with retiring rooms, somewhat as in our Capitol at Washington. Adjoining the Forum was a building of marble and limestone which is supposed to have served as a kind of stock exchange and tribunal of justice combined. It had a statue of Justice in it, a part of which remains.

There are several ruined temples in Timgad. One was devoted to Victory and another to the Jupiter of the Capitol. The walls of the latter are six feet in thickness, and are made of great blocks three or four feet in length. On a lofty platform overlooking the whole city some of the enormous columns which formed the back of this structure still stand. Each column is fifty feet high, is fluted and carved, and has a capital of wonderful beauty.

I climbed up to the base of these great pillars to take a bird's-eye view of the ruins. With the broken marble shafts here and there among them, the half-shattered buildings looked more like a palatial cattleyard of brick and stone than a city. The houses are now little more than walled pens, and the streets through them are like roads. This, however, is only a first impression. The ruins of the famous old city spring at once into view, and the wealth of the past everywhere strikes the eye. Just below me were great blocks of marble, pieces of broken statues. I could see the stone tables upon which the Romans offered their sacrifices, and beyond them the homes of the city. The columns beside me were as big around as a hogshead and rose above me to the height of a four-story house. They were made in blocks, each of which must have weighed many tons. They were probably chiselled out on the ground, but how they were raised so high without the aid of modern machinery I cannot imagine. This temple had twelve columns in front of it and twenty-two pillars of these enormous proportions on the platform above.

At the entrance of the Via Decumanus Maximus now stand the remains of the Arch of Trajan. The city, as I have said, was founded by Trajan, and this arch is a splendid monument to his memory. It must be eighty or one hundred feet in height. It is of sandstone with columns of marble. It is aged by the weather and as the sun shone upon it this morning it took on the colour of old gold and made a great gilded frame standing out against the blue sky. The arch has three entrances, two at the sides for foot passengers and one in the centre for carriages. The road through the central arch has been cut deep by chariot wheels. Birds were flying through this arch as I visited it and, looking beyond it over the plain, I could see the black tents of the Bedouins with the sheep feeding near them. They were grazing among the tops of ruined columns and on land covering a part of Timgad not yet excavated.

All the relics found at Timgad are kept in the musuem here and the collection gives live pictures of the old Roman days. Some of the rooms are walled with mosaics and contain enough broken-nosed statues to people a town. There are cases filled with gold coins and others containing jewellery of gold, some of which is set with precious stones. There are rouge pots like those discovered at Pompeii, and there are golden finger rings and earrings. There are surgical instruments, including pincers and forceps of steel wonderfully well made, knives of various kinds, and needles of all sizes. There are Roman lamps of bronze and of clay. There are bronze handles of vases and beautiful vessels and pieces of iridescent glass. Indeed, the collection is extraordinary; but it is shut up here in the heart of North Africa, twenty-five miles from the nearest railroad, so that few people ever behold it.

I have photographed some of the ruins and measured many of the columns and buildings. I also talked with the director of the excavations. He told me that the excavation has been carefully done and many articles of gold and precious stones have been found as well as remains of beautiful statues, mosaics, and antiques which throw a new light on Roman North Africa.

There are traces of the Roman civilization scattered all over this part of the world. Nearly every town in Algeria of any size has some relics of the Romans. I have seen the hand of old Rome in nearly every place I have been. It has left its mark upon Algiers, Oran, and Tlemçen. The latter city, which was ancient Pomaria, shows the remains of a great Roman aqueduct. I came across the old Roman military wall many times while exploring Algiers, and Constantine has some Roman ruins about it.

Lambese, seventeen miles east of Timgad, was built by the Romans 125 A. D. to form the headquarters of the Third Augustan Legion. The ruined arches of the gates outside the city show that it covered several miles. In its centre is a building of stone ninety-two feet long and sixty-six feet wide and some fifty feet high. The façade of this structure has a peristyle with handsome Ionic columns. Near it is a temple built during the reign of Marcus Aurelius and a great arch put up in honour of Septimius Severus. There are ruins of baths from which have been taken wonderful mosaics. The town had two forums, one of which measured more than half an acre and in one of which was a great temple surrounded by a colonnade.

On the site of Lambese the French have built an enormous barracks for such soldiers as they send to Africa for correction, and as I rode by I passed several companies of French troops going through their evolutions on the site of the old camp, just as the Roman soldiers did in that same place more than seventeen hundred years ago.

The walls of the Temple of Jupiter and Minerva were six feet thick, and from its platform, commanding a view of all the city, rose columns each fifty feet high.

The visitor finds life in the oasis town insufferably dull, but the Arabs seem to be entirely content so long as they can have their coffee and dominoes in a café or a shaded doorway.

CHAPTER XVIII

THE GARDEN OF ALLAH

ISKRA is the Paris of the Sahara. This oasis lies one hundred and seventy-five miles south of the Mediterranean Sea, in the midst of the desert. At one side of it great sand dunes roll on and on until they are lost in the yellow horizon. On the other side are the well-worn stones of the Oued, or dry river, Biskra, which becomes a flood during the short rainy part of the year but which is now so parched under this blazing sun that it would blister your bare feet to cross it.

Biskra is situated on a low plateau a little more than three hundred feet above the river. To the north of it is the mighty wall of the great peaks of the Atlas, which here rise a thousand feet higher than Mount Washington. In the crystal-clear African noon the mountains are of a pale yellow, the colour of the limestone of which they are made. A little later they will turn to hazy blue, changing, as the sun drops, to primrose and gold, and then dying out through a dark purple into the night.

This oasis is an island in the mighty sea of the Sahara. The mountain wall is a part of the shore and the great cliffs rise almost straight above it. With a glass one could find a break in those mountains known as the Gorge of Kantara. Here a river has burst through the wall, forming a golden gate to the greatest of deserts. One comes out from the mountains straight to the desert, passing through the little oasis of Kantara, a green key to that gate of gold.

Biskra has been rather voluptuously described in Hichens's novel, "The Garden of Allah." He makes it the chief scene of that story, painting all of its surroundings in more or less glowing colours. The Sahara becomes the Garden of Allah and Biskra its capital. It is, in fact, the European capital of North Africa, to which, every winter, tourists and health seekers by the thousands come over the railroad built by the French. There have been erected large hotels where one can live comfortably at reasonable rates. There are frequent concerts and many *cafés chantants*, while the casino steadily runs its roulette and *rouge-et-noir* tables; so that the place might well be called the Monte Carlo of the desert.

The season begins in November and lasts until May, being at its liveliest in February at the time of the races, in which horses, donkeys, and camels take part. There are long-distance camel races run by Arabs on *meharis*. These camels are so tall and lean that they seem to be all legs. They have saddles with high supports in front and behind, and the rider bobs up and down with a seesaw motion. The camel races are supposed to start from the oasis of Touggourt, two hundred and ten miles away, a distance which a fairly good camel ought to cover in less than ten hours. The horse races are run by Arabian steeds with Arab riders, who are splendid horsemen and delight in cross-country going, jumping everything on the way.

The city of Biskra is really composed of two towns, French Biskra and Old Biskra. The former contains about nine hundred Europeans and two or three times that many natives, while the latter is altogether native and, as is usual in these oasis towns, is ranked rather by the number of its palm trees than by the number of its inhabitants. It comprises six little mud villages scattered through plantations which support about one hundred and fifty thousand date trees.

The French town is surrounded by walls and entered by gates. It has several wide streets, the chief of which is the Rue Berthe, which runs from the railroad station past the public gardens and on out toward the oasis of Touggourt. It goes beyond the oasis of Old Biskra, two miles off, which is connected by street car with French Biskra.

Prices are much lower here in this far-away part of the world than at home. When I take a Turkish bath in the United States I have to pay at least one dollar, with twenty-five or fifty cents extra for fees. I had a Moorish bath here for twenty cents in a bathing establishment that would be considered fine in any American city; and this included a thorough massage and a cup of delicious Turkish coffee. The men who bathed me were brawny Arabs as yellow as gold and naked to the waist, and they spent something like an hour on the job. I do not mean to say that it took that much time to get off the dirt; but the hour was used in the massage and other extras. Biskra was a famous bathing place in the days of the Romans. It had a Roman name meaning "baths," which probably referred to the hot sulphur springs outside the city.

Biskra is the chief military station of the eastern Sahara and is called the *Territoire de Commandement*. One sees French soldiers everywhere, and there are French officers at the hotels and on the streets. They are fine-looking fellows, straight, broad-shouldered, and bronze-faced, who have been fighting with these tribes of the desert and show it. Some of the officers have the appearance of dudes and are noted for their extreme politeness, but no one dares to presume upon their foppishness.

The territory of Biskra, which is about as large as the state of Ohio, has, all told, a population of less than one hundred thousand, living in oases scattered over the desert. Biskra itself is commanded by a major, assisted by a captain, three lieutenants, and a military interpreter. The town has electric lights and schools for both French and Arabs. There is also a Negro quarter.

The French city is made up of flat-roofed white houses of one or two stories. Many of the roofs have walls about them. The women and children gossip and play on the roofs in the evening, and the people sleep there at night.

I wish I could take you through one of these Sahara towns. Even in French Biskra the scenes would seem strange. There are Moors sitting out in the street or on the sidewalks upon mats laid down for the purpose, quietly playing dominoes. They have little tables about as high as a footstool and, squatting with their bare feet under them, will move the blocks for an hour or more without saying a word. Many of the players are gray-bearded and gray-headed, but age does not affect their love for the game.

On every hand I meet the characters of the Bible. As I write these notes I can see in one group an old Abraham, with the aged Sarah beside him and the buxom Hagar behind. That little baby in Hagar's arms might be young Ishmael, and I observe that Abraham looks upon him with apparent love. At the same time Sarah seems

An American boy would think these stilts too low to be interesting, but they seemed entirely satisfactory to the Arab youth of Algeria.

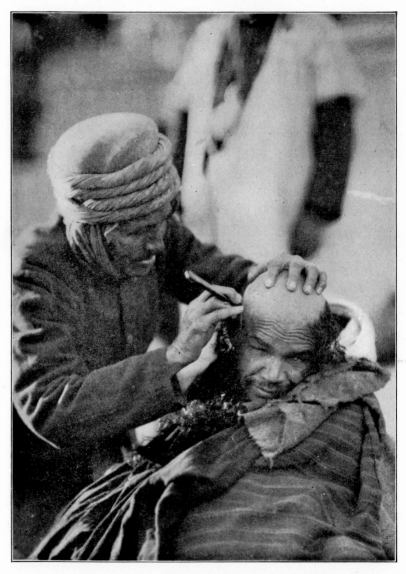

An Arab barber is a rough-and-ready worker, using only water and no soap when shaving the heads of the victims. Usually the customer must squat on the ground during the ordeal.

to be jealous, and glares at both baby and mother out of the tail of her eye.

That handsome Moor coming down the street might be Joseph, the friend of King Pharaoh. Observe his costly raiment of fine silk and wool; he walks with a strut and is evidently a man of authority.

On that donkey slowly pacing along is an old man whom one might easily imagine to be Balaam, and lo! the donkey stops, opens his mouth, and brays. His words, however, we do not understand, for he has not the power of speech like the ass of Holy Writ. And so I might go on, finding a character at every step which would correspond to one in the Scriptures. This is a bit of the Simon-pure Orient, where the natives are about the same to-day as they were in Bible times three or four thousand years ago. They are, however, all Mohammedans and believe only in Allah and the Prophet.

But let us go out to an oasis and visit the people who live under the palm trees. We drive along the Rue Berthe by walls of yellow mud inclosing date palms which rise high above them and are loaded with ripe golden fruit. The walls are as high as my head, and on their top dried thorn bushes, set in while the mud was still wet, protect the fruit like so much broken glass.

This oasis is fed by springs from the River Biskra, which is dry the greater part of the year. Wells have tapped the springs, however, and there is a flow of several thousand gallons a minute. The water is somewhat alkaline, but it puts the sugar into the dates and the sun is so hot that the fruit is delicious. According to the Arabs, to make good dates the head of the tree must be in the burning sun the greater part of the year. The thermometer here, even in midwinter, never falls below sixty, and the climate seems just right, although it is not so at Kantara, thirty or forty miles farther north. Biskra is annually producing something like ten million pounds of dates, enough to furnish a handful to every boy in the United States and leave some to spare. As we ride into the oasis we can see men picking dates, or rather cutting them. The fruit is not good until it is dead ripe. I bit into some green dates to-day and they puckered my mouth like unfrosted persimmons.

In the oasis of Biskra water rights are often sold in perpetuity but there are also leases at so much per year, and even at so much per hour. Not long ago the price was two hundred dollars for a perpetual stream half an inch wide and as deep as the rainfall would afford, and eight hundred dollars for a stream of four inches. Where the water is let out by the hour, so many times per week, an Arab watchman with an hour glass stands at the hole where it flows out and when the sand has run through, he shuts off the supply.

I cannot describe the dreariness of everyday life in these Saharan oases. About the only green thing one sees in the streets is the palm leaves overhead. Inside a garden, there may be patches of vegetables and grass, with trees bearing various kinds of fruit; but in the villages themselves everything is as bare as the middle of the road, notwithstanding the fact that this is a land which might be a tropical paradise. The houses themselves have no gardens in or about them. They are joined close together, and are more like catacombs than places where people live, move, and have their being. During much of the day there are few signs of life. There are no windows facing the streets, the only means of ventilation on that side of the houses being little holes about the size of a paving brick up near the roof.

In villages so poor as these of Biskra, though the people look squalid and dirty, the dirtiest of them are loaded with jewellery. I photographed one middle-aged dame of swarthy complexion who had earrings as big as an after-dinner coffee cup and as she turned around I noticed that she wore anklets of white metal as wide as a pint cup is high. Indeed, they looked like tin cups without bottoms or handles. Even the children were loaded with jewellery. Some of them were not averse to being photographed, and both women and children held out their hands for money as soon as their pictures were taken. The coffee houses look not unlike an American stable. Their only light comes in through the door and the people sit on the floor.

In "The Garden of Allah," the novel to which I have already referred, there are some vivid descriptions of the Château Landon, a wonderful date plantation belonging to a wealthy French nobleman. If one would know just how much water means in the desert he may learn by visiting this place. It contains about fifteen acres, including a wonderful botanical garden right here on the edge of the desert. It is a date forest interspersed with all sorts of tropical and sub-tropical fruit trees and shrubs. There are green hedges fifteen feet high, as carefully trimmed as those in the botanical gardens of Algiers, or in that of Buitenzorg, Java. About twenty Arab gardeners are busy keeping the plantation in order, and not even the leaves are allowed to lie on the paths or walks. Here and there in the garden are houses of Arab architecture, the homes of the owner, and in one place there is a great circle cut out under the trees where dances may be held in the open.

Have you ever heard of Sidi Okba?

He was a famous Arab general who conquered the whole of North Africa from the Nile to the Atlantic. All whom he conquered he converted to Islam by telling them that they must die if they did not espouse the Mohammedan religion. It is said that when he reached the sea he rode into it, exclaiming that if it were not for this barrier he would make every people beyond it worship Allah or die.

This man was one of the great Moslem heroes. The people look upon him as a saint, and they have named towns, oases, and other places after him. One of the most important of these is Sidi Okba, which lies twelve miles from Biskra, in the midst of the sands. There is the shrine of the saint, and the mosque containing it is said to be the oldest Mohammedan building in Africa. The town is the religious capital of this part of the world, so holy that the people make pilgrimages to it as they do to Kairouan in Tunisia, and to Mecca and Medina in Arabia. I rode across the desert to visit it. The way is over a country covered with a scanty vegetation of thorny scrub, through sandy and stony wastes, and by the oases of Filiach and Chetma.

Sidi Okba has sixty-five thousand palm trees, and the town has six thousand inhabitants. The plantations are surrounded by mud walls like those of Biskra, but the houses are better and some of the streets are so wide that one can drive through them. On our way there we passed caravans of camels and donkeys and saw many tent villages and great flocks of black goats watched by shepherds. Entering the gate, we rode between the mud walls to the

The villages about the oasis of Biskra are connected by a tramway which is popular with the Arabs. Sometimes the cars are drawn by horses and sometimes by camels.

The mosque of Sidi Okba, named for the conqueror of North Africa, has a school on the roof where Arab boys are taught to shout verses from the Koran.

The moats of feudal castles were mere furrows compared to the rocky-walled gorge, one thousand feet deep, encircling Constantine. The bridge into the city is seen in the background.

public square, which is surrounded by the typical petty stores or bazaars of the Sahara, low and boxlike, outside of which the customers must stand as they haggle with the venders. There was considerable industry going on. Here men were weaving, there they were making ploughs, and farther on they were constructing saddles. In the street of the tailors I saw several men using American sewing machines, but nowhere did I see any American goods. On the sides of the streets were mud ledges built out from the mud walls filled with white-gowned men working, chatting, or sleeping. Some were reeling cotton and some were sewing. At night these ledges are filled with sleepers.

Many of these poorer Arabs have no homes. They eat at the cafés and sleep in the streets. This is especially true in the cities. The men always sleep with their heads and faces covered. One reason for this is the number of flies which fairly swarm in all the oases, making one pray for the Caliph Adalmelic, the father of flies, to breathe upon them and drive them away. This old caliph was so fatal to flies that every one that flew over his mouth dropped dead.

Like every traveller in Biskra, I visited the famous mosque. It is an ordinary building with perhaps half a dozen rooms, including the place of worship. It was filled with worshippers when I entered it and I heard Moslem boys singing out verses from the Koran in the schoolrooms on each side. I spent some time watching the men at their prayers, and although it is known here that I am a Christian, I was not molested.

CHAPTER XIX

A CITY OF THE AIR

IF WE could take one of our American towns of fifty thousand inhabitants, crowd its houses together so that they would not cover more than the area of a half-section farm, and then lift the bed rock on which they stand straight up into the air for twenty-three hundred feet, we should have some of the conditions which exist here at Constantine, Africa's famous city of the air. It lies in the heart of North Africa about three hundred miles east of Algiers, fifty miles south of the Mediterranean, and one hundred and twenty-five miles north of the Desert of Sahara. It is built upon an enormous rock at an altitude of two thousand feet above the sea, and nearly encircling it is a mighty gorge a thousand feet deep. The houses stand on a huge stone platform on three sides of which rocky walls drop down precipitously to a valley almost twice as deep as the Washington Monument is high. A rushing, foaming river flows through the gorges thus made. On every side lies a rolling country ending in the desert-like mountains of the great Atlas chain. I doubt whether there is another such city on earth. The Arabs call it "The City of the Air," and it is the mightiest roof garden known to man.

But Constantine is far more than a roof garden. It is a fortification as well. For almost three thousand years it has been the site of a camp or barracks for soldiers, and

its adventurous story is written in blood. It has successfully withstood eighty sieges. When the French took it,
about 1837, they employed an army of ten thousand men.
At that time hundreds of its Arab inhabitants, who tried
to escape by letting themselves down over the rocks, were
dashed to pieces in the gorges below, and so many Mohammedan women committed suicide in that way that
the river ran blood.

The *kasbah* or citadel, which was then the chief fort of
the Arabs, is now occupied by several thousand French
troops. It commands the highest point on the rocky
plateau and is above the most precipitous part of the
gorge. In it there are stone cisterns and granaries built
by the Romans, while not far from it is a great stone aqueduct which the Romans made to supply the place with
water.

Constantine was a city in the days of the Phœnicians,
and under the name of Cirta it was the capital of a Carthaginian province ruled by Hannibal's brother-in-law.
Later on it became the capital of Numidia, which furnished
the famous Numidian lions for the gladiatorial shows of
old Rome. A little more than three hundred years after
Christ it was called Constantine, in honour of the Roman
emperor of that date, and when the Arabs came in it was
made one of their capitals.

Though once so invincible, the city could now be easily
battered to pieces. Modern guns, placed on the opposite
heights, could shatter the buildings, and in a few hours
sweep the rock clear of houses and people. In the warfare
of the past, however, it was almost impregnable, and the
great canyon by which it is surrounded formed a barrier
which no army could scale.

If you would realize how great the barrier was, come with me down into the gorge. Steps have been gouged out of the rocks by the French. There are hanging walks along the sides of the cliffs so that we can climb a thousand feet down to where the River Roummel, known also as the River of Sands, races and froths on its way to the Mediterranean Sea.

We take carriages and drive far up the valley, and then cross to get to the ladders. The way is rough and tiresome, but we climb down, down, down, until at last we are near the water, far below the city. On both sides of us rise sheer black walls stained by drains and springs and roofed by the sky.

The gorge is about two hundred feet wide, narrowing in places to one hundred and fifty feet or less. The rocks rise almost straight up from the river, and we make our way through a narrow canyon along this foaming stream. Down here in the gorge the noises of the city are unheard, and nothing breaks the stillness but the whirring of the wings of the crows, storks, and other birds, as they fly across to their nests in one wall or the other, and the roaring of the hurrying river as it dashes on through the rocks. The gorge changes in character as we go along. Here the cliffs are mighty pillars of stone five hundred feet high; there they look like great battlements, and farther on they almost meet overhead.

At the lower end of the canyon, almost under the *kasbah*, is a natural bridge, somewhat like that of Virginia. Across it runs an aqueduct built by the Romans, and at the same place are the remains of the Roman road which joined the city to the mainland. This old bridge is still in good condition. It is right under the iron bridge of Kantara, which now forms the chief highway to the city on the rock.

I came here from the Desert of Sahara by transferring at El Guerra to the railroad from Algiers to Tunis. This landed me on heights opposite the city and in a cab I crossed the Kantara bridge over the gorge to the rocky plateau. I am living in a comfortable hotel situated on a street so narrow that a carriage cannot turn round in it. I am only a short distance from where the ledge drops into the depths, and were I a sleep walker I might find my way out of the house and dash myself to pieces in the depths below.

In one part of the town there are many fine buildings. The French have put up a city hall at a cost of several million francs. There are some excellent stores, and at the north, reached by bridges, a European city has been constructed on a modern scale by a syndicate of capitalists from Lyons, in France. This settlement has now more than twenty-two thousand French residents and nearly three thousand other Europeans.

Constantine has about thirty-two thousand souls who believe in the Prophet Mohammed, and in addition something like eight thousand Jews. The Mohammedans are the controlling native element. Living at this place, they might be said to have in reality "mansions in the skies." I wish you could see their homes. They are along the usual narrow streets where you can stand in the middle and touch the walls on both sides. The streets wind this way and that. There are many blind alleys, and the maze of crossing ways is often so confusing that one might wander about a long time and learn his location only when he came to the edge of the plateau and looked down into the gorge.

These houses are squalid and rough. They are usually of two or three stories, made of brick and stone covered with stucco. They are painted blue or white, with roofs of the same hues. The roofs are flat, and each has a low wall about it. Few of the houses have windows facing the streets, and all windows are covered with an iron network for fear the ladies of the harem may be seen by others than their husbands.

The Arab women here are quite as secluded as those of other parts of Algeria or of Morocco. They wrap themselves in shawls when they go out of doors, and wear pieces of white cotton tied tightly about their faces so that one sees only their eyes. So far I have not observed a single pair of the voluminous trousers so common in the streets of Algiers. The gowns of these Constantine ladies fall clear to the feet, and the female population looks like so many big fat bundles waddling along upon slippers. The Arab men, on the other hand, are gorgeously dressed and spend much money on their clothes.

The Jews here differ from their race in Europe or America, so that what I write is not to be considered as applying at all to our Hebrew population. There have been Jews in Africa since the time of the Carthaginians. They are a people of their own class but quite as African as the Arabs themselves. At Constantine they dress like Arabs. The men wear rich jackets elaborately embroidered and full trousers tied in at the knee. They have red fezzes which are often bound with great turbans. Some wear gowns, but now and then one is to be seen in European clothes. The faces of these Israelites are darker than those of other countries but they have the same Jewish features, and many of them are fine looking.

I like especially the appearance of the Jewish women, although I sadly fear that some of them are no better than they should be. They look at men boldly and without shame. To-day is Saturday, the Hebrew Sabbath, and, as it is also a fête day, the people are all out in their fine clothes. The streets are swarming with Jewish girls loaded with jewellery. Their arms are bare to the shoulders, their wrists and forearms are adorned with bracelets of silver and gold, and their fingers sparkle with rings. Many of them are dressed in silk gowns over which lace shawls are thrown. Their heads are tied up in silk handkerchiefs and on the top of them are red velvet caps embroidered with gold. These caps are much like cornucopias. They are about four inches in diameter and are worn on the crown of the head. They are fastened on by silk bands tied under the chin, and these bands are often decorated with gold coins. Sometimes gold chains are used. Nearly all of the Jewesses wear earrings; some have brooches set with diamonds and many have strings of pearls about their necks.

I have visited the chief synagogue, which is situated near the gorge in the heart of the city, and it seems to be very well attended. When I entered, it was filled with Hebrew men wearing the same dress as the Arabs. Each had also a white shawl and all kept on their fezzes during the service. The rabbi, who occupied a pulpit in the centre of the synagogue, intoned the Scripture with a nasal twang from parchment scrolls, and the worshippers followed him with their Hebrew Bibles. Every man and boy had a little velvet bag decorated with Hebrew characters in gold or silver for carrying his books of worship. As far as I could see the books themselves were well thumbed.

The Jew stores are closed to-day, but the Arabs are carrying on business as usual. This is one of the industrial centres of eastern Algeria, and the native quarter fairly hums with men working at their trades. Constantine is famous for its leather work. It makes shoes, saddles, and harness, and also leather bags and cushions, beautifully embroidered. Each trade has its own street. One will be filled with shoemakers, another with blacksmiths, and another with weavers. About a hundred thousand *haicks* and *burnouses* are made here yearly, as well as a great deal of cloth for the tents used by the Bedouins. This work is all done upon hand looms, in rooms which look more like stables or cellars than factories.

I spent some time this afternoon in the street of the blacksmiths, watching them make hoes and ploughshares. The latter are for all the world like the long sharp trowels used by our masons save that they are about a quarter of an inch thick. They are of wrought iron and are so bent at one end that they can be fastened by an iron band to the forked stick which forms the rest of the plough.

The blacksmiths are Arabs, dressed in enormous trousers and jackets. Their sleeves were rolled up and they pounded away at the anvils just like our blacksmiths at home. The average shop of this kind is only big enough to hold the anvil, the furnace, and two or three men. It is a sort of a hole in the wall about six feet wide, twenty feet deep, and perhaps twelve feet in height. At the back are a rude bellows and furnace. In the centre the men work at the anvil while at the front is a counter upon which the plough-points are displayed for sale.

In one street I found scores of Arab cobblers making red

Constantine, the "City of the Air," is the world's mightiest roof garden. Its houses stand on a lofty stone platform which in the past enabled it to withstand eighty sieges.

A great cascade of stone has been formed by the limestone dissolved in the hot springs of Hammam-Meskoutine, on the railway not far from Constantine.

slippers for women, and in another place men sitting cross-legged embroidering leather in gold.

There are many restaurants and coffee houses in these localities. The coffee is always made to order and costs only about two cents a cup. The restaurant is usually in or back of the kitchen. The latter faces the street, and the cooking goes on in full view of the customers.

One of the oddest of these establishments sold nothing but boiled sheep heads cooked on an oven right next the sidewalk. In a kettle filled with boiling water sheep heads were bobbing up and down, their glazed eyes staring at the passers-by. The heads had been skinned and, as I looked in, the long white teeth of the sheep appeared to grind themselves together in rage. On the floor were a number of heads still unskinned. They had just come from the butchers, and the blood from them ran out into the street. My dragoman told me that the cooked heads were delicious and begged me to step in and try one, saying that we could get a whole head for twelve cents.

Many of the heads are sold to be carried home, and I find that sheep head is frequently on the bills of fare at the hotels. After what I saw to-day I shall eat them no more. This cook shop reminds me of a dog-and-rat restaurant of Canton in south China, and of a horse-meat restaurant which I once visited in Berlin. Both of them were cleanly in comparison.

I spent some time in the palace of the Bey. It is now the headquarters of the French army officers, but for a long time it was the residence of the Turkish rulers of Constantine and their harems. From the outside it looks like an ordinary two-story building, but its interior is wonderfully decorated and rich in marbles, mosaics, and

carvings. The palace consists of an acre or so of buildings, with galleries above and below built around beautiful gardens. The walls of the galleries are of porcelain
tiles and their roofs are upheld by marble pillars beautifully cut.

The old Bey who built the palace is said to have brought
much of the material from the ruins of Carthage. The
porcelains came from Genoa and the carvings from the
houses of the wealthy residents of Constantine. If a man
was noted as having an especially fine door or window the
Bey ordered him to send it to his new palace, and if there
was any furniture that he especially desired he got it in
the same high-handed way.

One of the strangest features of the arcades looking out
upon the gardens is a series of paintings of Mohammedan
cities. These are spread upon the walls without regard to
harmony or art. The colours swear at each other, the
drawing is faulty, and perspective is lacking. As it is
contrary to the Koran to make pictures of men, there is
no sign of human life in the paintings. This work was
done by a French shoemaker who was in prison in Constantine when the palace was building. The Bey wanted
some pictures on the walls, and he said "the dog of a
Christian" might do the work. The shoemaker objected,
saying he was not a painter, but the Bey's officials replied:
"Every Frenchman is an artist, and you must paint for
the Bey. If you do not, you will be flogged with twenty-
five lashes for every day you are idle."

The result was a series of remarkable representations of
Algiers, Cairo, Jerusalem, and Constantinople. When
the potentate saw them he was delighted. He paid the
man well and sent him back to Paris loaded with presents.

A CITY OF THE AIR

It was this same Bey, El Hadj Ahmed, who punished one of his wives for plucking the forbidden fruit of the palace garden. It was his custom to sit every afternoon in a little kiosque in the centre of a court filled with fruit trees and flowers. Here the bands played, and here betimes the women of his harem walked up and down and paraded themselves, while His Highness looked on. His four wives and three hundred concubines were all dressed in their finest clothing as they walked in single file around the court with their arms crossed upon their bosoms, not daring to look at their lord. They were allowed no liberties whatever, and one regulation was that they were not to touch the flowers or the fruit overhead. One day a new houri, a fair, red-headed Georgian girl, just in from the wilds of the Caucasus, who had not yet fully learned the dangers of her situation, reached up and snatched off an orange after she had got past the Bey. She was reported by one of the eunuchs, and about three hours after was brought to the tree she had rifled and fastened there by two nails driven through the backs of her hands.

This old Bey and the others who succeeded him had quick and summary methods of divorce. Such of their wives as were faithless, or such as they wished to get rid of for other reasons, were sewed up in sacks, carried to the edge of the gorge, and heaved over into the River of Sands a thousand feet below.

CHAPTER XX

WALKS ABOUT TUNIS

TAKE a seat upon one of the magic carpets of the Arabian Nights and fly across the Atlantic Ocean and over the Mediterranean to the shores of North Africa. Direct your genii to set you down beside me on the top of the *kasbah*, or citadel, in the snow-white city of Tunis and let us travel together through this, one of the oldest populations of the oriental world. Before we start cast your eyes over the expanse of buildings below you. You are high above the city, which stretches out in every direction, looking like a collection of great blocks of ice, with here and there the white dome of the shrine of a *marabout* or Mohammedan saint, or the square, marble-faced towers of a mosque rising above them. That reddish-brown section of buildings lying on the edge of the water is the French quarter; and that wide, gleaming avenue is the canal across Lake Tunis built to bring the ocean steamers right up to the town. There are blue mountains on our right with white buildings upon them, while away off to the left over the lake we see the snowy houses of Sidi Bon Said and the cathedral of the "White Fathers," which marks the site where old Carthage once stood. More than twenty centuries ago that was a mighty city; but Tunis, above which we are standing, was founded even before Carthage, throve until it was supplanted by its Phœnician rival, and then lived on to see Carthage crumble to dust.

178

From the Mosque of El Zitouna the call to prayer echoes over snow-white Tunis, which had already passed its youth when the Phœnicians landed here twelve hundred years before Christ.

Gold-embroidered cloths are much used by the tailors of Tunis to make gorgeous jackets and vests for both men and women.

Dates cut from the trees in great clusters are everywhere for sale. These African dates are far juicier and sweeter than those sold in American stores.

The Tunis of to-day is rapidly growing and it is one of the most cosmopolitan towns of the world. It contains, with its suburbs, in the neighbourhood of two hundred thousand souls. It has something like forty-four thousand Italians, twenty-six thousand Jews, far different in costume and appearance from the Israelites of our country, and thousands of Maltese, Sicilians, and Spaniards. Its French are somewhat fewer than the Italians, but they include a large garrison of soldiers, dressed in gay uniforms, who form striking figures wherever they go. The most important part of the Tunisian population, however, is the Mohammedan element. This numbers at least seventy thousand, and its members form the chief inhabitants of old Tunis, the great snowy town under our feet. They are Orientals of the Orientals, and live in a world of their own. They do not like Christians and tolerate us only because they must. Their town is shut off from the rest of the city by an enormous wall, and under French rule they are allowed to have their own customs and do about as they please. A person dares not enter any one of the hundred-odd mosques where they go daily for prayers; he must not visit their schools, while he who would attempt to go into one of their houses without permission might be killed. And if he were, I doubt whether the French would object.

I have visited most of the great cities of the oriental world; I have travelled through India, Turkey, and Egypt, and I have yet to find a section so strictly Eastern as the streets of old Tunis. They are narrow and winding. In some of them the fat Tunisian Jewesses have to suck in their breath in order to squeeze through. The white houses which wall these streets are almost windowless, and the few windows there are perch so high above the street that a field glass would not enable one to look in. They are covered with meshes so small that a lead pencil would not go through them. The doors are kept closed, and outside the business section there are only blank white walls on both sides. Many of the houses are built over the streets so that one goes through vaulted passages from one part of the town to the other.

Let us step down into the city and see for ourselves. We shall spend most of the time in the bazaars, which are stranger than those of Constantinople or Cairo and of greater extent than those of Damascus or Fez. There is an entrance near the *kasbah*, and a three minutes' walk will take us out of the sun and into a mammoth cave far stranger than that of Kentucky. This Tunisian cave is composed of a labyrinth of covered passageways lined with stores and filled with Arabs buying and selling. We shall meet all the characters of Eastern tradition and see them doing business in the same way as for centuries past. The streets of the bazaars are roofed so that they look like mighty vaults extending on and on until the eye is lost in following them. The roofs are of stone coated with whitewash. These are lighted only by grated holes cut here and there, but the sun is so bright that there is plenty of light, and under its rays the white ceiling itself shines like the stalactites of the cave of Luray. Some of the passageways are roofed with boards. They remind one of the old covered bridges of Venice or Florence which had shops upon them, save that the Tunisian bazaars extend for long distances and their shops are like nothing to be found outside the Orient. In addition there are smaller bazaars running off in every direction, until the whole is a sort of

Rosamond's Bower for business, in which we lose ourselves again and again in trying to find a way out.

Let us examine the construction of the bazaars. Pillars and stones taken from the remains of old Carthage have been used everywhere. At the sides of each little shop are marble columns, some of which have beautiful capitals. There are hundreds—yes, even thousands—of these columns to be seen, and, sad to relate, the Arabs have painted the snowy marble with stripes of yellow, red, green, and black. Similar columns are to be found in the residential quarters, for a large part of Mohammedan Tunis has been built from the near-by ruins of the old Punic city.

In the bazaars each trade has its own quarter. There are long streets filled with cells, where the Arabs make nothing but shoes and others in which the shops are devoted to weavers. In some silk thread is sold, and in others only perfumery or groceries. There are also bazaars of coppersmiths, booksellers, and tailors.

The bazaar of the tailors is not far from the *kasbah*. We push our way through the white-gowned, fezzed, turbaned Mohammedan crowd and take a look at it. We are in a covered street about twelve feet in width paved with stone blocks worn smooth by the bare feet and slippers of thousands. It is walled with shops extending fifteen or twenty feet back on each side.

The average shop is not more than eight feet in width. Its floor is about two feet above the street, and the tailors sit cross-legged upon it before tables eight inches high, upon which they cut and sew. They wear gowns or jackets and voluminous trousers, with fezzes or turbans upon their heads. Many of them work away with the goods on their knees and their bare feet and bare calves plainly seen. At my right is a shop where they are sewing upon a *burnouse* of the finest white wool for some Arab gentleman, and at my left is a man making a pair of elaborate trousers for some lady of wealth and fashion. Other tailors are working on gorgeous jackets and vests for both men and women. They use silk- and gold-embroidered cloths. Indeed, many of the garments are exceedingly costly, as you may see by the richly clad customers who stand in the street outside and bargain for clothes.

At ten o'clock in the morning there is an auction of second-hand clothing in this tailor street, when gray-bearded men go about holding fine garments high over their heads. They sing out the prices and quality of the goods, and beg the people to buy. I found hundreds engaged in that way and the crowd was so great that I could hardly make my way through.

But let us go on to the *souk* of the perfumers. The word *souk* is used as a term for the bazaars; so when one asks to be shown the Mohammedan business centre he tells his guide to take him, not to the bazaars, but to the *souks*. The Moslems are fond of perfumery. Their great Prophet once said that there were two things which especially delighted him—one was the society of a beautiful woman, and the other was sweet perfume.

The Tunisians have some of the best scents of the world. We can buy essence of jasmine, of violet, or of verbena that is worth its weight in gold; and a quart flask of the attar of roses sold in this *souk* would cost a king's ransom. Some of these essences are so valuable that the merchant measures them out by squeezing them drop by drop from a bit of cotton which he takes from his ear.

As we enter this bazaar, several Arab boys come and

Some of the finest perfumes come from Tunis. The Tunisians scent not only their garments but their baths, their food, and even their tea. The perfumer treated us to coffee before he would talk business.

Wooden sandals or loose leather slippers are convenient footwear for Moslems, who take off their shoes at home, in the mosques, and even in the cafés, just as a Westerner would remove his hat.

try to induce us to purchase at certain shops for which they are touting. We select one where sits a gray-bearded old Abraham in costly raiment. He is in a little pen surrounded by bottles and boxes, with a great string of candles hanging from a pole over his head. Outside his shop there is a bench upon which we sit down and have a cup of coffee with him before he asks us to buy. The coffee is as black as ink, as sweet as molasses, and almost as thick as chocolate. It is made of the beans pulverized by pounding them in a mortar and is brought in hot from the coals. After we have drunk, he begins to show his perfumes. He takes out a cork and touches it gently to the backs of our hands. The next bottle is tried on the wrist, and the next by pulling up our sleeves to the elbow and pressing the cork upon the forearm. Indeed, he stamps us with so many brands that when we leave we are walking perfume shops ourselves, and the scents are so pungent that they last for hours. The Arabs use perfumery not only on their clothes and in their baths, but also in their food and drink. They have an essence of orange flowers which is sold here with tea, and other perfumes for various foods.

I have spent some time to-day among the shoemakers. There is a long street devoted to their shops where there were hundreds of men and boys at work. They were cutting out shoes of bright red and yellow leather and sewing them into shape. The yellow shoes were for men and the red ones for women. They were also making many shoes for children. Nearly all the footwear of the Mohammedan world is made by hand, and perhaps some day a bright American shoemaker will set up a factory here and supply the trade.

The Tunisian cobbler's bench is not at all like that of the American. These cobblers cut and pound upon a section of a tree like a butcher's block raised upon legs. They do not use hammers, but pound the leather with pieces of brass so moulded that they can be easily held in the hand. They are not unlike brass paper weights. The leather work of Tunis is famous and the shoes are sold everywhere. Though they are all hand-sewed, a good pair can be bought for seventy-five cents.

Another street near that of the shoemakers is devoted to the saddlers, others to jewellers, and some to the sellers of cottons and of silks. There are also bazaars filled with old and new carpets and many which have fine brass work, embroidery, and furniture inlaid with mother-of-pearl.

All trading among these Mohammedans is by bargaining. There are no fixed prices, and the merchants always ask more than they expect to receive. I usually offer one half or one third, and am surprised to find that the dealer often comes after me and gives me the goods just after he has refused the price I named. This is especially so with the Jews, who have shops in the *souks*. Since they give a commission of five or ten per cent. to the dragoman, the first thing your guide does when you enter the bazaars is to lead you into one of these shops. He pretends that he works in your interest, but he is really a confederate of the shopkeeper, getting a rake-off from every sale he brings in. The first day I visited old Tunis I took along a Maltese named Gaouchi to act as interpreter. He warned me that I must expect the merchants to ask more than they would be satisfied to get, and said that when I saw him draw his handkerchief across his lips I might know the

price was too high. The first Jew shop we entered had
some magnificent rugs, for each of which the man asked
about one hundred dollars, but Gaouchi's handkerchief
remained in his pocket. In the next room I was shown
Tunisian silk dresses for which the man wanted twelve
dollars apiece, and still there was no sign from Gaouchi.
Notwithstanding, I found that I could have bought the
rug for one fifth of the price asked, and I did buy a silk
dress for a little over five dollars.

The *souks* fairly swarm with boys and men who beg you
to come into the shops and look at the goods. They will
say they want you not to buy, but only to see, and will
gesture to show what they mean. They point to their
eyes and catch you by the hand, trying to drag you in.
I have learned the words for "go away" and "get out" in
Arabic, and I now repeat them in that language and in
French, German, and English whenever one of these pests
becomes over-persistent.

Many of these bazaars are run by corporations, and
there is a great semi-religious trust company that owns
and rents out a large number of the shops. This is called
the Habous. I think the Bey of Tunisia is connected
with it and also some of the leading sheiks. This institution has been in existence for a long time, and its funds
amount to many millions. It has had considerable sums
dedicated to it with the understanding that they are to be
used for certain religious or charitable purposes. One
rich Mohammedan, for instance, left his money to the
Habous in order that it might supply free drinking water
to a certain locality. Though this was many years ago
the water still flows. Men sometimes leave fortunes to
this trust with instructions that it is to handle them in

185

the interest of their wives and children, and, in short, it does much the same sort of business as do our American trust companies.

The Habous owns buildings all over Tunis as well as extensive tracts of land outside the city. It possesses so much property that the French authorities are afraid of it, and they would like to have a safety valve created that would prevent its money from being turned to improper uses. The company's officers pretend that they desire nothing so much as an investigation, but when the French make their inquiries they learn nothing. There is always the fear that some Mohammedan fanatic may declare a holy war, in which event the Habous might become dangerous by furnishing a war chest for the Arabs.

During my wanderings through Tunis I have seen many of the shops owned by this corporation, and to-day I went into the building containing its offices. It is within a stone's throw of the bazaars on the Rue d'Eglise, in the very heart of the old city. It consists of many large rooms surrounding a court walled with marble and has so many clerks that it looks like a government department.

In striking contrast with the Arab parts of this city is the section in which the French have their residences and chief business houses. This is outside the walls of old Tunis, extending from them down to the harbour. Less than a generation ago the ground there was a swamp and considered fit for nothing. It now contains the finest buildings in Tunis and is worth hundreds of dollars per front foot. There are large hotels, banks, and stores upon it. It has wide and well-paved streets, and were it not for the Arabs, Jews, and veiled women in the crowds which parade it you might think it a part of Paris, Lyons, or Marseilles.

French Tunis is growing rapidly. It stretches far out into the country, one of its best avenues reaching to the Belvedere, or municipal park. This is lined with fine houses and there are other good residential streets. The main business thoroughfares of the French city are the Avenue de France and the Avenue Jules Ferry, formerly called the Avenue de la Marine. They contain the chief banks, shops, and cafés, and also the Casino and the principal hotels.

French Tunis prides itself on being an up-to-date town. It has electric lights and trolley lines, which now go all around the old city and reach to some parts of its interior as well. It has several large banks, two or three department stores, and a great many restaurants and cafés. The Casino is devoted to vaudeville shows, with a gambling department, and during the winter it becomes a little Monte Carlo, patronized by both native and tourist. This establishment has seats for something like two thousand spectators. Its audience room consists of a pit and boxes, and the people can have coffee, beer, or wine served while the actors are playing. At the right of the audience room is a large parlour in which several roulette tables are kept going both during and between the acts, while on the left there are rooms for private gambling and public places for *rouge et noir*. When I visited the gambling rooms during the intermissions last night I saw crowds about the tables. The stakes at roulette were from a franc upward, and the tables were well covered with silver. The *rouge et noir* rooms were deserted, but I understand they are well patronized in the winter, when many tourists are here.

Tunis has also a summer theatre at the Belvedere Park, and the military bands give frequent concerts in the public squares.

The most interesting theatrical presentations in this part of the world are plays with Phœnician characters and scenes acted in a ruined theatre excavated on the site of old Carthage. Several dramas have been written by French playwrights especially for Tunis, to be acted in the open air in the same surroundings and upon the same site where the plays of Carthage were presented when it was the capital of Africa and a rival of imperial Rome. The heroine of one of these plays takes the part of a beautiful woman whose statue was found in the ruins and is now in the museum of Carthage.

CHAPTER XXI

AMID THE RUINS OF OLD CARTHAGE

I HAVE spent the whole of to-day among the ruins of Carthage. The French have excavated them and made many valuable discoveries. Lying on the shore of the Mediterranean Sea beyond the lake on which Tunis is situated, the ruins cover some thousands of acres. The centre of old Carthage was about twelve miles from Tunis and the Phœnician capital reached even to Tunis itself. To defend its landward side the city had a wall twenty-three miles long. In the height of its glory it is said to have had more than a million inhabitants and even when it was destroyed, after its long war with Rome, it contained more than seven hundred thousand people. During that war it furnished armies of enormous size. When Hannibal went from Spain to invade Italy he took ninety thousand men and forty elephants with him over the Pyrenees and the Alps; and during the First Punic War a fleet started out from Carthage with three hundred and fifty ships of a capacity of one hundred and fifty thousand troops. Each of the ships had an iron beak to ram the boats of the enemy and was manned by sailors who were the best of ancient times.

That was during the closing days of Carthage the Mighty. Shortly afterward the Romans destroyed it and ploughed up the ground upon which it stood. Later still they founded another city upon its site, which they made their capital of Africa, and which was for a long time the third city of the world.

The ruins of Roman Carthage are still to be seen here, but far more interesting to me is Carthage the Mighty, that famous city favoured by Juno, Jupiter's henpecking wife, and founded, tradition says, by Dido, the Semitic princess of Tyre. After Dido's husband had been assassinated by her brother Pygmalion, she fled to this part of North Africa. Like Jessica, old Shylock's daughter, she did not go away empty handed. Her ship was loaded with her treasures from the royal palaces of her brother and herself and she took enough people to found a new empire.

When she first set foot on African soil Queen Dido bought land of the natives, and by a real estate trick obtained for a song this big tract upon which Carthage stood. When our forefathers purchased the site of New York from the Indians the price was a peck of glass beads and brass buttons; it is said that all Chicago was once offered for a pair of old boots, and that the ground upon which Melbourne, one of the richest cities of Australia, now stands was sold for two old woollen blankets. The thrifty Dido bought the site of this greatest city of antiquity at a somewhat similar rate. According to tradition, she told the natives that she wanted only a patch of land big enough to be inclosed in a bull's hide and they made a contract of sale on those terms. But Queen Dido cut the bull's hide into leather shoestrings and, tying them together, took in what seemed to the natives all out of doors. The tract ran around a beautiful harbour, inclosing the whole peninsula between the lake and the sea. It was gently sloping, with a little hill here and there, and with

In these tombs of the Phœnician cemetery of ancient Carthage have been found little stone boxes of ashes, supposed to contain the remains of Carthaginian babies burned in the red-hot arms of Moloch.

From one end of North Africa to the other Moslem women are seen shrouded in haicks with only a narrow slit or a tiny hole left for the eyes.

great rocky mountains in sight in the rear. The land itself was exceedingly rich, and the country about it produced so abundantly that it was for centuries one of the world's great wheat lands.

As I drove out to Carthage to-day I saw American windmills on great towers of steel agitating the air inhabited by the ghosts of the old Carthaginians. The windmills came from Chicago, but the city on whose site they now stand once ranked as far greater than Chicago. Punic Carthage was the chief business centre of the old world, and its captains of industry and trust magnates were as powerful as those of Chicago now are. Founded in 822 B. C., it was prominent when Athens was young, and long before Rome had begun to be.

The Carthaginians had their colonies throughout the known world. They owned the greater part of Sicily and many other Mediterranean islands, and had large settlements on the Spanish peninsula. More than two thousand years before Bartholomew Diaz or Vasco da Gama started out to explore Africa, Hanno the Carthaginian had sailed out of the Strait of Gibraltar with sixty ships and some thirty thousand men. He made his way down around the west coast of this continent to the Gulf of Guinea, bringing back stories of the ebony Negroes, the mighty elephants, and the gorillas. For centuries thereafter many tales of his were thought to be lies, but they have since been proved true. The Carthaginians established colonies on the west coast of Africa. They sent their ships to Great Britain. They had commercial centres everywhere. They were among the richest people of the world and about the best traders. They carried on business as a close corporation, allowing no foreigners to deal with their colonies. Such as dared do so were captured and drowned. As time went on, they sent caravans across the Sahara to the Sudan and over the Libyan Desert to the Valley of the Nile.

Lying before me as I write is a picture of old Carthage, the Carthage that Rome conquered, reproduced by a French antiquarian. The city, which was of vast extent, was somewhat like the great oriental capitals of to-day. Its buildings were white and flat-roofed. About it was a wall twenty miles in circumference and loftier than the Great Wall of China. It was over fifty feet in height, while the towers at regular intervals upon it were many feet higher. This wall was used for defence as well as for barracks to contain the army. Built into it were stalls for three hundred war elephants and four thousand war horses, storage places sufficient to supply them all with food, and quarters for tens of thousands of soldiers.

Old Carthage had a forum, a market place, and magnificent public buildings. It had an artificial harbour, restored in miniature by the French, which was so arranged that the entrance could be shut at night by chains. The door leading into it was only sixty feet wide, but this admitted the ships to two ports so connected that the vessels could sail from one to the other. It was a city of fine houses and cultured people, who owned quantities of gold and precious stones, their jewellery being equal to any sold in our best stores to-day, as one can easily see from the collection in the museum which stands on its site.

The Carthage I have described was utterly destroyed one hundred and forty-six years before Christ, and almost a century passed before another city began to rise on its ruins. This was the Carthage fostered by Julius Cæsar and Augustus, which in time became the Roman capital of North Africa. It had many theatres, the remains of which stand to-day on the ruins of the old Phœnician city. It was a city of gladiatorial shows, where Christians were eaten by lions, gored to death by wild bulls, and slaughtered by gladiators. On the hill where the museum is now I saw the tombs of Saints Perpetua and Felicitas, two young women who were killed in the arena.

Later yet, when Rome was converted, Carthage, still holding its place as one of the great ports of the world, became the chief Christian city of Africa. Here St. Augustine studied and preached, while near here St. Cyprian, the martyr, was killed. When the Vandals invaded Africa they made Carthage their capital. It remained a great city until the seventh century, when the Mohammedan Arabs came in and destroyed it.

Since then Carthage has been a quarry for the artistic material of all the palaces along the Mediterranean Sea. In the great mosque of Santa Sophia, at Constantinople, I saw marble columns that came from here; many of the wonders of architectural Rome originated in Carthage, and shiploads of its ruins have gone to Palermo and other Italian cities. The palaces of the Bey of Tunisia are built of Punic marble and, as I have noted, the bazaars of Tunis are flanked with Carthaginian marble columns which the Arabs have painted over in red, yellow, and green stripes, so that they now look like barber poles. Many of the houses of Tunis contain materials from the same source, and the ruins here have been furnishing building stone of all sorts for more than one thousand years.

During recent centuries the various museums of the world have been robbing this ancient city. Even travellers have been allowed to pick up and carry away what they pleased. This is no longer permitted. The French have established two great museums, one on the site of old Carthage and the other at the Bardo, in the palace of the Bey, and are trying to preserve what is left.

Some books about Africa will tell you that there is nothing of Carthage now to be seen except a few broken-down cisterns which once supplied the city with water. This is not so. The French have made excavations ever since they have had Tunisia under their control, not only here but in all parts of the country. They have unearthed ruins that will compare with those of Athens and Rome.

Suppose you could blot from the face of the United States either Boston, Philadelphia, or St. Louis. Suppose you could destroy all the buildings and cover them with earth. Then let them lie for decades and build other great cities on top. Then destroy those cities, and let the storms and dust of a thousand years settle upon them, and you may have some idea of the condition of the ruins of Carthage. You must add, however, the tombs in which the ancients were accustomed to put jewellery and other relics, and imagine that the destruction was such that many of the belongings of the people were left in the débris.

It is now more than twenty-seven hundred years since the first buildings of Carthage were erected, and many of the objects I have seen here are over two thousand years old. As I went over the ruins I observed the Arab farmers turning up fragments of pottery and pieces of marble which were parts of houses twenty centuries ago, and I have been bothered all day by dark-faced Mohammedans begging me to buy Carthaginian coins in use long

Before a devout Moslem goes into the mosque to pray, he visits the
fountain in the courtyard and washes his hands and face.

Even for camels dates are the chief food in the oases as well as the money crop of the inhabitants.

Among the desert people dwarfs are believed always to remain children. The holder of the wooden slate has been reciting the Koran in school for forty-five years, or ever since he was three years old.

before Christ, and cameos the size of my fingernail which were probably worn in the rings of Punic maidens when all the world was young.

I can't begin to describe the extent of the ruins. By this I do not mean the remains of great temples and palaces, of theatres and tombs. These are comparatively few; but there are vast tracts covered with scraps of pottery, pieces of broken marble, half ground up bricks, and bits of mosaic. The sheep and goats feed among them, and they are ploughed and harrowed and pulverized by cultivation to fertilize the crops of the present day.

My trip to Carthage was over an excellent road which runs around the bay. The scenery is beautiful and the flamingoes wing over the water, showing their pink plumage as they doubtless have done for centuries. All along the roads we saw Arabs cultivating their little farms. Here and there was a camp of Bedouins watching their flocks; and when we left the road and drove across the ploughed fields we passed through a lot of fat-tailed sheep and black goats driven by natives.

Nearly all our way was over the ruins of Carthage, and part of it through what was almost the heart of the ancient city. The ground was so covered with marble and pottery that we felt like getting out and looking for relics, and, indeed, during the whole day my eyes have been searching among the stones in the hope of finding treasure. We have had opportunity to purchase all sorts of coins and clay lamps, some of the time of the Romans and some dating back to the days of the Phœnicians.

We first visited the amphitheatre where the gladiatorial shows were held. It lies near an Arab village and as I stood in it, I heard the shrieking of a spanked baby filling the air which once resounded with the cries of the Christian martyrs. The cages for the wild beasts can be plainly seen, also the great vaults below in which the martyrs waited. The arena, which is elliptical in shape, covers more than an acre. I paced it from one end to the other and according to my estimate it was about three hundred feet long and two hundred feet wide. This space now lies about twenty-five feet below the level of the ground. It contains marble columns broken and battered. Some of the seats and a few of the arches are still to be seen.

This theatre was described by an Arab historian who was here eight hundred years ago. According to his account, there were five galleries and the building was the most beautiful of its kind ever known. To-day I saw sheep and goats feeding on the edge of what must have been at one time the second gallery, and a donkey was braying while I paced the arena.

The oldest and best known of the Carthaginian ruins are the great cisterns built to supply the city with water. There were two sets of them, one at each side of the town. They were of vast dimensions, enormous barrel-shaped caverns four hundred and forty-three feet long and more than eighty feet in diameter. They were surmounted by cupolas and were connected with pipes for distributing the water. The largest of these cisterns are near an Arab village and are now used as stables and dwellings. They number twenty-four and cover many acres. I went down into some of them. In one I found a tiny gray donkey with a little Arab girl standing beside it, and in another an old hen with a flock of small chickens feeding about her. A part of one cistern has been walled off as a haymow;

another is now an Arab house, and in a third I saw a Bedouin woman grinding meal upon two stones that rested on the floor.

The dust of ages has filled these great caverns, which now make an excellent protection from the weather. As I made my notes within them I heard the cry of prayer from a Mohammedan tomb near by: "There is no God but Allah and Mohammed is his Prophet!" As I listened I thought of the people who drank the water from these cisterns five hundred years before the Christian Era and more than one thousand years before Mohammed first saw the light of day in the deserts of Arabia.

Later in the day I visited the reservoirs on the other side of the town. They are twenty-five hundred years old, but the French have repaired them and they now supply water to the villages and towns about. The water, which comes from Tunis, is pumped in by steam engines. The cisterns are thirty feet deep and something like six hundred feet long. The engineer told me that he had about six million gallons in them at the time of my visit.

These cisterns, as used by the Carthaginians, were first filled with rain water, but later on they were supplied by an enormous aqueduct erected by the Roman emperor, Hadrian. This brought the water from Dougga, about eighty miles away. It carried six million gallons a day and the water passed through underground canals and over valleys on magnificent arches to Carthage. The remains of this aqueduct can be seen in many places, and at present parts of it have been so restored that it now supplies Tunis with water. The restoration, which cost millions, was done by a French engineer. Iron pipes have been used instead of the arches, but the old masonry still upholds much of the works. The water supply is far greater than it was in the days of the Romans.

I have spent considerable time wandering through the old Carthaginian cemeteries. Many tombs have been excavated, and the dead of a dozen generations have been taken from their graves to be shown to us, the heathen tourists of the present. Some of the tombs were far below ground and others almost at the surface. From one cemetery they have taken two hundred and eighty-nine epitaphs, and from another eight hundred, including the names of librarians, schoolmasters, doctors, soldiers, nurses, dancers, and slaves. Some of the oldest tombs are triangular in shape; others contained marble sarcophagi, and in some were bodies of men and women loaded with jewels.

During my visit to the museum I saw many little stone boxes which were found full of charred ashes and bones. They date back to the days of Carthage the Mighty, and are supposed to have contained the ashes of children sacrificed to Moloch. This brazen Punic god was made red hot at the times of sacrifice, and the children were placed in his arms. It was the custom to give him not only little children, but also young men and maidens. The victims rolled down from his searing arms into the blazing furnace below.

The museum at Carthage is filled with treasures which have been found in the ruins. There are dice, razors, spectacles, surgical instruments, and thousands of clay lamps and casks of all kinds. As far as ancient Phœnician exhibits are concerned, it is, I doubt not, the greatest storehouse in the world; and in its relics of the Roman period it compares favourably with many others more

The vaulted bazaars of Tunis are flanked with marble columns from Carthage, which the Arabs have painted over in red, yellow, and green stripes, so that they look like barber poles.

Many of her North African sisters would regard this unveiled woman of Constantine as a brazen creature, but the lady herself considers that with her earrings and anklets she is quite ready to face a critical world.

famous. I was especially interested in the jewellery and other things which once belonged to the gay girls of the Carthage of twenty-five hundred years ago. There is a lock of hair from the head of a fair Punic maiden, there is a box of rouge with some of the paint still in the bottom, and there are alabaster cases holding perfume and also pins, mirrors, trinkets, and other gewgaws.

There are golden necklaces of beautiful workmanship and hundreds of gold rings of all sizes, from one small enough for a two-year-old baby to some which may have been wedding rings for twelve-year-old brides. Many of these rings are set with cameos and stones. There are gold earrings by the hundreds, and beautiful they are. As I looked at them I asked the Catholic White Father beside me about the maidens who wore them so many centuries ago, mentioning the mortality of all things earthly. In reply he pointed to the shelves under the cases. I looked and saw skulls and bones in great quantities; remains of men, women, and children all mixed together. Then, taking me to a marble sarcophagus near by, he showed me the bones of a young Punic beau who lived centuries since. I measured his skeleton and found it was six feet two inches in length. On the finger of one hand there was a beautiful ring, evidencing the vanity of its owner. He may have been a friend of Hanno or Hannibal, or perhaps only some newly rich man of the time! Who knows?

CHAPTER XXII

WHERE THE WOMEN WEAR TROUSERS

ACCORDING to the Koran, every Moslem has the right to four wives upon earth, and when he goes to heaven he will receive in addition seventy-two black-eyed houris, ever beautiful and ever young. There he will have children or not, according to his wish, and the offspring will grow in an hour to the stature of their parents. The Prophet himself is said to have had about twenty wives while on earth. When he died he left nine, each of whom had her own house not far from the mosque at Medina. Mohammed started out by marrying a widow named Cadijah, whose money gave him his first boost into prominence. He was about twenty-five years old at the time and one of the finest looking young beaux of Arabia. Cadijah was forty, and it is alleged that it was she who popped the question. He lived with her for twenty-five years, during which time he took no other wife. A month after she died, however, he was betrothed to a girl of seven who became his wife two or three years later. This second wife was the beautiful Ayesha, whom to the day of his death he preferred above all others.

These facts form the basis of the Mohammedan's idea of marriage. He believes that the Prophet had the right to more wives than his followers, because he was favoured of God and there was a chance that he might generate a race of prophets to succeed him, though this chance failed. The Moslem still sticks to the limit of only four wives, and the Arab judges of Tunisia and Algeria will not recognize as legal any more than that number.

The French in Algeria, who are now trying to cut down the size of the harem, will not allow such of the Arabs as become naturalized to have more than one legal helpmate. I heard of a young man in Oran, the son of a sheik, who thought that it would be fine to be a French citizen. He took out his papers and shortly thereafter wanted to marry. As he already had one wife, the license was refused. Upon this, he became disgusted and said he wanted to be a pure Arab once more.

Down in Figig, on the edge of Morocco, I was told that it is the custom for the Moor of that region to marry at eighteen or twenty years of age, taking a wife of thirteen or fourteen. About ten years later he adds another young maiden of the same age to his household. When he gets to be forty he takes a third spouse and at fifty a fourth, so that he has always one young wife to wait upon him throughout his earthly career. As the new wives come, the older ones step back and act as their servants.

But with the advancement of modern civilization these plural marriages are steadily decreasing in number. This is true in all Mohammedan cities. Here in Tunis most of the natives have but one wife, while in all the cities of Algeria monogamy is becoming the rule. One reason for this is the fact that the cost of living is always increasing and the women demand more and more. They are patterning after the French ladies in their tastes, until now it is only the rich man who can keep more than one wife.

Moreover, where several wives are thrown together

under the same roof and in the same quarters, there is sure to be discord, so that it means both peace and economy to have only one. The Arab women of the better classes are a dead load on their husbands, for they are seldom more than children in character. They have no real education and they must have servants or slaves to wait upon them. The husband is expected to furnish a dower for each wife, and if he is rich he must give from two to ten thousand dollars to get her. This money goes to the girl's family, and a quartet of wives thus paid for requires a large sum. With people less rich, the dowries are smaller; but every husband must pay something for his wife, even down to the porter, although the latter may get his bride for five or ten dollars.

As a rule, the Mohammedan husband makes his matrimonial investments after the old fashion of buying a pig in a poke. Marriages are made at an early age. Girls wed at fifteen or sixteen and young men at twenty or twenty-five. There is no such thing as courtship, the matches being usually arranged by the parents of the respective families. In a marriage among wealthy families there are always preliminary presents and rites. The groom sends dates and other fruits to his sweetheart, and the prospective bride puts herself into training in order that she may look her best at the wedding. She takes frequent steam baths, and for a week before the marriage has one every day. At the same time her cheeks are painted with rouge, and her fingernails, toenails, and even her feet and the lower parts of her arms and legs, are decorated with henna, a red colouring matter in common use throughout the Orient.

While I was in Tangier I saw a number of wedding

processions. The ceremony usually takes place on Friday, the Moslem Sabbath, and consists chiefly in the couples joining hands while prayers are said over them. On her wedding day the bride is carried about in a covered chair or box on the shoulders of the slaves, amid music and dancing. Her girl friends keep her company, and there is a wedding feast which lasts almost all night. This is followed by other feasts throughout the next week or more.

I am told that a Moorish husband's first duty is to unbraid his wife's hair, and that, thereafter, she puts on the special dress of the married woman. The ordinary Mohammedan marriage is, I understand, moderately happy. It is said that the stronger character usually rules the household.

Divorces are easily accomplished in all Mohammedan countries, where a man can get rid of his superfluous wives far more easily than the American can divorce his only one in Idaho or Nevada. There are now in Algeria every year almost half as many divorces as there are marriages. All that a Mohammedan has to do to secure a separation is to point his wife to the door and say, "I divorce you! I divorce you!! I divorce you!!!" and out she goes. It is not much better with the Tunisian Jews, the chief difference being that the Moslem has the right to four wives while the Jew can have but one.

There is no place on earth where the females are so much secluded. There are millions in North Africa who are never seen by any other men than their husbands. In the city of Tunis the ladies of the wealthier classes never go out on the street except in closed carriages. They know nothing about shopping, and never visit the bazaars or stores. The carriages are brought into the courtyard of their homes, and after they have been put in by their servants and the doors tightly closed, the grooms come out and hitch up the horses. If they are calling upon a lady friend, the carriage is taken into the courtyard restricted to the women of the household, where the horses are unharnessed, so that the men may take them away before the ladies step out.

Every fine Mohammedan house has its harem. The rooms are built around courts, there being usually one court for the men and another for the women. In the latter only the master of the house is permitted to enter, and in less pretentious homes a male visitor will always make himself heard before he comes in, so that the women may flee. The women have their own private staircases to the roofs, which are their special quarters. These are usually flat and form the loafing and gossiping places for the feminine part of the household. They are surrounded by walls so that one cannot see the girls at all from the street.

In Tunis the women of the middle classes go out so wrapped up in veils that not a bit of their faces is to be seen. Over their heads they have long scarfs that fall to their knees. These scarfs are black, embroidered with red and white stripes, and so thick that it is impossible to see through them. The wearers hold them up with their hands as they walk, looking out for a step at a time. They sometimes wear shawls over the veils. As such women seldom visit the stores, if they are seen on the street they are probably on their way to the mosque or to the cemeteries or to visit their friends.

The women of the poorer classes look stranger still.

WHERE THE WOMEN WEAR TROUSERS

They dress in white garments of cotton or wool which cover the whole of their persons, excepting their faces. The latter are wrapped around with a thick black crêpe in which two holes are cut out for the eyes. In the distance they look like the blackest of Negroes, with features wrinkled like a washboard. As they come closer, their veils are seen to be masks and their bright, dark eyes shine out of the surrounding blackness.

The woman of Algiers generally wears a wide white band across her face to conceal it; sometimes a veil of white is fastened tightly over the bridge of the nose, the upper part of the face being hidden by the *haick* or blanket-like shawl common all over that country. In Morocco and in western Algeria the woman holds her *haick* tight over her face, leaving a little three-cornered hole, not much bigger than a finger ring, out of which one eye peeps as she goes waddling along.

It is impossible to see how the fair sex is dressed in Morocco. When they go out in the streets they bundle themselves up in blankets so that they look like bags walking on slippers. In Algeria and Tunisia nearly every female wears trousers of some kind with the overgarments so arranged that the pantaloons can be easily seen. They are worn enormously full and are tied in at the instep or at the calf. The *haick* or head shawl does not fall far below the waist, and these trousers are one of the features of the afternoon parade in the Rue Bab Azoun. The breeches of the Arab women in Tunisia are somewhat more hidden, but those of the Jewesses are always in evidence.

It is only for the streets that the Arab woman dons these very full trousers, which are removed as soon as she comes home. In the house she affects loose knee-pants made of silk or China crêpe. In addition, she has on a chemise which is tucked into her trousers, and above this a jacket of brocaded silk. She wears a silk sash wrapped about her waist, and may have several vests of gay colours fastened with bright buttons. Her headdress consists of a small velvet cap which comes to a point over the crown, and on her feet are slippers embroidered with gold.

All African women are fond of jewellery and the well-to-do Mohammedan girls have their necklaces of pearls, earrings of precious stones, and bracelets and anklets of gold. The poorer ones wear silver, while those who have nothing will load themselves down with brass.

Indeed, I am surprised at the number of ornaments which even the common Arab girls wear. Little tots of six and seven have heavy silver rings on their ankles, and gold rings as big around as the saucer of an after-dinner coffee cup not only in the lobes of their ears but also in the ear rims all along to the top. The Bedouin girl, especially, adorns herself lavishly and frequently carries the wealth of her whole family on her person. The Kabyle woman covers her breast with jewellery, and often wears enormous earrings and anklets and pins which will weigh a pound or more each. One reason why the women are so bedecked is the fact that the men don't like to put their money in banks, preferring to turn their surplus into ornaments for their wives and daughters.

During my trip into the western desert I had to spend a night in a first-class car with a rich Arab chief and his wife and their two little girls. When the woman came in she was so bundled up that one could tell nothing about her clothes. As the night wore on, however, her overgarments were thrown back and I observed that she was

Fourteen yards of stuff are required to make the baggy trousers worn by the women of North Africa when dressed to appear on the street, which many of them are permitted to do only once a week.

In addition to the usual Mohammedan veils the wealthy ladies of Tunis also cover their heads with long embroidered scarfs, which they hold out far enough to enable them to watch their steps.

dressed like the Queen of Sheba in her glory. She had half-a-dozen bracelets on each of her arms, her fingers sparkled with diamonds, and there were great gold rings in the sides and lobes of her ears. On her head was a little cornucopia cap of red velvet embroidered with gold, and she wore a spangled shirt waist over a white chemise of fine wool. She was tattooed on chin, forehead, and cheeks. Her lips were painted with rouge, her fingers stained red with henna, and her eyelids blackened with kohl.

I have spoken already of the fair-skinned Kabyle women of eastern Algeria. As a rule the Kabyle husband has but one wife and the women are allowed to go about as they please. Their ordinary dress is a gown that reaches from the neck to the feet and is fastened at the shoulder with a great pin of silver or white metal. On ceremonial occasions they wear gowns of bright red and yellow stripes strapped in at the loins with belts of bright-coloured leather. They sometimes wear a headdress of black silk, but their feet are usually bare.

Since the Jewish men think a woman beautiful according to her amount of flesh, a likely Hebrew girl of three hundred pounds or so has no trouble in getting a husband. As a maiden approaches the marriageable age she is stuffed, much after the manner of a Strassburg goose destined for *pâté de foie gras*. The Jewesses have their own way of eating to increase their fat and their own foods for putting on weight. One of our Agricultural Department experts tells me that they use a certain grain which surpasses any that we have in its fattening qualities, and also that the Department expects to introduce this grain into the United States. If so, it will be a boon to our thin, scrawny girls,

who worry because they cannot rise in avoirdupois. I
have before me a photograph of the two biggest Jewesses
of Tunis, who are simply mountains of flesh. One of them
weighs more than four hundred pounds.

These Jewesses have the homeliest costumes I have ever
seen upon women. Both on the street and at home they
wear breeches over which are short, loose sacques falling
to the waist. Some of them have their trousers loose
about the hips and tight at the calves and others wear
them equally full all the way down, loading them with
embroidery of silver and gold. Some pairs of breeches are
made entirely of gold thread, and I hear of money-lenders'
daughters who have trousers that cost two hundred dollars
a pair. As such garments are reserved for home use, they
are not to be seen on the streets. Other girls have pantaloons of velvet loaded with bands of gold and silver, a
girl thus carrying a whole fortune on her trousers. They
all wear jewellery, coming out on public occasions or fête
days in pearls and diamonds and gold without limit.

The Jewish men dress like the Arabs. The majority of
the women have what we would call brunette complexions,
although there is no sign of the mulatto about them.
They have black hair, beautiful eyes, and not infrequently
prominent Hebrew noses. Some of them are pretty, but
more are not; and with their outlandish costumes, the
homely ones are about the ugliest of their sex.

The Jewesses marry young. A girl is often wedded at
twelve, and she becomes a mother at fourteen or fifteen.
Marriages are usually preceded by a contract in which
there is often a forfeit put up against divorce. If the
man does not carry out his contract he has to pay damages,
while in the case of divorce he usually gives back half the

property which his wife brought him. A divorced wife always gets an allowance.

If his wife has no children, the Tunisian Jew has the right to add a second wife to his family, and a dead man's brother is expected to marry his sister-in-law even if he is married already. I am told that marriages sometimes occur between uncles and nieces, and that families combine to keep the fortunes in their own clan as far as possible.

About a week before the wedding the public festivities begin, and from that time on the girl has to go through a number of ceremonies without power of resistance. The older women of the family take possession of her. They first put her in a bath, where her body is covered with an ointment which, when dry, is peeled off, leaving the skin perfectly clean and as soft as when she was born. Her hair is then anointed with jet-black pomatum which gives it a gloss, her eyelids are blackened, and her eyebrows are pencilled and joined by a thick line of red paint. At the same time her fingernails are covered with henna and even her toenails are made red.

These Jewish marriages are usually made by the rabbis, at the house of the bride. Here the rabbi puts the young couple under a veil and directs the groom how to put the ring upon the bride's finger.

After marriage the woman becomes to a large extent the servant of her husband. If she is poor she cooks the meals, and no matter how well off her husband is, she is expected to make his bed and wait upon him. She always eats at a second table, for in the ordinary Jewish household of Tunis there are always two meals, the first of which is for the men.

Notwithstanding these customs, the course of true love runs as smoothly over the caravan tracks of Sahara as it does along the automobile roads of the United States. I am told that many of the marriages of Mohammedans, Kabyles, Jews, and Bedouins are happy ones and the literature of all of them has its love stories and its love songs. One of the most beautiful poems written by Bayard Taylor was the love song of a Bedouin. Whether or not it was an English rendering of something he heard in his travels I do not know. It reads:

> From the Desert I come to thee,
>   On a stallion shod with fire;
> And the winds are left behind
>   In the speed of my desire.
> Under thy window I stand,
>   And the midnight hears my cry:
> I love thee, I love but thee,
>   With a love that shall not die
>   Till the sun grows cold,
>   And the stars are old,
>   And the leaves of the Judgment
>   Book unfold!

> Look from thy window, and see
>   My passion and my pain!
> I lie on the sands below,
>   And I faint in thy disdain.
> Let the night-winds touch thy brow
>   With the heat of my burning sigh,
> And melt thee to hear the vow
>   Of a love that shall not die
>   Till the sun grows cold,
>   And the stars are old,
>   And the leaves of the Judgment
>   Book unfold!

This old man is not the girl's grandfather but her husband. A girl of the desert is often a bride at twelve, though the groom may be five times her age.

In the Jewish cemetery at Tunis shrouded women sit atop the graves and bob up and down and wail for their dead. At funerals women are hired to moan loudly for the deceased.

WHERE THE WOMEN WEAR TROUSERS

My steps are nightly driven,
  By the fever in my breast,
To hear from thy lattice breathed
  The word that shall give me rest.
Open the door of thy heart,
  And open thy chamber door,
And my kisses shall teach thy lips
  The love that shall fade no more
  Till the sun grows cold,
  And the stars are old,
  And the leaves of the Judgment
    Book unfold!

The Jews here are very particular in their religious observances. Their shops are shut up on Saturday and their wives do not cook or sweep on that day. They are also devoted to one another, and a Jewish funeral with its accompanying mourning is one of the remarkable things to be seen in Tunis. The Jewish cemeteries are nothing like ours. They have no tall monuments. The vaults, which are dug out so that their tops rest even with the surface of the earth, are covered with marble slabs of the same size and height, so that the whole surface of the cemetery appears to be one great marble floor.

Upon each slab are carved Hebrew characters giving the names and ages of those who lie below. When the women go out to mourn, they sit down on the slabs over their dead and bob up and down as they wail out their grief. I visited one of the largest of these cemeteries this afternoon. Its marble floor seemed to be spotted with white tents, but as I got closer I could see that each of these was a Jewish woman shrouded in white mourning her dead.

There was a chapel at one end of the graveyard from

which came a great noise. I entered and found that a funeral was being conducted. In one room was a coffin standing upright against the wall and beside it on the stone floor lay the corpse of a man covered by a sheet of bright red silk. About him were a number of Jewish men in Arab clothing weeping softly; while in the next room were the hired mourners, who are brought in for such occasions at so much per wail. These mourners were Jewish women ranging in age and size from a plump maid of eighteen to a weighty old lady of sixty or more. They numbered fifteen, and I venture to say they would pull down the scales at a ton and a half. They sat on the marble floor with their feet under them, and swaying back and forth, bowed their heads to the ground as they fairly howled out a chorus for which the fat old lady kept time. As the mourners saw me making a note, the wailing subsided for a moment, but when one of the bereaved family came in it burst out louder than ever. Such mourners are common in all oriental countries, and they are employed here by the Arabs as well as the Jews.

CHAPTER XXIII

KAIROUAN THE HOLY

KAIROUAN is the Mecca of North Africa and one of the holiest cities of the Mohammedan world. It was founded by the famous general Sidi Okba in 669 A. D., and until 1881, when the French took it, no Christian had ever gone into it and come out alive. A half century since it would not have been safe for any foreigner to enter it. In 1830, when Sir Grenville Temple came here, by permission of the Bey of Tunis, he had an escort of soldiers but was allowed to go out only after sunset, in the disguise of an Arab. It was not until after its conquest by the French that Kairouan was open to Christians, and even to-day they are looked on with hatred. The town is in charge of French soldiers, and has a French controller to direct the skeiks how to govern. By means of a card from him I am able to make my way about and visit the mosques.

The fact that "Christian dogs" and "infidels" may enter the mosques of this, the Holy City of North Africa, is said to be due to a curious bit of Tunisian history. It was taken by the French without the firing of a single shot, because a famous holy man had prophesied years before that the city would be taken by the French, and the people believed that its conquest was preordained. When they entered the city, the French, needing a clean place for a hospital, took for the purpose the chief mosque of Kai-

213

rouan, the Grand Mosque of Sidi Okba. Once that had been profaned by the presence of infidels it did not matter if they continued to come to see it. And if they entered the Grand Mosque they certainly could go into the others.

The city is so sacred in the minds of the Mohammedans that they make pilgrimages to it just as they do to Mecca and Medina. There are now pilgrims scattered through the various mosques and one may see them praying in the desert not far away. Many of them come for hundreds of miles to worship at the shrines here. They sleep in the mosques and during certain seasons they overflow the city and their tents are to be seen covering the country outside the walls.

The Kairouan of to-day has twenty-two mosques and many tombs of Moslem saints. In the Middle Ages it had three hundred mosques, nine hundred baths, and six hundred hotels where caravans could stop, and it was celebrated all over the world as a seat of religion and learning. Its population then numbered a million. Now it has only twenty-five thousand inhabitants, and some of the greatest mosques are outside the present limits of the city.

Kairouan is situated on a hill and surrounded by walls as high as a two-story house. Entering through the gates, one finds a town of Mohammedan architecture with typical flat-roofed buildings of one or two stories standing along streets so narrow that few of them are accessible except on foot, on horseback, or on donkeys. The business is done in covered bazaars and the people are dressed in turbans and gowns and the strange costumes worn by the Arabs. The women are closely veiled when they are on the street, it being no uncommon thing to see one

The Arab women bring their children for miles across the desert to drink from the sacred well of Kairouan, supposed to cure all ills and keep away disease.

Of the twenty-two mosques in Kairouan the Holy, that of Sidi Okba is the chief. Until used by the French invaders as a military hospital, it had never been entered by any Christian.

Though in the desert there is no muezzin to call the Faithful to prayer, he never fails in his devotions. He faces toward Mecca and uses sand in place of water for his ablutions.

draped in black from head to foot, her face so covered that not even an eye can be seen.

I have gone through the principal mosques. One of the most interesting is that of the barber of the Prophet Mohammed. This saintly man is buried here and with him three hairs of the Prophet's beard, which make the mosque especially holy. These hairs were secured by the barber one day when he had shaved Mohammed, and he carried them about with him for the rest of his life. One he kept under his tongue, another over his heart, and the third pasted on his right arm. The Moslems revere anything that comes from their Prophet, particularly the hairs of his beard. I remember when I visited the mosque of Jama Mausjid in Delhi, India, that the greatest curiosity shown me was a hair from Mohammed's moustache. It was kept in a crystal box inside a safe and I was able to see it only by bribing the officials. The hair was half an inch long and bright red in colour.

The mosque of the barber of Kairouan is outside of the city. It is entered through a vestibule lined with tiles and lacelike carvings. The minaret is faced with tiles and the court is surrounded by arcades of white marble columns. The barber's tomb is covered with black velvet, while hanging about it there are ostrich eggs, bags of earth from Mecca, and other offerings given by the pilgrims.

The Grand Mosque of Sidi Okba is situated just inside the walls. It is one of the largest mosques of North Africa and is imposing and beautiful. The building is of rectangular shape, with a great minaret at one side. It has arcades upheld by massive marble pillars running round a court of more than an acre, with an immense hall at one end. The latter has a ceiling of many arches supported by a forest of columns of marble and porphyry. The walls are decorated with mosaics of marble and lapis lazuli and with Moorish plaster work so carved that it looks like lace. The pulpit, which is of wood from Bagdad, has its panels chiselled with texts from the Koran. Many of the columns of this building were brought here from the ruins of Carthage, which city was taken by Sidi Okba just before he built Kairouan.

This is a good place to learn something of the Mohammedans and their religion. In North America and Europe, where one sees mostly Christians, it is hard to believe that there are millions upon millions who look upon us as heretics and think we are on the straight road to Hades. Every man I see here considers me already damned, and for the last three months I have been travelling among people who in their souls call me a Christian dog and feel that they would have a sure passport to heaven if they could put me out of the way. I have before me the figures representing the religious divisions of the world and I observe that more than one seventh of all the people on earth are Mohammedans. Here is the account in round numbers:

Total world population . . .	1,700,000,000
Mohammedans	221,000,000
Christians	563,000,000
Confucians and Taoists . . .	300,000,000
Brahmans	210,000,000
Buddhists	138,000,000
Jews	12,000,000
Other religions	247,000,000

This means that if all the people on this big, round globe could be brought together in one place, one person in every three would be a Christian, either Protestant, Catholic, or Greek Catholic. One in every five would be a Confucian or Taoist, a Chinaman with yellow face and almond eyes. Out of every eight one would be a dark-skinned Brahman from India and one in every seven would be a Mohammedan. The rest would be made up of pagans, Jews, or the numberless small sects.

The Mohammedans are scattered all over North Africa. They form the bulk of the population of Morocco, Algeria, Tunisia, Tripoli, and Egypt, and there are millions of them in the Sudan. There are more than sixty million Mohammedans in India. Arabia is populated by them. They form the predominating influence in Persia, Asia Minor, and Turkey. There are more millions in China and the islands of the western Pacific Ocean. We have a degraded Mohammedan sect in the Sulu Islands and Mindanao in the Philippines, and there are many in Borneo, Java, and in other parts of the Dutch East Indies. Jerusalem was held by these people for many centuries and they now outnumber the Christians in the Holy Land. Mohammedanism as a religion is increasing rather than decreasing. Whole tribes are being converted at one time in this African continent.

There is no doubt that the Mohammedans believe in their religion. They teach charity and brotherly love. They preach against avarice and the lending of money at interest, and the orthodox Moslems do not drink intoxicating drinks. Their faith is quite as strong as ours and they practise it more religiously. I see men at their prayers here every day; they pray in their shops or out in the fields; and in going through the bazaars one often observes the merchants studying the Koran. Nearly every turbaned and gowned man I meet carries a rosary on which he counts his prayers as he goes over his beads. Five times every day I hear the shrill cry of the muezzin, or Mohammedan priest, as he stands on the minaret of a mosque, high over the city, and calls the people to come to pray.

The hours of prayer begin at daybreak. The second call is at midday and the third at about three o'clock. There is a fourth call at sunset and a fifth in the evening. The words of the call, which is in Arabic, are somewhat like these:

Allah is great. I testify that there is no God but Allah, and Mohammed is the prophet of Allah. Come to prayer! Come to worship! Allah is great! There is no God but Allah!

Another call is:

Prayer is better than sleep! Come to prayer! Come to prayer!

As these calls ring out one sees the Mohammedan men on their way to the mosques. Some of them carry prayer rugs under their arms, while others go without them, relying on the matting or carpets which are usually on the mosque floors to protect their clothing. They take off their shoes before they enter the mosques and generally prostrate themselves as they pray.

In every mosque there is a fountain or washing place, for the Koran requires that one wash himself before he goes in to pray. He cleanses his feet, hands, face, and other parts of his body, and he goes through the motions of doing so whether he has water or not. It is often impossible to get water in the Sahara and at such times the Faithful use sand.

As they pray, the Moslems always face toward Mecca.

218

They have their fixed motions for praying. They begin by raising their hands to the lobes of their ears; they next hold them a little below the girdle, and then bow their heads over. After this they get down on their knees and touch their heads to the floor and then sit up and pray, muttering the words laid down in the Koran. They have numerous prayers, but one of the shortest and most common, used as we use the Lord's Prayer, is as follows:

In the name of God, merciful and gracious. Praise be to God, the Lord of creatures, the merciful and gracious, the Prince of the day of judgment. We serve Thee, and we pray Thee for help! Lead us in the right way of those to whom Thou hast shown mercy, and who go not astray! Amen.

The Mohammedans believe in one God and in an infinite number of prophets. They have altogether more than two hundred thousand prophets, but the greatest of them all are Adam, Noah, Abraham, Jesus, and Mohammed. It rather surprised me to know that they believe in Jesus, but I am told that they consider Him one of the best of their prophets, although the greatest of all is Mohammed, who is also the last. They believe in a future state, and that Christ will unite with Mohammed on the day of judgment in sending mankind to heaven or hell. On the judgment day there will be a wire rope as fine as a hair running across from Solomon's Temple in Jerusalem to the Mount of Olives. Upon that hair all mankind will have to walk. The good will be upheld by angels and will go on to paradise; while the wicked will drop into hell.

The Faithful believe also in angels. They have their Gabriel, who writes down the decrees of God; their Michael, who fights the battles of the faith, and their Israfil, who will sound the trumpet on resurrection day. There are a multitude of secondary angels whose business it is to watch over mankind. Every man has one of these angels on his right hand and another on his left, who keep a record of his every word and action. At the close of each day they fly up to heaven to file this report in the great ledgers there kept for the time when man comes to judgment. At the end of every prayer the Mohammedan always turns his face to the right and then to the left, greeting his recording angels, who are supposed to be watching him, and by his motions suggests to them that they do not forget to put the prayer to his credit.

These people have also their Lucifer and great hordes of bad angels, who are always trying to pry into the secrets of heaven. To prevent their learning them, whenever they try to enter heaven the good angels pelt them with falling stars.

Predestination is a tenet of the Mohammedans. They think that every event which will take place was written down by God at the beginning of the world and that no man can change his destiny. For this reason they are strong in war, the soldier believing that he cannot be killed until his time comes and that it is already determined whether he is to die in his bed or on the field of battle. Besides, he is convinced that if he dies fighting for the faith he will go straight to heaven.

The Koran is full of descriptions of heaven and hell. According to its authority, Mohammed went to heaven during his lifetime, and when he came back he gave the full story of his adventures there and told how things looked. He was called up by Gabriel, who brought him a white steed with a human face and a body resplendent with gems and precious stones. It had wings and when Mohammed mounted it, it soared with him through the skies with the rapidity of lightning. By and by the gate of the first heaven was reached. This was of pure silver and the heaven had a sky in which the stars were suspended by chains of gold. It contained a mighty rooster, so tall that his comb reached the second heaven. This bird crows every morning and all mankind is awakened by him, the cocks below beginning to crow when he opens his mouth.

Mohammed met our first father Adam in the first heaven, Noah in the second, and Moses and Aaron in the fifth. Noah hailed him as the greatest of the prophets, while Moses shed tears at the sight of him. In the seventh heaven Mohammed was received by Abraham and met the Deity himself. At this time many of the doctrines of the Koran were given to him, among others the command that fifty prayers should be made daily by all true believers.

As Mohammed dropped down from the seventh heaven he met Moses, who asked him what the Lord had required. The Prophet replied that God wanted mankind to make fifty prayers every day. Moses told Mohammed that this was impossible, as he knew from his own experience with the children of Israel, and that he had better return and ask the Lord to reduce the number. The number was cut down to forty. Moses sent him back again and again, until at last it was made only five. Moses thought this was too many, but Mohammed replied that he had already asked the Lord's indulgence until he was ashamed, and so the prayers made by Mohammedans remain five to this day.

In the Moslem's heaven the ground is of the finest wheat flour strewn with pearls and hyacinths instead of sand and pebbles. The air is fragrant with perfume and cooled by sparkling fountains. Some of the streams are pure water, running between green banks enamelled with flowers, while others are of milk and honey flowing over beds of musk. Among the trees is one the boughs of which are laden with every variety of fruit and the shade of which spreads so far that a horse might run for a hundred years and not cross it.

The inhabitants of heaven are clothed in raiment sparkling with jewels. They have sumptuous palaces and voluptuous couches. Every believer will have hundreds of servants, who will bring him the most delicious food and drink in dishes and goblets of gold, and he will eat as long as he wishes without being full and drink without growing drunk.

For society he will have the learned of mankind to talk with him and the great of all time to amuse him. He will have the wives he had upon earth in their full beauty when they were brides, and will also be allotted seventy-two black-eyed houris by whom he may have children or not as he wishes. As the Mohammedans are fond of children, this is an important part of their heavenly dreams.

Another of their curious ideas concerns the age of men when they reach heaven. As they rise from their graves they will regain the prime of their manhood. Every one will be thirty and will have the stature of Adam who, according to their belief, was over fifty feet high and perfect in form.

The Mohammedan's hell is as horrible as his heaven is beautiful. It is composed of seven stages, one below the

The fanatical dervishes keep the Moslems stirred up with their talk of a combination of the Faithful of the world under the green flag of the Jehad, or Holy War, against their Christian conquerors.

In parts of Algeria the Tuareg desert policeman on his *mehari* is replaced by the Spahi mounted on a swift Arab horse. This one is on duty near Kairouan.

other, varying in the intensity of their torments. The first is devoted to atheists, the second to the idolaters of the time of Mohammed, and the third to the Brahmans. The Jews have their quarters in the fourth hell, we Christians are confined to the fifth, while in the seventh and lowest of all are those hypocrites who profess religion but practise it not.

The Moslem Sabbath is on Friday, at which time every good believer attends mosque. On that day the bazaars are nearly all closed. There is a sermon by the imam, or priest, and the people go out during the day to the cemetery and pray at the graves.

The Mohammedans have their Lent, which is known as Ramadan. It lasts for a month during which time a strict fast is observed. The Faithful then eat nothing at all from daylight until it is so dark that they cannot distinguish a white thread from a black one. They will not drink or smoke, and the most saintly of them will not even swallow their saliva. I had a dragoman at Constantine who was keeping Ramadan. Some of our days were full of hard work and he spoke again and again of how tired and hungry he was and how glad he would be when the night came. At the end of Ramadan is Bairam, or the time of rejoicing. This is a great festive occasion, corresponding somewhat to our Christmas or New Year. Parents give presents to their children and friends make calls upon one another. Everyone comes out in new clothes and the whole Mohammedan world gives itself up to holiday feasting.

CHAPTER XXIV

TO THE COLOSSEUM OF EL DJEM BY MOTOR

ACROSS Africa in an automobile!

Snorting and puffing through the silent deserts of eastern Tunisia; dashing along on the back of a "yellow devil" through crowds of superstitious Mohammedan Arabs!

Scaring the people, routing the donkeys and the camels, and turning the caravans into flying hordes of men and beasts!

These are some features of my eighty-mile journey from Sousse to Sfax by automobile.

From Tunis to Sousse we came by train. The journey, which is less than a hundred miles and all the way along the Mediterranean Sea, took us nearly six hours. Sousse lies on the Mediterranean away off here on the edge of North Africa. It is an old walled city of twenty-seven thousand Mohammedans made up of snow-white, flat-roofed buildings. The men in the streets are dark-skinned Arabs while the black-clad women are closely veiled.

A town of few foreigners, Sousse has all the aspects of the days of Haroun al Raschid. Its streets resound with the tales of story-tellers, with the high, thin voices of Arab schoolboys as they sing out the Koran they are trying to learn, and with the shrill cries of the imams from the minarets of the mosques as they call the Faithful to prayers.

It seems queer to see anything so modern here as an

224

automobile. Sousse is one of the oldest cities of the world, having been founded by the Phœnicians twenty-eight centuries ago. It existed before Carthage itself and was an imperial Roman city in the days of the Emperor Trajan. Under the Arabs it was for a long time the stronghold of pirates and corsairs.

A strange picture was presented at the time of our departure with the crowd that gathered outside the walls to see the "yellow devil" start off. The "devil" is a great golden automobile imported from Paris to carry first-class passengers from Sousse to Sfax. It is shaped like an old Concord coach, with three seats on the top, six inside, and one in front for the chauffeur.

Take a seat with me on the top and ride through the wild scenes of northeastern Africa. We are higher than the roofs of the huts by the roadside and away above the motley crowd of Arabs watching the start. The chauffeur cranks our "yellow devil." Now he blows his horn. Honk! Honk! We are off. Men and beasts in the road run to get out of our way.

We pass an encampment of Arab soldiers. The men are drying their wash and wave their wet garments at us as we go by.

Now we have left the suburbs of Sousse and are far out on the plains, travelling through olive orchards. They cover the country for miles. Sousse makes salad oil for shipment all over the world, and has been noted for its olives ever since the days of the Carthaginians. Indeed, most of the trees look old enough to have been planted long before the time of Christ. They are knotted and gnarled, but their wide-spreading branches are loaded with fruit. The orchards are interspersed with grain fields and pastures and the automobile startles the men at the ploughs and the animals that feed near the roadside.

See those black sheep, their fat tails flopping as they gallop over the fields! The ewes are running as fast as they can, with the little lambs tagging behind. Now we are passing a flock where the rams are butting the ewes to make them get out of the way.

See the camels cantering over the plain. They look like interrogation points on legs. Nearer the road are some harnessed to the forked-stick ploughs of the region. Their backs are turned to the automobile, but they see us and break away in a panic, dragging their rude ploughs after them. We meet others on the road carrying great burdens which they almost lose as they gallop out of the way. We see them hobbled in the fields and standing out like great yellow ostriches against the horizon.

Farther on we reach the edge of the desert. We pass Arab encampments. The low black tents become alive as we approach. Bedouin women clad in Turkey red gowns crawl out from under the tent curtains, and gaily dressed children loaded with jewellery stand and stare at our motor car. There are Bedouin girls whose silver anklets flash in the sun and whose enormous earrings gleam out against their rich copper faces.

Now we are passing a cemetery. It is filled with Arabs in white gowns and there is evidently a funeral going on. They rise from the ground about the tombs to gaze at us as we fly by. The tombstones are mere boxes of clay. Each has a stone at the head and one at the foot upon which the guardian angels of the deceased are supposed to sit watching their dead.

Notice the road. It is as smooth as a park drive in any

Sousse is one of the world's oldest cities. It was founded twenty-eight centuries ago by the Phœnicians, remains of whose civilization have been discovered in its ancient Punic catacombs.

Few Americans have ever heard of El Djem, yet here are the ruins of a great amphitheatre, surpassed only by the Colosseum at Rome. Thousands of Christians were thrown to the wild beasts in its arena.

Near the coasts of Algeria and Tunisia are thousands of miles of hard, smooth motor roads extending in straight lines across desert and plain.

American city and harder and better than most of them.
From our seats on top of the automobile we can see it
stretching on and on for miles through the desert, narrowing down to a pin point in the distance.   Tunisia and Al
geria have thousands of miles of well-kept highways and
one can travel from Morocco almost to Tripoli in a motor
car.   Our journey of eighty miles is everywhere equally
good.   As dusk comes on we fly along with the yellow
devil's eyes blazing forth their glare and have no fear of
bursting tires or of ruts that may cause a breakdown.
It is pitch dark as we make our way into Sfax and pull up
in front of a French hotel, where we stay for the night.

Comparatively few people have ever heard of El Djem.
It is the site of one of the most wonderful of all Roman
ruins, surpassed in size only by the Colosseum at Rome
itself.   The great amphitheatre situated about twenty
miles from the sea stands on a plain, rising high above its
surroundings.   The Colosseum at Rome is dwarfed by
other buildings.   El Djem stands out in the open and,
save for a little Arab village of mud huts ten feet high,
there are no other buildings in sight.

From the top of the automobile one can see the ruins
long before one comes to them.   At first they look like a
mighty bluff, a fortification, or the walls of a fortified town.
Nearer we observe that they are a huge amphitheatre.   As
we get closer still, the walls rise above us to the height of a
twelve-story apartment house.   One side of the amphitheatre has been torn away, but the greater part still
stands.   Climbing up from gallery to gallery, I wandered
through the arcades where men and women promenaded
in the days of imperial Rome while waiting for the gladiatorial shows to begin in the arena below.

The outlines of the arena are plainly marked. They enclose an ellipse of almost an acre and, according to my paces, they actually measure about two hundred feet long and one hundred and seventy-five feet wide.

The walls of this mighty structure, most of which still stand, are one hundred and twenty feet high and it is said that they were one story higher, but the upper story has been torn away. There are three galleries rising one over the other. Under the lowest gallery are the cells where the wild animals were kept and the rooms in which the gladiators waited until called into the arena to fight with beasts or murder the early Christians. This theatre saw the massacre of thousands and was even more noted for its lions than that of Rome. The wild beasts were brought from the Atlas Mountains near by.

The Colosseum at Rome seated eighty-seven thousand spectators. It is estimated that El Djem was about three quarters as large and had seats for sixty thousand. Looking at its galleries, I should say that this is undoubtedly true. The building has a ground floor of five or six acres and with the galleries it could have accommodated an enormous number of people. The circumference of El Djem is only two hundred feet less than that of the Colosseum while its width and breadth each measures within one hundred feet of the same dimensions in the Roman amphitheatre. El Djem as it stands is a little lower than the Colosseum, but with the missing story added the two amphitheatres would be of about the same height.

The Romans had an old saying:

While stands the Colosseum, Rome shall stand;
When falls the Colosseum, Rome shall fall;
And when Rome falls, with it shall fall the world.

I doubt not the Roman citizens of northern Africa thought the same of El Djem. But who can tell us anything of the people who sat in that mighty playhouse? We know only that there was a great metropolis here in the time of imperial Rome, that it was called Thysdrus, and that it must have been of enormous size to have required a theatre like this. During the third century it was one of the richest cities of northern Africa and the capital of a thickly populated country. There were other big cities close by. About eight miles away was one which had also a theatre and which still shows the remains of huge cisterns built for its water supply.

Thysdrus remained great up to the time of the Arab invasion, but the people around it were then governed by a Berber queen known as Kahena. The country was so rich that it was attacked again and again, and Kahena, thinking the matter over, came to the conclusion that the wealth of her people was the cause of the numerous invasions and that if she destroyed her cities her country would be let alone. She thereupon called her mountain tribes together and ordered them to cut down the orchards and level the towns. This was done all over the country, vast territories being reduced from riches to poverty. It had, however, the opposite effect to what she intended. The people who had lost their property sided with the invaders and Kahena was defeated. Her last stand was made in the amphitheatre of El Djem, the battered walls of which still show the effects of that siege.

Since then it has been robbed by the generations which followed. It has been a quarry for both Arabs and Christians, and the French have uncovered its mosaics and carried them off to their museums. To-day efforts are being made to protect what is left. I found parts of the ruins shut off by doors and wire fences, and masons were at work here and there repairing the damages of the vandals.

The day will come when northern Africa will be thronged with tourists and others studying the relics of its historic past. Most of the ruins here have until now been allowed to remain as they were, while those of Italy, Greece, and Egypt have been carted off to fill the museums of the world. There are acres of mosaics to be seen in the museums of Tunisia which will compare in beauty with any in Italy. The arena of this great amphitheatre was one solid mosaic which is now a part of the wonderful collection in the Bey's palace in the city of Tunis. There are other mosaics almost as wonderful in the museum of Sousse and others of great value in the Carthage museum.

A cemetery in Sousse has been excavated which dates back to the time of the Carthaginians. In it are tombs that were built when Hannibal was alive and I fingered the bone dust of some of these ancient heroes as I looked at the urns containing their remains.

Even more wonderful are the catacombs of Sousse, now exposed to the light of modern times. I had never heard of them until I came here. They are not mentioned in the usual books upon Africa and I doubt if they are known outside this part of Tunisia. Nevertheless, they are of enormous extent and of historic interest. They lie a mile or so outside the walls, with olive trees and other crops growing above them. They are reached by stone steps which take one far below the surface, and they extend over several square miles. We walked along gallery after

This street is crowded for an oasis village. At noon time not a human being is in sight. The occasional rain flows off the mud house-tops through pipes stuck through the walls.

Near the port of Tripoli is the sculptured white marble arch of the Roman Emperor, Marcus Aurelius. In the arch, now partly buried in débris, a cabaret has been installed.

gallery cut out of the solid limestone, lighting our way with candles. Now and then we had to stoop over, and I was warned to keep close to the guide, as there are so many cross-passages that one might become lost and wander long before getting out. The galleries are walled with tombs containing the remains of tens of thousands of human beings all lying in boxes cut out of the walls deep down under the ground. The tombs are, in fact, a series of pigeonholes, each hole containing a skeleton or bones and bone dust.

After the body was put in, the front of the tomb was walled up and an inscription was carved upon it giving the name and sometimes the story of the deceased. In many tombs gold and silver and precious stones have been found and in others articles which throw light on the life of the times gone by. Some of the tombs were those of little children. In one I saw the bones of a woman, the impression of whose buxom breast still showed in the plaster cast made by the soft limestone or clay. Upon a shelf over this I saw the bones of a baby perhaps two years of age, and in the niche below, the skull and foot of a man the rest of whose skeleton had disappeared.

I am writing at Sfax, the capital of southern Tunisia and one of the rapidly growing cities of North Africa. The town lies on a harbour which can be entered by the largest of ocean steamers and it has a considerable trade. It ships great quantities of phosphates and olive oil and millions of sponges gathered in the waters near by. The population of Sfax is about sixty-four thousand natives and sixty-five hundred Europeans, most of whom are Italians with a few Maltese. The European town lies between the Arab town and the sea. It contains a theatre, a post office, several hotels and banks, and a few business houses.

The native city, like all those of Tunisia, is surrounded by an enormous wall and entered by gates. The houses inside the walls are of Arabian architecture and the tortuous streets are too narrow for wheeled vehicles.

CHAPTER XXV

TRIPOLI

I WRITE these notes in the city of Tripoli, long the capital of that one of the old Barbary states which lies between Tunisia and Egypt on the Mediterranean Sea. I came here from Sfax, passing around the Gulf of Gabes and skirting the Libyan Desert the greater part of the way. Our boat was a little Italian steamer sailing from Genoa to Tunis and then going on to Tripoli and back to Naples via Sicily and Malta. We came to anchor in Tripoli harbour this morning and were brought ashore by boatmen as fierce looking as the pirates who fought here against our American sailors over one hundred years ago.

It was in this harbour that Uncle Sam had his first big naval engagement after the conclusion of the war which made him independent of Great Britain. This town was then a great piratical stronghold. It levied its tribute on all the ships of the Mediterranean and its soldiers not infrequently captured Christians and either held them for ransom or kept them in slavery. They had committed outrages upon our shipping during the last days of John Adams's presidency, so in 1801 we formally declared war, sending Commodore Decatur across the Atlantic and through the Mediterranean to punish the pirates. Decatur recaptured and burned the American frigate *Philadelphia* in the harbour here in February, 1804, thus teaching these semi-savages that even though they took their toll from the nations of Europe, our own little republic across the Atlantic must be left alone. It was this same Decatur who, later on, put the Dey of Algiers in his place.

Tripoli (or Libya) is for the most part nothing but sand. It is as long as from New York to Detroit, as wide as from Philadelphia to Buffalo, and contains altogether an area nearly ten times that of the state of Ohio. The only cultivated portions are a narrow strip of land along the Mediterranean Sea and the oases scattered here and there through the desert of Libya. The population is about six millions.

The foreign trade of the country is with the Sudan and Europe. Tripoli is the chief starting point for the caravans crossing the Sahara. There are half-a-dozen routes over the desert from here to the rich lands of Central Africa and great quantities of ivory, ostrich feathers, and skins are brought to Tripoli on camels from those regions. The trip takes several months. The caravans used to include in their freight female slaves for the Barbary harems. Millions of them have been thus carried over the desert and vast numbers have been sent from Tripoli to Tunisia and Turkey. The caravan routes are lined with the bones of slaves who died on the way.

The city of Tripoli lies in the Libyan Desert on the edge of the Mediterranean Sea. It is not an oasis of mud houses surrounded by mud walls, such as I have described in previous chapters on the Sahara, but is a desert city of seventy-three thousand inhabitants with great white buildings and walls of stone.

Approached from the sea, the town looks like a mighty fortification. It is built upon a sloping peninsula, the houses running around a beautiful bay guarded by rocky islands which rise like sentinels out of the blue Mediterranean. At one end of the bay is a huge fortification and at the other is the *kasbah*, a fortified castle containing the government offices. Between these two, inside the horns of the crescent, are white buildings, mixed here and there with structures of green, blue, and rose-pink, which rise almost straight from the water and form a great bow with the forts at the ends. Behind are other buildings of three and four stories, while over them all may be seen the tall minarets of the mosques with green caps on their tops. The houses are of Arabic architecture, and when one climbs to the highest roofs as I did to-day he sees that each house is built about a little court the walls facing which are painted bright blue.

As I stood on the housetop all Tripoli lay below me. It looked like a jumble of great goods boxes cast by the hands of the gods down into the midst of the desert. There are few trees in the town. At the right, facing the sea some distance away, is an oasis of date palms, but on the other side, as far as the eye can reach, there is nothing but the bare yellow sand of the desert of Libya.

Let us go down into the city itself and take a walk through the streets. The time is midday and the sun blazes like a furnace in this tropical sky of the desert. When we reach the open spaces it dazzles our eyes as the white buildings about us catch the rays and throw them back in an almost blinding glare. But in the chief streets there is no sun at all, for Tripoli is a city of caverns. Most of the streets are either covered with matting or boards, or are actually built over like great vaults and lighted here and there by holes in the roofs. It is like going through half-lighted tunnels, and we might wander about for hours bareheaded without fear of the sun. This is true especially in the business sections. The bazaars consist of streets ten or fifteen feet wide with white vaulted roofs, the light coming through holes each of which is about a foot square. Now and then there will be a break in these roofs, making a short open space where the sun shines, but after that the vaults begin again, so that one may keep under cover through almost the whole town. The business streets are paved with stone, while along the walls of the houses run ledges about three feet high upon which the shops face and where the customers sit as they haggle.

The chief shopping section of Tripoli consists of a mighty grape arbour. Here the street is roofed over with a lattice work upon which grapevines have been trained, their cool green leaves tempering the rays of the burning sun. This street is lined with shops some of which are about fifteen feet square. Such shops are considered great business establishments and their turbaned owners are among the nabobs of the city. The average store is not as wide or as long as a library table, while many are so small that the merchant within could not ask a friend to enter without moving his goods. There are very few streets through which wheeled vehicles can go, and some will not admit even donkeys or camels. Most of the freight is carried by porters who go about with great loads on their backs or heads. In the wider streets little donkeys are the chief beasts of burden, with camels carrying the heavier cargoes.

One of the most interesting features of Tripoli is connected with its water supply, which comes entirely from wells in or near the city. Some of it is carried in goatskins on the backs of men, some of it in clay jars on the heads of

women, and a great deal in barrels on the humps of camels.
The camels kneel down by the wells while the barrels are
filled. Each camel carries two barrels at a load, one on
each side of its hump, and on the horn of the saddle is
hung the measuring tub turned upside down. The water
is sold at so much per tub and the camel owner has his
regular customers to whom he furnishes their daily supply.

The only modern thing I have seen in Tripoli is the
American sewing machine, which is used in the street of
the tailors. As is the usual oriental custom, every business
here has its own section, and one long street is filled with
tailors sitting cross-legged on the floors of their little
cubbyhole shops as they sew. Some of them use hand
machines placed on little tables beside them, but some
have table machines of a well-known American make.
Where the full-sized machine is used it takes up half the
shop. Nevertheless, I have seen more than a score of
such machines in action. They are all exported by one
company which sells its machines everywhere over the
world notwithstanding the fact that we have equally
good makes that are never seen abroad.

Let us take a walk through the bazaars and observe
these ex-pirates at work. They are a busy people and have
many manufactures, although everything is turned out by
hand. For instance, here is the bazaar of the jewellers. It
consists of a street walled on both sides with little rooms
not much bigger than an upright piano. In the centre of
every room there is a tiny furnace kept going with a bellows
worked by a boy. Here is one in which a long-gowned,
dark-faced Arab holds a pot of molten silver over the fire.
When he takes it off he casts the metal into bracelets and
anklets. In the next shop a turbaned man sits flat on the

floor pounding a gold bar into earrings as big around as a saucer, while over the way are smiths making silver anklets each of which will weigh several pounds.

In the bazaar of the shoemakers I saw scores of cobblers at work upon slippers. The Arab gets along without shoe strings or shoe buttons. The shoe shops are small, and yet the ordinary cobbler often has three or four boys, sitting cross-legged, working away beside him.

Tripoli makes a great deal of cloth. There are streets filled with weavers where men are at work on hand looms in just about the same way that they worked in the time of Mohammed.

The city is the Minneapolis of this country and its roller patent process of making flour is a curious sight to an American. Its many mills are worked day in and day out the year through. Each mill looks more like a stable than anything else and, indeed, it is often stable and mill combined. In the centre of the place are two great stones as big around as a cart wheel and about two feet in thickness. There is a hopper above the top stone from which the wheat pours down into a hole in that stone and is ground as the two stones move about one on the other. The power is a shambling camel hitched to a long bar that moves the top stone. The camel has over his eyes two cups of closely woven basket work as big around as saucers, so that he plods around blindfolded. In addition to this kind of grinding, a great deal of flour is made with hand stones kept in motion by woman power. This is the custom in most of the oases, the grain being ground from day to day as it is needed.

Another Tripolitan institution, through which many families combine to cheapen their food, is the town baker.

Though a city of over seventy thousand people, Tripoli still depends on scattered wells for its supply of water, much of which is peddled about from barrels loaded on the backs of camels.

One of the few modern things in Tripoli is the American sewing machine, which is used in the shops of the tailors.

As in Tangier, this man is to be found in most of the streets
of Tripoli. The butcher and the candlestick maker, too,
have shops in Tripoli. The chief light of the dwellings
still comes from candles, and there is a regular business
of making candles for the trade. They are usually sold
by the perfumers.

The butchers are even more interesting. I spent some
time the other day in a big meat market just inside the
city walls. The chief meats sold are mutton and camel
flesh each of which has its own department and its own
butchers. The market is held out of doors and the killing
and selling are done on the same spot. I saw men slaugh-
tering sheep and skinning them while their customers
waited for the still smoking flesh, and beside them their
fellows were cutting up other carcasses and weighing them
preparatory to selling.

The Tripoli mutton is fine. It is tender and fat and the
carcasses have great flaps of fat at the tails. The Barbary
sheep have tails made of nothing but fat; they hang down
like great aprons over their rumps, a single tail sometimes
weighing fifteen pounds. Much of the mutton sold in the
market is decorated with gold paper to catch the eyes of
customers, while some is sprinkled with black and white
seeds.

A little farther on was the camel market. Here the
meat was also decorated with gilt paper, but as it came
from old and broken-down camels it was tough and jaw-
breaking and brought much less than the mutton.

Leaving the meat market, I visited a place where men
were selling perfumery in little bottles about as big as
one's thumb. They sat on the ground with their tables
before them and weighed out the scents at so much per

ounce. Close by I saw several Arabs peddling second-hand weapons. Most of the guns were of the old flintlock variety, some beautifully inlaid with gold, silver, and ivory. The flintlock gun is still in use here and even the flints are sold. In some of the shops flints are shown for sale side by side with cast bullets and cast shot.

CHAPTER XXVI

THE OASES OF LIBYA

I HAVE just returned from Mechia, the great oasis on the edge of the Libyan Desert, east of Tripoli. It faces the Mediterranean and is an island of green on the edge of this mighty ocean of sand. It contains more than a million date palms, fully as many olive trees, and vast groves of oranges and lemons. The oasis is cut up by roads much like the streets of a city. Each little farm has walls six or eight feet high and everywhere are to be seen the high frameworks of the wells by which the land is irrigated. Cows, camels, donkeys, and women furnish the motive power for raising the water. In many places tunnels or long inclined ditches beginning at the wells and sloping downward for several hundred feet have been dug, and in these tracks the cow, donkey, camel, or woman trots up and down, dragging the rope which passes over a wheel on the top of the framework and thus raises the water. At the end of the rope is a huge bag of skin open at both ends. This is dropped into the well and when it fills, the lower end is pulled together, thus forming a closed bottom, and the whole is dragged high up into the air. The bottom is now released so that the water pours out into the trough which carries it off into a reservoir. As one of these bags will hold about thirty gallons and the work goes on all day, the quantity of water raised is enormous.

241

During my stay I visited some of the gardens. They are of all sizes and are extremely well kept. One I remember was cut up by cement conduits running along on the top of the ground, so disposed that every little tract could be irrigated at will. Here and there under the rich orange groves there were beds of beautiful flowers, and in most places three crops were growing on the same soil. Over the whole, the ragged trunks of the date palms rose high into the air, their wide-branched, fan-like leaves quivering in the breeze and their honey-coloured dates shining like gold under the dazzling sun. The trees below were loaded with oranges, pale yellow lemons, flaming pomegranates, and even peaches and pears. On the ground itself vegetables were growing, and I saw alfalfa and grain of different kinds in some places. This garden was in charge of a Bedouin and several of his wives. Over a fire in the open the women were boiling dates in a pot about the size of an apple butter kettle, making date butter or date honey, or perhaps merely cooking the dates for sale in the markets. The women were loaded with jewellery. With a lira I bribed one of them to let me take her photograph. The others, more bashful, wrapped themselves up in their shawls whenever the camera was pointed their way.

The oases of Libya contain practically its whole population. Scattered over a territory one ninth as large as the United States, they have altogether a million or more people. A large number of the oases, such as Mechia, are found along the shores of the Mediterranean; others are farther south in the desert, in a great depression known as the Fezzan; while still others are in the beds of dry rivers, where the water supply comes from springs or artesian wells. There are caravan routes leading from Tripoli to

There are more Negroes in Libya than anywhere else in North Africa. They were brought up from the south as slaves, and not until very recently did this traffic entirely cease.

The Ouled Nails are the Geisha Girls of the oases, and may be seen in their dances at almost any of the Arab cafés.

all of these oases, as well as routes crossing the desert to the Sudan from one oasis to another.

Tripoli is in fact the commercial metropolis of the eastern Sahara. It lies almost directly north of Lake Chad and its routes across the desert are the shortest although they are by no means the safest. The roads over the Sahara lead not only to Lake Chad but also to Tuat and Timbuktu, so that Tripoli gets a share of the trade of the French Sahara as well.

The French have made every effort to divert the caravans to Gabes in southern Tunisia as their landing point, but with only a partial degree of success. There has been no ready market at Gabes for caravan goods because there were no merchants at hand to buy out a large camel train on its arrival. The caravans often transport goods to the value of tens of thousands of dollars, and a big capital is required to handle their trade. The journey to the Sudan, for example, takes many months, so the freight must be valuable to stand the cost of transportation.

I took a camel ride along one of the routes a few days ago and passed several caravans coming in and going out. The only roads I could see were the fresh camel tracks, which must be obliterated by every sand storm, and in some places there were for long distances no tracks at all. Nevertheless, the Arabs and Bedouins can travel two thousand miles over such wastes without once losing their way.

I have heard much about the great oasis centres from the merchants of Tripoli. They tell terrible stories of the horrors of the desert and of the desolate villages scattered through it. Between here and Fezzan there is a wide plain of hot stones where there is no water at all and upon which travellers almost roast as they hurry across it.

This plain, known as the Hammada, is about as big as Kentucky and has an altitude nearly that of the Blue Ridge Mountains in Virginia.

The Fezzan, which lies on the other side of the Hammada, also covers a large territory. It is a shallow depression in the desert spotted here and there by oases. It lies eight hundred miles north of Lake Chad in the path of the chief caravan routes to Kuka and Bornu.

The trans-Sahara trade of the past consisted largely of slaves. From Tripoli they were smuggled to Tunisia, Algeria, and Turkey, finding a ready market in the harems of those countries. They were often taken on the steamers as the nominal wives of their masters. Since no Mohammedan will tolerate any inquiry into his family arrangements, such a statement prevented investigation.

The capital of the Fezzan is Murzuk, a dreary city containing about eleven thousand inhabitants and dependent almost entirely on the caravan trade. Its climate is considered so deadly that foreigners compelled to live there think themselves lucky if they lose only their senses of smell and taste.

Another important caravan centre is the oasis of Ghat, which lies in the bed of a dry river, and a third is Ghadames in another dry river some distance farther on. Ghat is famous for its great fair, which is held once a year and brings together traders from all parts of the Sahara. In ordinary times the town has only about four thousand population and the fair is held on a great plain outside of it. The city is surrounded by walls and entered only by gates. Its streets are dark passages with houses built over them, so that getting through it is like travelling through the tunnels of a mine.

THE OASES OF LIBYA

Gha-dam-es—I hesitate to write the name, it sounds so much like swearing—is twice as big as Ghat. It has been a trading place since the days of the Romans, and the caravans of the Fezzan, Touat, Timbuktu, and Lake Chad all pass through it. It is surrounded by a wall three miles in length, but the people live only in one corner of the enclosure. The houses are box shaped and so laid out that the women can walk from one house to another on the roofs, which are reserved for their use.

Some of the most interesting parts of this region are along the Mediterranean Sea. To the eastward of Tripoli is the town of Benghazi, which was a thriving city in the days of the Phœnicians and the Romans. Still farther east is Derna, the only place on the African continent ever seized by Americans. In the spring of 1805 William Eaton, formerly American consul to Tunis, started off with a band of five hundred men, including a few Americans, about forty Greeks, and some Arab cavalry, to cross the Libyan Desert from Alexandria to Derna, six hundred miles away. His purpose was the restoration of Ahmet Karamanli to the throne of Tripoli and his action far exceeded the authority granted him by the United States Government. In the long march the camel-drivers and the Arab chiefs continually mutinied, and the expedition ran short of provisions. Yet Eaton struggled through, took the town of Derna, and held it for several months until peace with Ahmet's rival was concluded by the United States. He built a fort in Derna, the ruins and rusty guns of which are still to be seen.

The products of the desert are much more important than is generally supposed. The caravans bring in to Tripoli quantities of ostrich feathers and cotton, dates, tobacco, and grain, as well as the ivory and gold dust of the Sudan. The output of the oases themselves is greater than that of any similar area on earth. Outside of them there are vast tracts used for grazing millions of camels, sheep, and goats, as well as horses and cattle.

Of late years a new crop has been found which is bringing fortunes into the Sahara. This is the alfa grass, commonly called esparto by foreigners. It grows wild along the edges of the desert and upon the plateaus where there is only a slight rainfall. Not many years ago this crop went to waste, but now the Arabs are gathering it and bring it in from everywhere by car and caravan. I saw it stacked along the railroad in the deserts of Algeria and Tunisia; the trains were loaded with it, and there were mountains of it on the wharves of every port that I visited.

Here in Tripoli the alfa grass is brought in upon camels. It is picked by the Bedouins, Arabs, and Berbers, every blade of it being pulled from the ground. It is packed in great bags about four feet wide and eight feet in length. Two of these bags are slung over the hump of a camel and are thus carried for miles over the desert. When the grass arrives at Tripoli it is weighed upon steelyards and paid for at about ten dollars a ton. It is then baled up like hay and shipped on the steamers to England where it is used for the making of the best book and writing papers.

Some of the great newspaper companies of England have put up factories in Algeria for the handling of alfa grass. It is said that its value was originally discovered by the Lloyds of Lloyds' *Register*. It makes a much better paper than wood pulp, but as it is far more costly there is no possibility that it will displace the latter.

A large part of the caravan business at the ports is han-

In parts of the desert the only roads are fresh camel tracks, which are obliterated by every sand storm. Yet the Arabs and Bedouins travel thousands of miles over such wastes without once losing their way.

The alfa grass, used in making paper, is brought to the city in great nets slung on camels. As usual, the camel bawls over his load.

The shrewd and stingy Mozabites, known as the "Jews of the Desert," go off on long trading journeys. If a husband does not return within a fixed time, his wife may not only marry again, but may also take over all his property.

dled by Greeks and Italians. The alfa grass is bought
by Italians, acting for the English, who ship it to Liverpool
and London and bring back hardware and Manchester
cotton goods. The Italians handle also the date exports,
although the fruit is brought in by native tribes who
make a specialty of merchandising.

Distinct among the tribes of the Libyan Desert are the
Mozabites, who are sometimes called the "Jews of the
Sahara." The Arabs say that while it takes five of their
people to beat a Jew at a bargain, it requires at least five
Jews to get the better of one Mozabite. Indeed many
believe that the Mozabites are of Jewish origin. At any
rate, they outrank the Jews in their trading ability and
have monopolized certain kinds of trade in the desert.

The Mozabites have seven cities far down below Algiers
in the middle of the Sahara, at the point where the caravan
routes cross. They are engaged in commerce there as
well as in Algiers, in Tunis, and in nearly every trading
centre of North Africa. These men stay away from home
for two years at a time. Their laws require that they
come back at regular intervals, and their wives can claim
a divorce if they remain away longer. If a man is absent
more than two years his wife not only has the right to
marry again, but can take possession of all the property
belonging to the family and keep it.

I am told that the Mozabite women are true to
their husbands. They wear black while their lords are
absent and make great feasts when they come home.
Among the viands served on such occasions are barbecued
camels and sheep. At the same time a dinner is given
to the poor which, strange to say, takes place at the cemetery. Here the wife plays the Lady Bountiful, sitting on

the tomb of her parents while she hands out the soup and dispenses her alms.

I have seen many of the Mozabites during my travels. They are short, stout, and of light complexion, with a Jewish cast of features. They are noted for their stinginess. Most of them sleep in their shops where they sometimes do their own cooking, saving every cent to take home.

At ten a girl of the Sahara begins to primp and look at men and something is supposed to be wrong with her if she is not married at seventeen or eighteen. As for the age of the husband, that matters not. He may be sixteen or sixty and he may have several wives.

Sometimes a female matchmaker is employed by the groom to find out all the details of the character and wealth of the bride. This woman goes with her to the bath and investigates her beauty; she makes inquiries at home about her cooking and housekeeping ability, so as to furnish a full description of the girl's qualities. The groom is supposed to pay a certain sum for the bride and she is expected to bring him a small fortune in jewellery and household effects. On her wedding day the bride is wrapped up in so many veils that she looks more like a bundle than a woman, and in this shape she is carried on a camel or donkey to the home of the groom.

The new home of the desert bride is with her husband's family, but only when she is the first wife. If he has other wives she goes to the common tent where she takes her place as boss of the establishment. After holding this position for a year or so, she comes down to everyday life and does her share of the work. She aids in the cooking, in gathering fuel, and in weaving the cloth for the tents and the family clothing.

THE OASES OF LIBYA

Have you ever heard of the Ouled Nails? They are to be found in every oasis and there is a whole street given up to them in Biskra, the so-called Paris of the Sahara. They are noted for their beauty and are professional entertainers, much like the Nautch girls of India, the Ghawazi of Egypt, or the Geishas of Japan. Robert Hichens rather effusively described them in "The Garden of Allah," making them more beautiful than I have ever found them either in Biskra or here in Tripoli. The Ouled Nails sing and dance for money in the Moorish cafés. Any one who will pay for a cup of coffee can see them, and scores of these dark-faced, turbaned, long-bearded Arabs will sit and watch them for hours. The girls are paid by the owners of the establishments, but they also collect contributions from the foreigners present, coming to them and kneeling down at the close of each dance. Thereupon the foreigner wets a silver coin with his lips and presses it upon the forehead of the dancer. The coin sticks and the girl rises and goes through the wild abandon of another dance, moving her head so gently that the coin remains where it was placed.

The dance of the Ouled Nails is the well-known stomach dance in vogue throughout the Orient. It consists of a series of contortions of the hips and abdomen, while the remainder of the body remains stationary or perhaps sways back and forth. The girls are fully dressed; there is no exposure of the person, and they lack the tights of our wicked stage. Nevertheless, their actions are more demoralizing than those of the worst of our dance halls. Yet their profession is considered respectable by their own tribe and after a time they take the money they have thus made and go home to marry their lovers,

CHAPTER XXVII

THE ISLANDS OF MALTA

SAILING northward from Tripoli I have reached the Island of Malta where I shall get a ship for Alexandria, in Egypt, the next field of my travels. I made the trip to Malta on a little Italian steamer. Our thirty-six-hour sail ended at the port of Valletta, under the shadow of the great English fortifications which guard this, John Bull's outpost in the mid-Mediterranean.

Malta is just about half way between Gibraltar and Port Said. It is scarcely a fly speck on the map of the world, but it is one of the most valuable of all strategical points. It is in the centre of the most travelled sea, a great station on the busiest of our commercial highways, and just where the steamers stop to take on coal. Malta is now handling about a half million tons of coal a year. It is brought here from Great Britain to be retailed to the steamers. As we came in we saw several ocean liners taking on fuel preparatory to their start for the Far East. Most of the ships which go to Australia, India, and China by the Suez Canal bunker here, and the port has a fleet of several hundred lighters which are used for that purpose. Training vessels and other naval ships are coaling in the harbour, while a great English transport, which will leave for Suez to-morrow, lies at the wharves. Malta is a strong naval station and the chief base for the repairs and outfitting of the Mediterranean fleet, but the fleet has already outgrown its capacity.

First let me tell you something about the Maltese Islands. They are quite numerous, but the only ones of note are Malta, Gozo, and Comino. Altogether they have an area of only one hundred and eighteen square miles. They seem mere rocks cropping out of the sea, but they are covered with a thin rich mould which makes them among the most thickly populated parts of the globe. Malta, which is the biggest, has an area just about that of the District of Columbia. It rises right up out of the water, and as one looks at it from the steamer it seems bleak and bare. The slopes are precipitous, but the land is so terraced and held back by stone walls that all of it is cultivated. To look at it you would not think it could raise anything. It seems more like a stone quarry or a stone pile than a fertile region; nevertheless, everything that is planted grows, and Malta alone supports more than two hundred thousand people. This is over two thousand for every square mile and more, it is said, than any other like area on the globe.

The two chief towns of the archipelago are Valletta and Città Vecchia, which are both on this island. It is at Valletta that all the great ships stop. From the harbour the view of the city is beautiful. Great walls which look like forts rise up from the water, and back of these the houses mount the hills in terraces. Many of the buildings are painted in bright colours and under the glorious sun of the Mediterranean they shine out resplendent.

The town is built on a hill high above the sea. Its streets ascend at all sorts of angles, so that one has to climb up or down in going to any part of it. Lord Beaconsfield once said that the architecture of Valletta was equal to that of any city of Europe, but it seems to me he overdrew it. The buildings are much like those of Naples. The streets are narrow, with the tall stone houses extending out over them. Many of the houses have balconies from which the family washing generally hangs out over the streets. The wet clothes flap to and fro in the breeze, and now and then the passer-by is apt to be startled by a shower of pearly drops from a newly washed shirt spattering down upon his neck.

The city has some fine structures. It has an opera house in which Patti sang the first time she came to Malta. This was when she was still a girl, and the price she received was twenty-five dollars. Another building of note is the Church of St. John, containing the tombs of the grand masters of the Knights of Malta. This church, which is one of the most remarkable in Europe, is revered by the Knights throughout the world. It is now over three hundred years old, but it is still in excellent condition. It is gloriously decorated. The altar, which is magnificently carved, is fairly loaded with gold and silver, and the railing in front of it is made of virgin silver. Beneath it are kept the keys of Jerusalem, Acre, and Rhodes. Some of the paintings in the church were brought from Rhodes, and it has tapestries made in Brussels at a cost of thirty thousand dollars.

You have heard of the Capuchin cemetery in Rome the chapels of which are walled with the bones of dead monks. I visited a similar one some time ago during a trip to Palermo, the capital of Sicily, and I find here at Malta another evidence of the gruesome taste of the pious fathers of the past. There is a church here known as the Church of the Monks, in which the bodies of the deceased are put away unburied. Their skeletons are wrapped in the cloaks which they wore in life, and they will, I suppose, be thus clad until the day of judgment. The place is a hideous one, so hideous, indeed, that a visit to it sometimes affects people seriously. Not long ago a smart young fellow went through with his sweetheart. He thought he would have a joke on her, so when her back was turned he slyly pinned her skirt to one of the cloaks. As she started to go the skeleton was pulled forward and fell upon her as if about to embrace her. The girl was terribly frightened and it is said that the shock destroyed her reason.

I like the Maltese girls. They have large, soulful eyes, beautiful features, and complexions the colour of the dark moss rose. They wear great black hoods over their heads with long black cloaks hanging to them so that most of the person is hidden and little more than the face and eyes can be seen. This part of their costume is called the *omnella*. It is usually made of black silk, and the hood part of it is boned at the front over a thin piece of whalebone, which is drawn over the head, forming an arch. The left arm is usually covered by one part of this dress while the right is used for holding down the other side and bringing the two together.

In other respects the Maltese of the better classes dress much like the people of Europe, and it is only the peasants who have costumes at all out of the ordinary. The peasant women wear hoods. Their dresses are of a striped native cotton and they seldom have shoes. The men wear short pantaloons which leave the legs bare to the knee and are tied about the waist with a girdle of cotton or silk. Above this they have on cotton shirts and some-times vests ornamented with rows of silver buttons made of American quarter-dollars or English shillings. They seldom wear coats. Their heads are usually covered with caps of bright colours made in the shape of a bag so long that the crown of tne cap often hangs down to the shoulders. They sometimes carry their money and their tobacco in their caps.

Outside the cities the Maltese houses are of one story. They are usually stone huts built of the materials gathered on the ground. The doors and windows are made by the carpenters and the village blacksmiths supply the locks and hinges. The people have little farms on which they raise fruit and small quantities of grain. They grow oranges, figs, and grapes. Many of them have bees and raise the honey for which the island is noted. Among the chief domestic animals are the goats, of which there are thousands. I have seen the Maltese goats in Morocco, Tunisia, and Tripoli. They are considered about the best along the Mediterranean, being imported not only on account of their milk but as breeders. They give so much milk that the whole population depends upon them for its supply, and the few cows which are kept are not regarded with favour. Indeed, there is not enough pasture on the island to furnish good cow's milk.

These Maltese goats are the chief competitors of the Angora goat, and it is questioned whether they would not be more valuable for our country than the latter. There is a demand in all the American cities for goat's milk for babies, and young kids are said to sell at the price of lambs. Here in Malta goat's milk brings about eight or ten cents a quart. The average goat yields from two to

Scarcely a speck on the map of the world, Malta is one of the most valuable strategic points and an important station on the busiest inland sea.

From its founding in the sixteenth century, Valetta was a strongly fortified city. This old gate dates from the early eighteenth century, about the time when the Turkish prisoners and slaves of the Knights of Malta conspired to seize the island.

The narrow streets remind the visitor that Malta is among the most densely populated areas of the world, while drops from the family wash flapping on the balconies above tell him the city has few back yards.

two and one half quarts per day. The milk is not used for cheese or butter, although fresh butter and cheese made of sheep's milk are sold here. I see goats in the streets every morning. They are driven from house to house and milked at the doors. It is not uncommon to see rags tied about the goats' nipples, to prevent the kids sucking their mothers between milking times.

The islands of Malta are among the oldest in history. On Gozo lived Calypso, the nymph who enchanted Ulysses and kept him for seven years on the promise that she would give him perpetual youth and immortality if he stayed with her.

Malta once belonged to the Phœnicians and was colonized by the Carthaginians. Before that it was owned by the Greeks, and after the Punic wars by the Romans. Later on it was attached to Sicily, and after the Roman power was overthrown it was occupied by the Vandals, the Goths, and again by the Greeks. In the ninth or tenth century the Arabs took possession of it, and later on the Normans came in and ruled it under one form or other for hundreds of years.

But one of the most interesting things about this island is its story in connection with the Knights of Malta, who owned and governed it for many years. It was in 1530 that Charles V of Spain gave Malta to the order of the Knights of St. John of Jerusalem, who thereupon took the title of the Knights of Malta and fortified it. At this time they had not only Malta but also Gozo and Tripoli. Taking upon themselves the defence of the Mediterranean, they made war upon the Barbary pirates, fought the Turks again and again, and defeated the Sultan when he attacked them. They waged war with the Moslems for

generations; and it was not until Napoleon Bonaparte besieged them, on his way to Egypt, that they surrendered
their fortresses.   Altogether, they held the island for two
hundred and sixty-eight years.   When the French took it
they agreed to give the grand master of the Knights an
annual pension of about sixty thousand dollars and to
make every French Knight resident in Malta a yearly
allowance of one hundred and forty dollars.

The French occupation was followed by a blockade under the English fleet, aided by the Maltese, which lasted
two years.   During a part of this time there was a famine
in Malta.   Fresh pork sold for two dollars a pound, dogs
and cats were generally eaten, and even rats brought an
exorbitant price.

While the Knights had possession of the island they
lived in grand style.   Those of each nationality had a
particular post assigned them in case of attack, and there
were also palaces or inns for those of each language, where
all the members ate and assembled to transact business.
The palace of the grand master was surrounded by the
four principal streets.   It still stands and is now occupied
by the officers of the British garrison.   This building
covers more than two acres.   It has two entrances and
two courtyards, one of which is used as an amusement
court for the British officers.   The interior of the palace
is elegant, the chief halls and apartments being embel-
lished with paintings commemorating the battles of the
order.   One of the most interesting parts of the building
is the armoury.   It is a great hall running the whole length
of the structure and containing many warlike weapons
and trophies which belonged to the Knights of Malta.
In it there are now ninety complete coats of armour for

mounted knights, and a large number of weapons used by the infantry of the past. The complete suits of armour stand among the muskets of the garrison, looking like sentinels and giving the whole a threatening appearance. In one piece of armour several slight dents may be seen. They were caused by shooting at it with a musket at one hundred and eighty feet. The bullets failed to penetrate or break the steel.

Città Vecchia, the old capital of Malta, which is six miles from Valletta, may be reached by rail or carriage. It is there that the grand masters had their summer residences, and there they were inaugurated. They left Valletta early in the morning, escorted by a bodyguard and bands of music. When the grand master came near the city he was saluted by musketry, and one of the chief citizens came out and gave him a bunch of artificial flowers, making an appropriate speech and kissing his hands. When the potentate arrived at the gates he knelt down before a cross which had been erected there and the keys of the city were given to him. At the same time he swore that he would respect the privileges and franchises of the city. After this he went to the cathedral to mass and then on back to Valletta.

Città Vecchia is in the centre of the island and about on the top of it. It is so high that on a clear day the coasts of both Sicily and Africa may be seen from its walls.

According to tradition, St. Paul the apostle, accompanied by St. Luke, spent three months on the Island of Malta. During this time they lived not far from Città Vecchia in a cave over which a church was built about two hundred years ago. The cave is about thirty-six feet in diameter and eight feet high. In the middle of it is a marble statue of St. Paul before which lights are kept burning day and night. Among the relics of the church is a piece of the true cross upon which the Saviour was crucified. There are also relics of not less than six of the apostles and of other saints.

Malta has been a possession of the British since Thomas Jefferson was president of the United States. Nevertheless, the people do not speak English, and although they have been ruled for centuries by foreigners, they still have a language of their own. There have been attempts to make Italian the national tongue, but the Maltese object and still speak the same language that they have spoken in the past. There are a number of newspapers published in Maltese and the Maltese language is used to some extent in the schools.

The percentage of illiteracy is great. Most of the people are unable to read or write and many of the children do not go to school. Nevertheless, the island has common schools and private schools everywhere. There is a university, a lyceum, and a large school for girls. There is a public library in Valletta which contains more than sixty thousand volumes and which has many of the books of the Knights of St. John.

The religion of Malta is Roman Catholic. It has an archbishop and more than a thousand priests and monks. There are twenty convents and five nunneries on the island and these are conducted after the manner of the Middle Ages, the nuns seldom coming out of their seclusion. There are more than a hundred Catholic churches and chapels some of which are elaborately decorated. Many of the churches are rich. That of St. Paul is said to own more than one million dollars' worth of statues, altar ornaments, and jewelled robes.

To go anywhere in Valetta you must walk either up or down hill between stone buildings that look like forts rising out of the water.

For a thousand years the Moor scratched the ground with a pointed stick drawn by camel or donkey—the French are teaching the use of modern farm machinery and production is increasing many-fold.

CHAPTER XXVIII

A LOOK AHEAD IN NORTH AFRICA

THE life in these Moslem lands of North Africa remains much the same as before their Christian conquerors came across the Mediterranean bringing their unwelcome Western ways. Yet, partly as a result of the upheaval among the European nations, and partly because the great Powers are ever strengthening their grasp upon their African possessions, some changes have inevitably occurred. These are most marked in French Morocco, whose present-day administration will remind Americans of our own military governments in Cuba, Porto Rico, and the Philippines.

If we were to visit Morocco again next winter we should probably choose to cross from Europe by airplane. This land, chained so long to the traditions of the past and until recently steeped in anarchy, has the first of the international air-transport services with which France is binding closer her African colonies. Our airplane would take us on board at Toulouse at sunrise and land us at Casablanca before sunset, after a flight longer than from New York to the Mississippi River. Under French control, Casablanca has already surpassed Tangier as a commercial centre, modern docks and piers have been built, and its business is rapidly increasing.

If we like, we may fly down the coast to Agadir, the port famous for the naval demonstration of Kaiser Wilhelm

which nearly precipitated the World War several years before it finally came.   If we are very adventurous, we can
travel by air from the Moroccan coast to Dakar, the capital of West French Africa, near Cape Verde.   From there
it is only three days' sail to Pernambuco, Brazil, and the
French have a scheme for a combined rail-water-and-air
route through Spain, across to Morocco, down to Dakar,
and over the Atlantic to the easternmost tip of South
America.   This route will bring all Europe a week nearer
South America.

As we fly over the country we shall not find Morocco
greatly changed in appearance though the French have
made many improvements since they took it over.   We
know, however, that we can travel with safety anywhere
we please, riding on the little narrow-gauge railroad lines,
or motoring over the smooth, hard roads, even to the
sacred city of Fez.   Many miles of these new motor roads
were built by German prisoners sent over from France
during the World War.   As labourers they replaced the
thousands of natives, hundreds of them former rebels and
mutineers, who left their homes to fight for France.

Morocco has helped to feed France as well as to fight
for her.   Where formerly most of the grain raised by
rude methods on the little native farms was consumed
at home, during and since the World War Morocco
has furnished to France millions of bushels of wheat,
barley, beans, and corn, besides quantities of hogs, eggs,
and other foodstuffs.   The arable lands extend for about
three hundred miles along the coast and end with the
Atlas Mountains, yet if all the land now under cultivation
were put together it would form an area not larger than
Massachusetts.   There are rich possibilities in planting

grains, grapes, lemons, olives, and almonds. There is also a future in sheep-raising and in the development of the forests of cedar and cork oak.

In her minerals Morocco has a practically untouched source of riches. There are large deposits of iron, copper, lead, silver, gold, and platinum believed to contain ores sufficient to supply all Europe for years to come. Vast coal beds and underground reservoirs of fuel oil are also known to exist. It was a hint of this undeveloped wealth that made the Powers so eager to get control of Morocco and sustained the ambitions of France in manœuvres with rival nations.

The French are doing all they can to improve the farming methods of the natives, who have been accustomed to getting only ten bushels of wheat to an acre. At the agricultural schools the simplest rules of good farming are taught and experts go through the country teaching better ways of handling crops and live stock. Annual fairs and expositions are held in several places and mixed chambers of commerce and agricultural societies have been organized. Stimulated by cash prizes for the largest acreage cultivated with modern methods and machinery, the natives are giving up the plough made of a forked stick and the farm tractor is abroad in the land.

The French are also trying to revive among the people their ancient handicrafts, which were fast being forgotten. Specimens of native pottery, jewellery, rugs, metal work, and embroidery are to-day shown along with farm produce.

The visitor to the new Morocco need not feel that he is at the end of the earth or out of touch with the world. There are more than four thousand miles of telegraph lines, several radio stations, and daily mail service from European ports. The holy city of Fez, far in the interior, gets the wireless flashed every day from the Eiffel Tower in Paris, while there is a telephone even on the walls of the Sultan's harem. There are over six hundred miles of new railways and motor buses, and private cars are available for trips across the country into Algeria.

Even so recently as during the World War, there was not a wheeled vehicle in all Morocco, there were no roads outside the towns, and freight transportation was limited to what could be carried on a camel's back, and that at prohibitive rates. Only yesterday fifteen miles was a day's journey; now one can go fifteen times as far between breakfast and supper and will find little hotels and eating places along the way. Near the towns the roads are lined with tiny tents where candy, tobacco, and all manner of goods are offered for sale and the barber and the blacksmith are ready to ply their trades.

While the French programme of railroad construction is far from complete, already they have linked up Casablanca with Fez and have established rail communication with Algeria by means of the Fez–Taza line. The narrow-gauge railways built for military purposes are being replaced as rapidly as possible with standard construction.

The recent remarkable progress of Morocco is largely the work of one man—the French Resident General, and the real ruler of the country. I first met Marshal Lyautey when he was in charge of one of the provinces of Algeria, and doubtless this earlier experience in North Africa helped him to make his brilliant success in turbulent Morocco.

When the French took hold of the Moroccan mess, they

deposed Mulai Abd el-Hafid, the brother who had forced the abdication of Abd el-Aziz, and put in his place a younger half-brother, Mulai Yusef, Sultan still, but shorn of most of his power. Immediately bloody mutinies broke out at Fez. Yet within five months Lyautey reported pacification and immediately began the outlay of millions of francs on a programme of development and public improvement. He completely reorganized the administration of Moroccan affairs and undertook a general opening up of the country. Lyautey raised regiment after regiment to go to France to fight, yet at the same time, with the help of specialists sent from home, he built roads,. schools, and docks, and taught the natives how to cultivate their farms as never before. Instead of becoming, as was feared, a menace to France, the so lately chaotic Morocco was transformed into a source of men and supplies.

The people have been won by policies that made them more prosperous. The travel routes, once shunned by the natives for fear their crops and animals might be seized by the Sultan's agents or carried off by robbers, are lined with busy farms, and new villages have sprung up here and there. The population has increased to about six millions. The boys and girls of Morocco, for the first time in the history of the land, now have toys like their Western brothers and sisters and are learning to play, while their fathers and uncles who live in towns have acquired the moving-picture habit.

What the French have done in the area where they enjoy full control stands out in marked contrast to the confusion and lack of progress in Tangier, the ancient city just across the way from Gibraltar. Under international administration, it is one of the most mixed-up places in the world. There are French, English, and Spanish post offices and mail services. The moneys used and the languages spoken are equally numerous. Even the names of the streets are mixed, as each of the nationalities represented in the administration tries to impose its own preference on the city. There are three Sabbaths in the week, for Moslems observe Friday, the Jews Saturday, and the Christians Sunday. It is said that a German firm successfully made capital out of the conditions in Tangier by putting out some shirts especially designed for diplomats at social functions. Inside the cuffs were such conversational small change as: "Good afternoon, Madam." "How do you do, Madam?" "You are looking charming, Mademoiselle," etc., printed in more than twenty different languages.

In Spanish Morocco conditions are much like those I found in the days of Abd el-Aziz, even including the exploits of that historic trouble-maker, Raisuli himself. Largely for military purposes, the Spaniards have built some railways and motor-roads. A motor line operates daily between Tetuan and Tangier, and Melilla is connected with the French territory on the east by an excellent road. A short line of railway extends from Melilla through Hador to Estacion, but even the troops have to depend chiefly upon pack mules in the western section and camels in the east to bring up their supplies.

Algeria's prosperity has not only won for her the status of a French province, but every soldier who fought in the Allied forces during the World War may now become a citizen of France. The cash allowance made the families of men in the service, though small, seem like riches to them. Many of the natives who stayed at home grew wealthy in business connected with the war and are now living in luxury that the Prophet himself might have envied. Numbers of the chiefs enlisted in the army received in France a training and education almost equal to that of the French officer. There is a wholesome increase in the native population and a growing willingness on the part of capitalists and French colonists to invest in the future of the country.

In Tunisia, less progress has been made, though the French have long been in control and now dictate the policies of the native Bey. Since the war political agitation for more self-government has increased among the natives, while the Italians, who make up a considerable number of the population, have strengthened their hold on the fishing industry and other commercial enterprises. The country has over one thousand miles of railroad, chiefly along the coast, part of an elaborate system being developed by the French to link up their North African possessions from the borders of Tripoli to the Atlantic coast of Morocco. Tunisia furnished many soldiers to fight for France, and its foreign trade amounting to about one hundred million dollars a year is a valuable asset.

Tripoli, taken from the Turks by Italy, has cost its latest conquerors a pretty penny and yielded little in return. While France and England have large assets in Africa; Italian Libya must be regarded as one of Italy's liabilities. Imagine a line from New York to Norfolk as the only railroad in the United States and you will have a picture of rail transportation in Tripoli, which has less than two hundred miles of track. The capitals of the two administrative districts of Italian Libya are Tripoli and Benghazi, both on the coast, and the combined population of the two cities is less than that of Wilmington, Delaware.

Italy had to fight to get Tripoli. During the World War she had to fight again, not only Turks and Arabs, but Germans as well, in order to keep it. Disorders in the interior and French and British competition have caused a falling off in the once important caravan trade. The country has not yet fully been pacified and organized for modern administration, and it will undoubtedly be a long time before it is developed on a profitable basis.

THE END

BIBLIOGRAPHY

GENERAL

THE British Foreign Office publishes diplomatic and consular reports annually which give trade statistics for the countries of North Africa, and also a miscellaneous series of reports which from time to time contain exhaustive studies of special countries. "The Statesman's Year Book" gives the latest information on each country, with a bibliography attached. The French Government publishes a similar handbook, "Annuaire Générale de la France et de l'Etranger," of which there is an English translation. There is issued in Algiers an "Annuaire Générale de l'Algérie, Tunisie, et Maroc." For guidebooks there are the "Guides Joanne" published in Paris, Murray's, Baedeker's, and Cooks' guides to Algeria and Tunisia, and references to these countries and to Morocco in general guidebooks to the Mediterranean coasts. There are numerous books in French on the African lands belonging to the republic, and general descriptions in such travel books as Arthur Bullard's "Barbary Coast," New York, 1913, and Cyril F. Grant's " 'Twixt Sand and Sea; Sketches in North Africa," London, 1911. There are historical and geographical accounts of all the countries mentioned in this volume in Herbert Adams Gibbons's "The New Map of Africa," brought up to the date of its publication, 1916.

BIBLIOGRAPHY

MOROCCO

ASHMEAD-BARTLETT, E. "The Passing of the Shereefian Empire." London, 1910.

BALCH, THOMAS WILLING. "France in North Africa." London, 1906.

CHEVRILLON, ANDRÉ. "Marrakesh." Paris, 1919.

DESROCHES, GEORGES. "Le Maroc." Paris, 1921.

FRASER, J. FOSTER. "The Land of Veiled Women." London, 1911.

GEORGES-GAULIS, BERTHE. "La France au Maroc." Paris, 1919.

GOULVEN, J. "Le Maroc." Paris, 1919.

HARRIS, W. B. "Morocco that Was." London, 1921.

HOLT, G. E. "Morocco the Piquant." London, 1914.

KANN, R. "Le Protectorat Morocain." Paris, 1921.

LOTI, PIERRE (pseudonym of Viaud, Julien). "Morocco." London, 1914.

MACKENZIE, DONALD. "The Khalifate of the West." London, 1911.

MEAKIN, BUDGETT. "The Land of the Moors." London, 1901.

MOREL, E. D. "Morocco in Diplomacy." London, 1912.

PIQUET, VICTOR. "Le Maroc," Paris, 1918. (Crowned by French Academy.)

STERNBERG, GRAFT VON (trans. by Ethel Peck). "The Barbarians of Morocco." London, 1908.

WHARTON, EDITH. "In Morocco." New York, 1920.

ALGERIA AND SAHARA

AUGIÉRAS, ERNEST M. "Le Sahara Occidental." Paris, 1919.

AYNARD, RAYMOND. "L'Œuvre Français en Algérie." Paris, 1913.

BAENSCH, A. "Algerien und die Kabylie." Zurchk, 1914.

BETHAM-EDWARDS, MATILDA B. "In French Africa." London, 1913.

CASTERAN, AUGUSTIN. "L'Algérie Française de 1884 à nos jours." Paris, 1900.

FURLONG, CHARLES W. "The Gateway of the Sahara." New York, 1914.

GAUTIER, E. T. "L'Algérie et la Métropole." Paris, 1920.

HILTON-SIMPSON. "Algiers and Beyond." New York, 1906.

HILTON-SIMPSON. "Among the Hill Folk of Algiers." New York, 1921.

KING, W. J. HARDING. "A Search for the Masked Tawareks." London, 1903.

BIBLIOGRAPHY

LAURIE, GEORGE BRENTON. "The French Conquest of Algeria." 1909.

MÉLIA, JEAN. "La France et l'Algérie." Paris, 1917.

PHILLIPPS, L. MARCH. "In the Desert." New York, 1909.

SOMMERVILLE, MAXWELL. "Sands of Sahara." Philadelphia, 1901.

STANFORD, CHARLES THOMAS. "About Algeria." London, 1912.

STOTT, M. D. "The Real Algeria." London, 1914.

VISCHER, HANNS. "Across the Sahara from Tripoli to Bornu." London, 1910.

WOODBERRY, GEORGE E. "North Africa and the Desert." New York, 1914.

TUNISIA

"Annual reports" on Tunisia to the president of France.

"Atlas touristique. Tunisie," published by the P. L. M. Railway Company. Paris, 1921.

BESNIER, PROF., and others. "La Tunisie au début du XXme siècle." Paris, 1904.

LANESSAN (DE). "La Tunisie." Paris, 1917.

PETRIE, GRAHAM. "Tunis, Kairouan and Carthage." London, 1908.

RITTMEYER, M. "Bilder aus Tunisien." Wolfenbüttel, 1909.

SLADEN, DOUGLAS. "Carthage and Tunis." 2 vols: I. Carthage; II. Tunis. London, 1907.

TRIPOLI (LIBYA)

BRAUN, ETHEL. "The New Tripoli." London, 1914.

"Bulletins" of the Ministerio delle Colonie, Rome.

FURLONG, CHARLES W. "Tripoli in Barbary." New York, 1911.

GIAMPICCOLO, E. "Colonie Italiane in Africa." Catania, 1914.

McCLURE, W. K. "Italy in North Africa." London, 1913.

MEHIER DE MATHUISIEULX, HENRI. "La Tripolitaine d'Hier et de Démain." Paris, 1912.

RHOLFS, G. "Tripolitania." Milan, 1913.

SFORZA, A. M. COUNT. "Esplorazione e prigionia in Libya." Milan, 1919.

TODD, MRS. MABEL LOOMIS. "Tripoli the Mysterious." Boston, 1912.

INDEX

271

INDEX

INDEX

Sahara, travel in the, 76.

Sand dunes, formation of, in Sahara Desert, 81.

Sewing machines, American, in Tripoli, 237.

Sfax, capital of southern Tunisia, 231.

Shoemakers, of Tunis, 183.

Sidi Bel Abbes, French settlement in Algeria, 65.

Sidi Okba, desert town of, 166; Grand Mosque of, at Kairouan, 214.

Sousse, automobile journey to, 224.

Spanish colonies in Africa, 42.

Tafilelt, group of oases in Sahara Desert, 83, 89, 105.

Tangier, and its people, 3; backwardness of, 263.

Tarla, oasis in Sahara Desert, 101.

Tea drinking in Sahara oasis, 99.

Tell, the, principal agricultural section of Algeria, 51; being rapidly settled by Europeans, 66; one of the granaries of the ancient world, 67.

Thysdrus, ancient city of, 229.

Timgad, excavations by the French at, 148.

Tlemçen, ancient city of Algeria, 57.

Touat, group of oases in Sahara Desert, 104.

Transportation, difficulties of, in Morocco, 20.

Trans-Saharan railroad, construction of, 106, 107.

Tripoli, city of, 233; Italy's difficulties in, 265.

Trousers, worn by Arab women, 205.

Tuaregs, now employed as desert police by French, 85, 86; tribal customs, 87.

Tunis, the city of, 178.

Tunisia, recent progress in, 265.

Valletta, Island of Malta, 251.

Wady Saoora, underground stream in Sahara Desert, 101

Wheat raising in the Tell, Algeria, 51, 67.

Women, of Morocco, the, 9; Mohammedan, seclusion of, 203; customs in dress, 204.

Zenaga, oasis town in Sahara Desert, 95, 97.